BEER LAW

Beer affects the law, and the law affects beer. The regulation of beer goes back thousands of years, and beer laws have shaped society in both obvious and unexpected ways.

Beer Law provides a fun and accessible account of the complex interaction between law and beer. The book engages with a broad range of beer law topics including:

- Health
- Intellectual property
- Consumer protection and unfair competition
- Contract
- Competition
- International trade
- Environment
- Tax

The book also provides a detailed description of beer, brewing, beer as a product, and the brewing industry, as well as an overview of some broad lessons from the regulation of beer. Given the importance of understanding law in context, the book also explores beer, beer culture, and beer laws in more detail, with a focus on Belgium, the Czech Republic, Germany, the Nordic countries, North America, and Britain and Ireland.

Dan Jerker B. Svantesson is Professor at the Faculty of Law, Bond University. He has written extensively on international aspects of internet law and data privacy. He is also an award-winning amateur brewer, including a Chocolate Baltic Porter being 'Best of Show' amongst 580 competing beers in the 2022 Queensland Amateur Brewing Championship.

William Van Caenegem is Professor of Law at the Faculty of Law, Bond University, QLD Australia and an Honorary Visiting Professor at the University of Gothenburg, Sweden. He holds masters and doctoral degrees from Cambridge University, and previously published the monograph *Intellectual Property and Innovation* with Cambridge University Press. He has written extensively on IP law, brand protection, and competition issues.

Anthea Jane Gerrard is an assistant professor at the Faculty of Law, Bond University. She studied commerce, law, and accounting in South Africa, the United Kingdom, and Australia. She is an associate member of the Tax Institute of Australia, previous editor of the *Revenue Law Journal*, and taught taxation and constitutional law covering the varying roles of excise duties between different jurisdictions for over twenty years.

Radim Polčák is Professor at the Institute of Law and Technology, Faculty of Law, Masaryk University. He founded the Institute of Law and Technology at the Faculty of

Law, Masaryk University, where the law of specific production (including beer law) has been taught and researched, among other fields of technology law. He has written extensively about the theory and philosophy of technology law.

Alain Strowel is a professor at UC Louvain, where he teaches courses in intellectual property, IT, and media law. He is also an attorney at the Brussels bar. He graduated in law, economics, and philosophy at the UC Louvain and the University of Amsterdam. Today his research focuses on data governance, artificial intelligence, and the regulation of online platforms.

Andreas Wiebe is Chair for Civil Law, Intellectual Property and Unfair Competition Law, Media and Information Law at the Faculty of Law, University of Göttingen, Germany. He has several publications on unfair competition law and IP in German and English. He has been co-editor of the *Commentary on Unfair Competition Law in Austria* since 2007; he organizes annual conferences on IP and unfair competition law in Germany and Austria, is an active member of the German IP Association (GRUR), and is director of the LLM Programme on European and Transnational IP and ICT Law at University of Göttingen.

Beer Law

DAN JERKER B. SVANTESSON
Bond University, Queensland

WILLIAM VAN CAENEGEM
Bond University, Queensland

ANTHEA GERRARD
Bond University, Queensland

RADIM POLČÁK
Masarykova Univerzita v Brně, Czech Republic

ALAIN STROWEL
Université Catholique de Louvain, Belgium

ANDREAS WIEBE
Georg-August-Universität, Göttingen, Germany

CAMBRIDGE
UNIVERSITY PRESS

CAMBRIDGE
UNIVERSITY PRESS

Shaftesbury Road, Cambridge CB2 8EA, United Kingdom

One Liberty Plaza, 20th Floor, New York, NY 10006, USA

477 Williamstown Road, Port Melbourne, VIC 3207, Australia

314–321, 3rd Floor, Plot 3, Splendor Forum, Jasola District Centre, New Delhi – 110025, India

103 Penang Road, #05-06/07, Visioncrest Commercial, Singapore 238467

Cambridge University Press is part of Cambridge University Press & Assessment, a department of the University of Cambridge.

We share the University's mission to contribute to society through the pursuit of education, learning and research at the highest international levels of excellence.

www.cambridge.org
Information on this title: www.cambridge.org/9781009632577

DOI: 10.1017/9781009632560

When citing this work, please include a reference to the DOI 10.1017/9781009632560

First published 2025

A catalogue record for this publication is available from the British Library

Library of Congress Cataloging-in-Publication Data

NAMES: Svantesson, Dan Jerker B., author. | Caenegem, William van, author. | Gerrard, Anthea, author. | Polčák, Radim, 1978- author. | Strowel, Alain, author. | Wiebe, Andreas, author.
TITLE: Beer law / Dan Jerker B. Svantesson, Bond University, Queensland; William van Caenegem, Bond University, Queensland; Anthea Gerrard, Bond University, Queensland; Radim Polčák, Masarykova Univerzita v Brně, Czech Republic; Alain Strowel, Université Catholique de Louvain, Belgium; Andreas Wiebe, Georg-August-Universität, Göttingen, Germany.
DESCRIPTION: Cambridge, United Kingdom ; New York, NY : Cambridge University Press, 2025. | Includes bibliographical references and index. | Summary: "Lawyers will enjoy learning about beer and how the law has shaped the brewing industry over the years, while brewers and beer drinkers will find an accessible overview of the complex laws that impact beer and brewing"– Provided by publisher.
IDENTIFIERS: LCCN 2025016423 (print) | LCCN 2025016424 (ebook) | ISBN 9781009632577 (hardback) | ISBN 9781009632591 (paperback) | ISBN 9781009632560 (epub)
SUBJECTS: LCSH: Beer industry–Law and legislation–Europe. | Brewing industry–Law and legislation–Europe. | Brewing industry–Law and legislation–North America | Liquor laws–Europe. | Liquor laws–North America. | Beer–Taxation–Law and legislation–Europe. | Beer–Taxation–Law and legislation–North America.
CLASSIFICATION: LCC K3651 .S83 2025 (print) | LCC K3651 (ebook) | DDC 343.407/866342–dc23/eng/20250404
LC record available at https://lccn.loc.gov/2025016423
LC ebook record available at https://lccn.loc.gov/2025016424

ISBN 978-1-009-63257-7 Hardback
ISBN 978-1-009-63259-1 Paperback

We dedicate this book to all the friends with whom we have shared a beer, or two, over the years.

Contents

Figures

Tables

Foreword

The many books devoted to beer that occupy the ranks of brewers' libraries are essentially devoted either to the history of beer, to the major families of brewers, or to manufacturing methods, styles, and very often to tastings, if not to the descriptions by brand or style. Let's not forget the many books on recipes and food-pairing, which also haunt our kitchens, and which demonstrate the social and cultural character that beer occupies in our daily lives.

Only a few books, dedicated to specific legal issues or explaining the main principles of law (in commercial, distribution, intellectual property, taxation law, etc.) refer, in one or other of their chapters, to examples and situations related to products containing alcohol, but very little to the brewing sector in particular.

Personally, when I took my first steps in the world of brewing in 1999, the first image I had of this sector was very far from the world of law because beer stands more as a symbol of conviviality, sharing, and culture. However, I quickly realized that behind this emblematic drink hides a complex legal universe, often unknown, that deserves to be explored. As my experience in the brewing world progressed, I learned to no longer consider beer only as a beverage but also as a field reflecting ever-changing business practices, epic battles around intellectual property, and a fast-moving regulatory framework.

In a world where traditions and innovations intertwine, this book teaches us how the law has evolved with the development of beer consumption. Brand protection, supply chain regulation, and consumer rights issues are addressed from a brewing perspective, as well as taxation, the economy, and health regulations.

The legal issues surrounding beer are not limited to commercial considerations. They also touch on public health issues, quality standards, fairness in business practices, and even ethical issues. Whatever the size of our breweries, how can we navigate the maze of legal rules to assert our place in the market? How do you find your place in a changing environment while remaining 'within the limits'?

This book offers answers to all those questions while shedding light on the contemporary challenges facing the brewing industry wherever we are in the world.

More than just a beverage, beer is fertile ground for exciting legal debates and reflections on the social responsibility of industry players. If being a brewer is an exciting adventure, it is nevertheless an activity that is part of a complex industrial, commercial, and legal environment.

As producers, our responsibility has always been to offer healthy and quality products while meeting consumer expectations. But it is undeniable that we are increasingly evolving in a regulated and controlled environment. This environment cannot be ignored if we want to make the right strategic choices.

As consumers, we live in an era where the slightest of our actions, related to our consumption and therefore to our health, is scrutinized, judged, and even controlled. Where does our individual freedom still stand in the face of regulations? How can we judge our behaviour in the face of countless studies that sometimes contradict each other?

It is therefore important that the framework in which we operate is better known so that brewers, on the one hand, and consumers, on the other, act with full knowledge of the facts.

This book employs a rigorous analytical approach, aimed at raising awareness among professionals, law students, and beer enthusiasts of the importance of legal and ethical considerations in this ancestral, traditional, but nevertheless innovative world that is the brewing sector.

I invite you to raise a glass to an enriching exploration, where beer and law meet to unveil a fascinating and often unknown panorama. May this book be a source of inspiration for those who wish to understand the legal issues related to one of humanity's most universal pleasures.

Welcome to this world where beer and law intertwine, revealing unexpected stories and challenges to be met.

Philippe Henroz
Directeur Général, Brasserie d'Orval s.a.

Acknowledgements

The authors express their sincere gratitude to all the beer brewers, maltsters, hop growers, yeast propagators, beer writers, beer judges, distributors, and pub operators of the world, now and throughout history; whether they are/were innovators or guardians of tradition and quality.

We sincerely thank Philippe Henroz, CEO of the Orval brewery, for his elegant and insightful foreword.

We are indebted to Dr Michal Koščík of Masaryk University for his insightful contribution to the health law chapter, and to Jean-Marc Deltorn, Professor at the Centre for International Intellectual Property Studies of the University of Strasbourg, for his contribution on beer-related patents. We also are very grateful to Jannik Scherer from the University of Göttingen for his valuable input in the country section of Germany. Further, we sincerely thank Helena Vingtoft for her helpful feedback on aspects of the book.

We thank Bond University Faculty of Law for the generous support funding the initial editing and formatting assistance, and we thank Caitlyn Douglas, Isabel Cepero, and Duncan Croker for their fine work. We also thank Dr Glen Pumuye for his valuable research assistance with aspects of Chapter 9.

The book would, of course, not have been possible without a publisher and we are extremely grateful that Cambridge University Press was willing to publish on this 'new' (yet very old) and developing legal field. In particular, we thank Sharon McCann, Matt Gallaway, and Gemma Smith for their support. In this context we also thank the anonymous reviewers that endorsed our project.

In addition to the above, Dan thanks his wife Bianca, children Freja and Felix, and dog Fenris for their boundless patience, and for their support during the project (and beyond).

Radim thanks his wife Petra and son Jan for tolerating his passion for beer, law, and beer law.

Anthea thanks John, Catherine, and Alexandra for their constant encouragement and enthusiasm in listening to her new insights on all aspects of beer.

William thanks his colleagues, family (in Australia, the US, and Belgium) and friends for their patience and support while this project was coming to fruition.

Alain thanks all those who have drawn his attention to many stories about beer (and shared many more beer glasses), including Dan, the Bond University team, and Jean-Marc Deltorn.

Andreas thanks Agata and Janek for their patience, backing, and inspiring suggestions.

Skål – Cheers – Prost – Na zdraví – Santé!

1

About Beer, Beer Brewing, and Beer Law

1.1 BEER + LAW = ?

Is there any connection between beer and law? And can we speak of 'beer law' as a distinct field of law? These two questions are clearly related. But they will not necessarily generate the same answer.

The answer to the first question is clearly 'yes'; beer and law are connected in many ways. The production, distribution, and sale of beer have, of course, been regulated in most parts of the world and for long periods in history. In the most extreme of cases, brewing and drinking beer has been illegal, and in that way, the law has aimed to stop the production of beer. Just think of 'Prohibition' in the US in the early 1900s, or the Icelandic ban on beer lifted as recently as 1 March 1989.

Even though the law has failed to prevent the consumption of beer (even during times of prohibition), the very fact that the law has sought to regulate this product to such a degree is rather strong evidence of the connection between law and beer. But there are many others, as we will demonstrate and discuss throughout this book. Tax law, for example, has an obvious impact on beer production and has indeed led to certain styles being favoured over others. Put simply, tax law has played a major role in deciding what beer you drink. The law also affects matters such as the design of beer glasses and bottles, as well as how and where beer is marketed and sold, and so on.

What we have said so far has focused on how law impacts beer. But there is also reason to consider the reverse; that is, how beer impacts law. Court decisions on beer-related disputes have advanced the law in several fields, such as competition law and intellectual property. Furthermore, societal concerns about the consumption of beer have driven legal developments in public health law, and the law in some states has changed to accommodate changes in the beer industry – primarily the so-called craft brew revolution. These are merely some examples. Others are discussed throughout the book.

So, what about the second question raised above: can we really speak of 'beer law' as a distinct field of law? The answer to this – in a typically lawyer-like manner – is that it depends. Determining what is seen as a distinct area of law is not a particularly scientific exercise. Rather it is highly subjective. Is it justified to speak of 'internet law' as a separate area of law? What about 'sports law', 'space law', and 'food law'? You can decide for yourself, but for us it is obvious that 'beer law' can be approached as a distinct field of law.

Beer is a distinct and prominent product and there is a long tradition of specific laws for beer, such as the world-famous German *Reinheitsgebot*, or '(Beer) Purity Law' dating back to 1516.[1] Indeed, this means it has been applicable for over half a millennium. How many other laws can you think of that can make such a claim?

But beer laws are much older than that. For example, while slightly more famous for other reasons, the Magna Carta of 1215 addressed the issue of a standardization of beer and wine quantification.[2] Furthermore, brewing ordinances aiming at consumer protection, security of supply, organization of the brewing industry, beer trade, and means of beer inspections date back to 1156 for Augsburg and 1268 for Paris.[3] Indeed, the Code of Hammurabi (a set of 282 laws inscribed in stone by the Babylonian king Hammurabi (r. 1795–1750 BCE)) provides specific rules for the serving of beer. In essence, 'Law 108 had to do with those tavern keepers who poured "short measures" of beer in return for cash instead of grain (which could be weighed and held to a measure) to cheat their customers; they would be drowned if caught doing so'.[4]

Importantly, some laws on beer have had societal implications going far beyond beer. For example, one of the functions of the beer ordinances noted above was to prioritize the use of grains for baking over brewing at certain times, such as during famine. Indeed, Meussdoerffer observes that '[d]uring severe famines brewing was interdicted altogether, as in London during the great famine of 1315'.[5] Thus, beer laws have doubtless saved lives in more than one way. Further, the Beer House Act 1830, that we discuss in more detail later in this book (Chapter 12), has been described as 'one of the most extraordinary pieces of all nineteenth-century legislation'[6] and as potentially 'more revolutionary in its immediate social consequences than any other of the reform age'.[7] All this suggests that it is useful to study beer law as a distinct field.

1 L Narziss, 'The German Beer Law' (1984) 90(6) *Journal of the Institute of Brewing* 351, 351.
2 See Magna Carta 1215, cl 35.
3 Franz G Meussdoerffer, 'A Comprehensive History of Beer Brewing' in Hans Michael Eßlinger (ed), *Handbook of Brewing: Processes, Technology, Markets* (Wiley-VCH Verlag GmbH & Co KGaA, 2009) 1, 14.
4 Joshua J Mark, 'Beer in the Ancient World', *World History Encyclopedia* (Web Page, 2 March 2011) www.worldhistory.org/article/223/beer-in-the-ancient-world/.
5 Meussdoerffer (n 3) 15.
6 TR Gourvish and RG Wilson, *The British Brewing Industry, 1830–1980* (Cambridge University Press, 1994) 3.
7 Ibid 7, citing William Laurence Burn, *The Age of Equipoise* (Norton, 1964).

There are already books and university courses on 'wine law' so why not 'beer law'? And if we have 'food law', then surely 'beer law' is a sub-discipline of that? Sceptics may here intervene that in that case we might also speak of 'coriander law', 'bacon law', and 'cos lettuce law'. But such an objection arguably lacks sting as it is conventional to delineate legal fields along the lines of distinct major industries; that is, while speaking of beer law is justifiable by reference to the size and nature of the beer industry, the same does not necessarily hold for the coriander, bacon, and cos lettuce industries.

Having said that, we would not necessarily be 'up in arms' should anyone want to write a book about 'coriander law' or 'the law of pickled herring', and ultimately, the question of whether a given topic can be described as a distinct field of law ought to be determined by reference to whether doing so provides any value. And with this book, we seek to demonstrate that beer law not only *can* be approached as a distinct field of law, but that doing so provides value.

1.2 ABOUT BEER, BREWING, AND THE INGREDIENTS

There are already many books that discuss the brewing process, and the common (and not so common) ingredients in beer. Some of them are highly technical,[8] and others emphasize accessibility. We do not seek to compete with any such books. But we do not presume that the reader has already spent time on such literature and, in our view, a book about beer law needs to start with a discussion of beer and brewing.

Sure, most of us may already be well acquainted with beer, its smell, its taste, how it looks; and if you are picturing one right now, you are probably getting quite thirsty. But a surprisingly large proportion of beer drinkers seem to have little more than a cursory knowledge of beer ingredients and the brewing process. It is consequently our aim to introduce beer as a product, the brewing process, and the ingredients used. However, we also use this section to hint at the important economic and societal roles of beer and brewing and we do so while linking into, and flagging, the legal issues that are discussed in detail in the rest of the book.

At its core, (modern) beer consists of four ingredients: malted barley, hops, yeast, and water. Sounds simple or even simplistic, right? But even where brewers stick to just these four ingredients, they can create a highly diverse range of styles of beer with flavours varying from full-bodied Doppelbocks, Irish Extra Stouts, and American Barleywine at one end of the spectrum, to the most flavourless and watery light beers at the other end.

The brewing techniques used may, as discussed below, significantly impact how the beer tastes, smells, and looks. However, the other key reason that these four ingredients can generate such diversity is found in the diversity within each type of

8 See, eg, James S Hough, *The Biotechnology of Malting and Brewing* (Cambridge University Press, 1985).

ingredient. Just as there are many different types of malt, there are many different types of hops and of yeast. As most people probably are already aware, even water tastes different in different locations. The mineral composition obviously impacts the beer as well. So let us now look briefly at each of the four key ingredients of modern beer before turning to all the other things that brewers may put into their products.

Interestingly, of the four ingredients, only three are essential, two have been banned, and one was unknown until relatively recently.

1.2.1 *Malt*

Malt is perhaps both the most well-known and the least understood ingredient in beer. Everyone knows that beer is made from grains. Grains could be said to be the main characteristic ingredient in beer just as grapes are the main characteristic ingredient in wine, apples are the main characteristic ingredient in cider, and honey is the main characteristic ingredient in mead. So far so good. But what then is malt?

To make possible the use of grain for beer brewing, the grains must be 'malted' (Figure 1.1). The complex malting process involves several steps. First, the grains are soaked in water to initiate germination. This step – 'steeping' – hydrates the grains and activates enzymes. Second, the soaked grains are spread out in a controlled environment with set temperature and humidity. During this step – 'germination' – enzymes are produced, converting the starches stored in the grain into fermentable

FIGURE 1.1 Barley malt.

sugars. The grains start to sprout during this stage. Third, the germinated grains are dried in a kiln to stop the germination process. The temperature and duration of this third step of 'kilning' varies, affecting the malt's colour and flavour profile. Fourth, after kilning, the malt undergoes cleaning to remove rootlets and other impurities. It is then graded based on colour, size, and quality – 'cleaning and grading'.

The term 'grist' refers to the milled malt and other cereal ingredients of the mash. The standard type of grain used in the grist for beer is barley, and more precisely two-row, or six-row, varieties. There is a range of reasons why barley has come to be the dominant grain for beer production, including its genetic traits and ability to grow well in large parts of the world. However, other types of grains are also used depending on style.

Wheat beers – such as German Weissbier and Belgian 'witbier' – unsurprisingly use wheat as part of the grist. Laws, or at least style guides, may regulate the percentages of wheat that must be included in such styles. For example, under German law a beer sold as a 'Hefeweizen', 'Weizenbier', or 'Weissbier' must include at least 50 per cent wheat.[9] Wheat is also commonly used in a range of other 'modern' styles, such as Pacific Ale and XPA.

Rye is a key ingredient in some styles, including German Roggenbier, with the flavour of the malted rye often described as 'spicy'. Further, oat is a typical key ingredient in modern 'hazy' beers such as New England Indian Pale Ales (NEIPAs), as well as some more traditional styles such as oatmeal stout. A range of other grains – for example, rice commonly found in Asian beers – may also be used in beer brewing.

The malt performs many different roles in beer. Most importantly, it is the sugars from the malt that the yeast converts into alcohol ('dizziness') and carbon dioxide ('fizziness'), and the malt also contributes significantly to the flavour and aroma of the beer. Furthermore, the choice of malt has a strong impact on the beer's colour. The colour density of beer is measured either in Standard Reference Method (SRM) or European Brewery Convention (EBC), where a higher number indicates a darker beer.

In the most basic form, malts may be separated into two different categories: that is, 'base malts' and 'speciality malts'. However, when brewers discuss malt, they commonly place the speciality malts within at least three categories: caramel and crystal malts, toasted malts, and roasted malts.

Base malts are the primary malted grains used in beer brewing. They typically provide the majority of fermentable sugars needed for the brewing process. Base malts are lightly kilned, resulting in a relatively light colour and a subtle or neutral flavour profile. Common types of base malts include pale malt, pilsner malt, Vienna

9 Horst Dornbusch and Garrett Oliver, 'The Oxford Companion to Beer Definition of Weissbier', *Craft Beer & Brewing* (Web Page) https://beerandbrewing.com/dictionary/84fU3qNtk5/.

malt, and Munich malt. Brewers use the base malts as a foundation and may add speciality malts to achieve specific flavour, colour, and aroma characteristics in the final beer.

Caramel and crystal malts are kilned with a higher degree of moisture to allow the sugars in the malt to partially dissolve and caramelize inside the grain. This process results in malts with a range of colours and flavours, from light caramel to dark toffee. Caramel and crystal malts contribute sweetness, body, and caramel-like notes to the beer, and may be used in various beer styles to enhance flavour, mouthfeel, and colour.

Toasted and roasted malt undergo a longer and more intense kilning process compared to base malts. This extended kilning imparts a range of flavours, and results in darker colours to the malt. They can contribute to the beer's roasted, caramel, chocolate, or coffee-like flavours and aromas, and are often used in stouts, porters, and other dark beer styles to add complexity and depth to the beer's flavour profile.

In addition to these widely used types of speciality malts, there are other – less common – types. For example, some beer styles – most famously so-called Rauchbier – utilize smoked malt. Such malts pick up the smoke character of the wood it is kilned with, and the character is then transferred into the beer. The types of the wood used may vary, but some common types include beechwood, oak, maple, and manuka. Some malt is peat smoked. While only a very small percentage of beers sold today utilize smoked malt, historically malt was kilned over an open fire and all beers would have had a degree of smoke flavour.

Before leaving our discussion of malts, we wish to emphasize something that is implied in the above – that is, there are several ways to categorize malt. We may primarily do so by reference to type of grain, variety, terroir, brand, and malting process.

1.2.2 *Hops*

Prior to the use of hops, 'brewers used a large variety of herbs, known as gruit [or "grut", discussed in more detail in Chapter 2] in medieval Europe, as well as strange items such as oxen gall, soot, bark, and mushrooms to spice their beers and sometimes to cover up off-flavors'.[10] But today, we take for granted that beer contains hops.

The exact history of the use of hops for beer is somewhat controversial and partly shrouded in mystery.[11] Furthermore, in some places at some points in time, brewers have been banned from using hops. We will get to all that, but let us first look at what hops are and the functions that they fulfil in beer.

[10] Victoria Carollo Blake, 'The Oxford Companion to Beer Definition of Hops', *Craft Beer & Brewing* (Web Page) https://beerandbrewing.com/dictionary/VnEcZ72c86/.

[11] We also discuss this in Chapter 4 in the context of the Nordic countries.

Hops (*Humulus lupulus*) provide the bitterness that we are familiar with in beer. While the level of bitterness varies greatly between different styles of beer, the presence of hop-derived bitterness is typically seen as a crucial component as it balances out the sweetness of the malt.

A beer's bitterness is commonly measured, and expressed, in International Bitterness Units (IBUs)[12] – an internationally agreed-upon standard for measuring bitterness in beer. The IBU expresses the measurement of the number of specific bittering compounds (isomerized and oxidized alpha acids, polyphenols, and other select bittering chemicals), that contribute to making beer taste bitter. Very bitter beers have a high IBU while beers with low bitterness have a low IBU.

But bitterness is not the only flavour derived from hops. Hops also provide many other flavours, such as the citrus and tropical fruit flavours of many India pale ales (IPAs) and the grassy, spicy, herbal notes of many lagers.

While the focus so far has been on the flavours provided by hops, the first contact beer drinkers typically have with hops is in the beer's aroma. Hops – typically sold in pellets, as hop cones, or extracts – are critical for, and dominant for many styles of, beer aroma.

In addition to the impact hops have on the beer's flavour and aroma, there is another strong reason why they are added to beer: hops are antiseptic, making beer resistant to microbial infection. In fact, few other food products are safer from this perspective. This has seemingly had a direct impact on beer styles. For example, it has been argued that the characteristic hoppiness of IPA stems from the aim of making the beer safe for the long voyage involved in exporting it from England to India and elsewhere in the 1800s.

Before moving on to consider the hop varieties and some legal issues, we may also note how hops impact the visual appeal of beer – while foam stability is also affected by other factors (such as the type(s) of malt used) – hops significantly contribute to foam stability.

When brewers speak of hop varieties, they typically divide them into three categories: bittering hops, aroma hops, and dual-use hops (Figure 1.2). However, as is discussed below when we turn to the brewing process, hops may also be categorized based on how they are used rather than on what the hop variety is primarily grown for; that is, even when a hop variety is grown primarily to be used as an aroma hop, it may still be added early in the boil with the aim of imparting bitterness.

Another way in which hops are commonly categorized is by reference to their origin. While different types of hops may be grown in all regions of the world, continental European hops – predominantly grown in Germany and Czechia – are often described as earthy, spicy, peppery, and woody.[13] English hops are associated

[12] An alternative is found in the European Bittering Units (EBU), which is roughly the same as the IBU.

[13] Specific examples of these hops include Saaz, Hallertauer Mittelfrüh, Spalt, and Tettnanger.

FIGURE 1.2 Hops in pellet form.

with descriptors such as minty, floral, grassy, and tea-like.[14] American hops are commonly characterized as being citrusy, pine-like, floral, and producing stone fruit aromas.[15] Beyond these regions covered in the book, the only other significant hop-producing region is Australia and New Zealand. Hops from Australia and New Zealand are associated with intense tropical fruitiness, including characteristics such as passion fruit, peach, orange, mandarin, lime, lychee, melon, and gooseberry.[16]

As we will come back to throughout this book, the law has directly impacted hops in very different ways over time and place. The French King Louis IX issued a decree in 1268 stipulating that only malt and hops could be used for beer making in his realm.[17] Henry VIII – perhaps best known for his habit of executing his wives – has been said to have decided to ban the use of hops in ale, thus maintaining a separation between unhopped 'ales' and hopped 'beers'.[18] Around the same time (from the 1400s), growing hops was a legal obligation in Sweden – one that lasted until 1860.[19]

[14] Specific examples of these hops include East Kent Golding and Fuggle.

[15] Specific examples of these hops include Cascade, Centennial, Citra, Chinook, Amarillo, and Mosaic.

[16] Specific examples of these hops include Galaxy, Eclipse, Nectaron, and Nelson Sauvin.

[17] Blake (n 10).

[18] See also Charles W Bamforth, *Grape vs. Grain: A Historical, Technological, and Social Comparison of Wine and Beer* (Cambridge University Press, 2008) 43.

[19] Mårten Larsson, 'Did You Know That... There was a Law on Growing Hops in Sweden?', *Skåne Plus* (Web Page, 10 August 2023) https://skaneplus.se/visste-du-att-det-var-lag-pa-att-odla-

To all this may be added that some hop varieties, as well as the names under which they are sold, are protected under intellectual property laws. We discuss this further in Chapter 5.

1.2.3 *Yeast*

There is an often repeated, but somewhat misleading, saying that 'brewers make wort, yeast makes beer'. In many ways this is like saying that bakers make dough and yeast (combined with heated ovens) makes bread. However, the saying still has merits in the way that it emphasizes the central role that yeast plays in beer-making. And the yeast is, after all, the only living organism involved in the brewing process apart from the brewer.

As noted, yeast converts sugars derived from the carbohydrate of the malt (or adjuncts) into alcohol and carbon dioxide. The simple reality is then that, without yeast, there will be no beer. So given this great importance, yeast must obviously always have been the brewers' treasure, no doubt protected by the law? Wrong. In fact, the world's most famous beer law – the previously mentioned *Reinheitsgebot* – actually banned the use of yeast (at least implicitly) when taken literally.

It is commonly said that yeast was 'unknown at the time' the *Reinheitsgebot* was drafted, and the result is that in prescribing that only the ingredients known at the time – malt, hops, and water – were allowed in beer, the world's most famous beer law bans the use of yeast. Funnily enough, then, a law aimed at regulating the production of beer actually – if complied with – would have made beer-making impossible. Perhaps modern lawmakers – not least those working with technology-related law – may wish to take onboard some lessons from this. For example, at the minimum, it highlights the risks of making laws in relation to something we do not fully understand from a technical perspective.

While this book is focused on beer law and not brewing techniques as such, it is worthwhile to pause and consider the mystery of why the *Reinheitsgebot* does not mention yeast. Writers such as Lars Marius Garshol have pointed to convincing evidence suggesting that yeast was intentionally added in the beer production well before the *Reinheitsgebot* was introduced.[20] Strong support for the existence of a very conscious use of yeast at the time is also found in the inter-guild Munich Baker–Brewer Dispute between 1481 and 1517.[21] This conflict stemmed from the fact that

humle-i-sverige/#:~:text=I%20Sverige%20har%20humle%20odlats,en%20viktig%20ingrediens%20i%20%C3%B6l.

20 Lars Marius Garshol, 'When Did People Start Reusing Yeast?' *Larsblog* (Blog Post, 29 April 2018) www.garshol.priv.no/blog/390.html.

21 Franz D Hofer, 'The Munich Baker–Brewer Dispute: Yeast and the Emergence of Lager', *A Tempest in a Tankard* (Web Page, 23 April 2024) https://tempestinatankard.com/2024/04/23/the-munich-baker-brewer-dispute-yeast-and-the-emergence-of-lager/.

bakers bought their yeast from the brewers and when brewers started brewing 'Bohemian beer' (hoppier beers based on lager yeast), the harvested yeast that was delivered to the bakers required a lower active temperature, resulting in longer rise times for bakers, and thus making it less efficient for bread-baking than top-fermenting yeast was. Adding to this, the harvested yeast from the 'Bohemian beer' was intermixed with more hop matter than the yeast from the lower-hopped top-fermented beer. This added hop matter resulted in greater bitterness, which, the bakers claimed, had a detrimental effect on the taste of their bread.[22] So, while they may not have been getting along so well, clearly both brewers and bakers actively and consciously worked with yeast. Indeed, in parts of Germany, there was a specific 'yeaster guild', or in German 'Hefener guild' (and no, it has nothing to do with 'Playboy' apart from the founder's surname, Hefner, stemming from the job Hefener).[23]

The mystery of the lack of reference to yeast in the *Reinheitsgebot* seems to stem from a matter of definition – how very lawyerly! It has been suggested that yeast, although well-known and understood from a functional perspective, was not regarded as an ingredient at the time that the *Reinheitsgebot* was drafted:

> 'The yeast is in fact not mentioned; that is correct.' Trum, who studied history while earning his brewing degree at Weihenstephan, points out that brewers of the day were well aware of yeast's existence. 'In the Middle Ages, they had a profession called the "hefener", so they knew exactly. The purity law lists ingredients, right? Yeast I put in there and I get more out of it. I harvest the yeast at the end and I put it into the next batch. And that was actually the job of the hefener.' It's actually hard to imagine how they couldn't have known about it. Why? Because after you brew, you end up with a fluffy layer of stuff at the bottom of the fermenter: 'Zeug. Zeug was the German word, which is "stuff". The hefener's job was to harvest the yeast from the batches, to press out as much remaining beer as possible, which was sold at a low price to the poor, and then the yeast was added to the next batch. You started with a smaller amount of yeast and then you ended with a bigger amount of yeast.' An ingredient, Wilhelm's logic went, was something that stayed in the beer.[24]

But also this explanation might be incomplete.

> The documents surrounding the dispute [the Munich Baker–Brewer Dispute] help dispel the persistent notion that since yeast wasn't mentioned in the Reinheitsgebot of 1516, Central Europeans had little idea about yeast before Pasteur. But if we have documentary evidence that Bavarians already knew about yeast, why did the Reinheitsgebot of 1516 omit any discussion of yeast? Aside from speculation that brewers and lawmakers viewed yeast more as a result of the brewing process than as

22 Ibid.

23 Mark Dredge, *A Brief History of Lager: 500 Years of the World's Favourite Beer* (Kyle Books, 2019).

24 Jeff Alworth, 'The Complex, 500-Year-Old Story of Reinheitsgebot', *Beervana* (Web Page, 6 April 2021) www.beervanablog.com/beervana/2021/4/6/the-complex-half-millenium-story-of-reinheitsgebot.

> an ingredient in its own right, the answer lies with numerous city ordinances from the fourteenth and fifteenth centuries that fed into the Bavarian law code (*Landesordnung*) of 1516. What we now call the Reinheitsgebot is but a small section in this compendium. In a word, the authorities didn't need to reinvent the wheel of previous ordinances. The law code of 1516 was a set of ordinances for an entire duchy that had only recently been reunited. Brevity in particular matters covered (like brewing) was likely a virtue. And besides, the nascent brewing industry was already familiar with the *essence* of the brewing prescriptions contained in the 1516 compendium.[25]

In other words, the fact that the 1516 *Reinheitsgebot*, applying to all of Bavaria, builds on previous law is argued to have affected the wording adopted. This obviously makes logical sense and is fully in line with how laws generally develop. In fact, Dredge states that, when making the law that includes the *Reinheitsgebot*, 'Wilhelm IV is thought to have compared his father's Munich purity law [of 1447] to the more extensive Landshut one [*Biersatzordnung* of 1493] and had to pick one of them: he went with his father's simpler one, and this became the new Bavarian law'.[26] Interestingly, while the more detailed *Biersatzordnung* of 1493 also excluded yeast from the list of ingredients, it did make reference to how brewers could sell their yeast, and it specifically distinguished between beer yeast and wine yeast![27]

This allows us to conclude that, at the time the 1516 *Reinheitsgebot* was drafted:

1. Brewers did not understand the physiology of yeast, such as that it is a living organism.
2. Brewers did, however, understand the function of yeast in brewing (and baking).
3. Brewers were also aware of different yeast types.
4. Brewers intentionally and systematically added yeast as part of the brewing process.
5. Yeast might not have been regarded as an 'ingredient' in brewing.
6. There were already local laws addressing the ingredients to be used in brewing.
7. The 1516 *Reinheitsgebot* was developed based on the local laws that preceded it.
8. In 1551 yeast was added in an updated version of the Bavarian *Reinheitsgebot*.

At any rate, the types of yeast used in brewing today fall into two main categories; ale yeasts (*Saccharomyces cerevisiae*) and lager yeasts (*Saccharomyces pastorianus*).[28]

25 Hofer (n 21).
26 Dredge (n 23).
27 Ibid.
28 Interestingly, key questions such as the origins of lager yeasts are still being debated today. See, eg, Mathias Hutzler et al, 'A New Hypothesis for the Origin of the Lager Yeast Saccharomyces Pastorianus' (2023) 23 *FEMS Yeast Research* 1.

We discuss this distinction when delving deeper into the discussion of ales versus lagers.

These days, breweries add a carefully calculated amount of yeast cells to the wort to make beer. However, that was not always the case. As noted by Bamforth:

> the ancients learned empirically that the addition of fruit to the brew would trigger the fermentation process . . . as would the transferring of the brew to containers that had previously been used to store fruit. More importantly, they realized that mixing a little of the old brew with a new one would kick the process into life. Some people refer to this by the somewhat unpleasant term 'back slopping'.[29]

In other words, the way yeast is introduced into the wort has varied, but yeast has always been a necessity for beer production. As a side note, it may be pointed out that the unpleasant sounding practice of back-slopping remains a useful cost-cutting tool for homebrewers.

While hops cannot be reused and spent grains are disposed of, for example as animal feed, breweries commonly harvest yeast from one batch, and reuse it for the next. Despite this, to maintain quality, new yeast is normally used after five or six successive fermentations. Once no longer reusable in the brewing process, the yeast may still have value. It is, for example, used in products such as Australia's Vegemite and the UK's Marmite.

1.2.4 *Water*

What is the main ingredient in beer? Well, given the heading here it is not too difficult to figure out the answer to that question. However, despite clearly being the main ingredient in beer, the reality is that water is often overlooked as an ingredient. Yet the importance of the water cannot be overstated. First of all, proximity to a water source was one of the traditional essentials for choosing a brewery location. Huge quantities of water are required both as an ingredient, as we discuss here, and for cleaning brewery equipment. Furthermore, before the steam engine, breweries often relied on water power for the operation of the brewery.

The profile of the water is key for giving beer its characteristics. Indeed, several of the world's most famous beer types are strongly associated with the character of the water used. For example, the famous Czech pilsner needs to be brewed with very soft water, while some of the most distinctive English ales are brewed with the very hard water of Burton-upon-Trent. Hard water contains more minerals (such as calcium and magnesium) than soft water, while soft water may have higher salt concentrations.

While minerals occur naturally in water, brewers commonly add brewing salts, such as calcium sulphate and calcium chloride, to manipulate the water chemistry

[29] Bamforth (n 18) 15.

according to the style they are brewing. For example, the 'chloride to sulphate ratio' is an important aspect of a beer recipe, with more chloride giving a softer body and more sulphate accentuating hop bitterness. It is, of course, true that these minerals can be seen as adjuncts and should thus be discussed in the relevant section below rather than here. However, since even the strict German *Reinheitsgebot* allows the addition of some minerals, it seems more logical to note them here.

1.2.5 *Traditional, and Non-traditional, Adjuncts*

The idea of adding adjuncts – ingredients beyond the quartet of malt, hops, yeast, and water – in the brewing process may seem unappealing. Purity is attractive and purity sells. This is so also beyond Germany's strict purity regime.

Nevertheless, the reality is that many of the most popular beer styles from around the world not only benefit from, but depend upon, the use of adjuncts. American Lager commonly contains adjuncts such as rice and corn, and you cannot brew a Belgian witbier without adding spice (commonly coriander and bitter orange zest). Autumn beers maintain a respectable position despite containing various spices, and a Fruit Lambic would not be possible without, well, fruit. Indeed, for anyone who has been following the 'craft beer scene', one thing is clear; you can put just about anything in beer.

Looking at the most common adjuncts, we may usefully start by observing that some adjuncts are only adjuncts from a certain point of view. While a beer *must* contain malted grains (unless mashing enzymes are added[30]), it *may* also contain unmalted grains. Such unmalted grains are typically seen as an adjunct. Whether viewed as an adjunct or not, unmalted grains may contribute in a variety of ways. For example, unmalted wheat may add a strong grain flavour, create a cloudiness, and improve head formation.

Another adjunct that we may not instinctively think of as an adjunct is CO_2. At least for the bigger beer brands, it is an almost universal practice in many countries to add carbonation to beer before packaging. Strictly speaking, CO_2 added in that manner is an adjunct. Those seeking to truly comply with the *Reinheitsgebot* must rely on natural carbonation; that is, they must capture the CO_2 produced during fermentation and use that to carbonate their beer.[31]

Sugar may be added to a range of beers. Some styles are the way they are due to a clever use of added sugars. This is particularly the case with a range of strong Belgian beers (such as Duvel, and many of the Trappist beers) that get their higher alcohol level, dryness, and thinner body in large parts due to the added sugars. Indeed, in the

[30] Shiwen Zhuang et al, 'Brewing with 100% Unmalted Grains: Barley, Wheat, Oat and Rye' (2017) 243(3) *European Food Research & Technology* 447.

[31] Alworth (n 24).

case of darker beers using caramelized sugars, the sugar also adds colour and contributes to the distinct flavours.

Before leaving the topic of sugar, it should be noted that not all sugars are the same and the different sugars have different impacts on the beer. Many of the Belgian styles referred to above utilize so-called candi sugar or candi sugar syrups. Another specific type of sugar that has its particular effect on the beer is lactose, used for example in milk stouts. Since lactose is not fully fermentable by beer yeast, it leaves a residual sweetness in the beer.

Looking at additives, it has also been noted that 'small amounts of inorganic and organic materials used as preservatives (e.g. sulphur dioxide) or for preventing turbidity (e.g. papain, a proteolytic enzyme)'[32] may be added to the beer. In this context, reference may also be made to substances such as isinglass used for fining and stabilizing the beer.

Rice is used as an adjunct, or indeed the primary ingredient, in some beers, not least in many Japanese and Taiwanese beers, but also in the well-known American Lager beer like Budweiser. In fact, '[t]he single biggest use for rice in the United States is for the production of Budweiser products'.[33] Where rice is used instead of barley, the beer may be gluten-free.

Maize, or corn, may also be used as the primary source of carbohydrates. This is the case in some traditional beer-like alcoholic beverages, particularly in Latin America and Africa. More commonly, corn may also serve as an adjunct for mass-market beer production throughout the world. Finally, many native African 'beers' are produced with malted sorghum and millets as key ingredients.

Before leaving the topic of adjuncts, one final point must be made: the addition of adjuncts is one way in which the beer industry shows innovation – innovation that commonly clashes with tradition (a theme we explore further throughout the book). To take one example, 'Phantasm' is a powder made from sauvignon blanc grape skins from the Marlborough region of New Zealand. It is rich in the 'thiol precursors' (also found in certain types of hops) that help create tropical or citrus aromas in beer.[34] Particularly when used in combination with certain types of yeast (so-called thiolizing yeasts), the Phantasm powder can provide a strong tropical or citrus aroma. This is a great example illustrating that, despite its long history, real innovations still occur.

1.3 THE BREWING PROCESS

The brewing process is, of course, something one should experience rather than read about. But now that we are familiar with the ingredients, let us look at the

[32] Hough (n 8) 4.
[33] Bamforth (n 18) 121.
[34] Michael Donaldson, 'NZ Creation Phantasm Revolutionises Beer World', *Pursuit of Hoppiness* (Web Page, 1 September 2022) https://hoppiness.co.nz/nz-creation-phantasm-revolutionises-beer-world.

brewing process. Before doing so, however, it must be understood that different styles of beer require different processes. This is no doubt unsurprising and similar to how baking sourdough bread involves a different process to baking a traditional baguette. Thus, here we will primarily focus on describing the 'standard' brewing process used for most beers so that later on – throughout the book – we can make some remarks about variations of this process used to produce what somewhat imprecisely may be termed non-standard styles of beer.

Some view the malting of the grains as the first step in the brewing process, but assuming that the malting has been completed, the first step in the standard brewing process involves crushing the malt (the term 'milling' is often used). This makes possible the extraction of the sugars in the grains that otherwise would be inaccessible due to the hard surface of each grain.

In the second step, warm water and the milled grains are added in a vessel referred to as a 'mash tun' creating what is referred to as the 'mash'. Predictably the mash looks a lot like porridge. The ratio of water to grain may vary, but two to four litres of water per kilogram of grain is a common guide, at least for small-scale brewing. The water is then typically recirculated through the 'grain bed' for a period of time. The duration of this step depends on what type of mashing process the brewer has adopted. While there are others, the three standard types of mashing processes are:

- *Step mashing* – the mash temperature is progressively increased through a series of so-called rests. For example, by holding the mash at 35–45°C the brewer may carry out what is known as an 'acid rest' aimed at lowering the mash pH and to break down glucans, while holding the mash at rest at a higher temperature range (61–71°C) – the 'saccharification rest' – is necessary for converting starch into sugars.
- *Infusion mashing* – the mash is kept in the 'saccharification rest' for the entire mash process. With the quality of malts available today, this simple mash type has become prevalent for many styles.
- *Decoction mashing* – the brewer takes out a portion of the thicker part of the mash and brings that part to a boil. The boiled portion of the mash is then returned to the mash tun. This creates the Maillard effect. Decoction mashing is relatively rare these days but is an essential component in the making of a traditional pilsner.

The temperature of the mash impacts several things, including the fermentability of the resulting wort – a higher mash temperature may result in sweeter and more full-bodied beer, while a lower mash temperature provides a drier, crisper, and thinner beer.

After the mashing, in step three, the liquid – called 'wort' – is separated from the grains (now referred to as 'spent grains') and warm water is sprayed onto the grains to further extract the remaining sugars. This process is referred to as 'sparging', and after the sparging, the spent grains may then be used, for example as animal feed.

In step four, the wort is boiled in a so-called brew kettle.[35] Again, the duration may vary but a boil duration of 60 minutes is relatively common. During the boil, hops are typically added, but both the amounts of hops added and the timing of adding the hops vary based on style. As the oils in the hops are highly volatile, hops added early in the boil will typically only add bitterness, while hops added later in the boil may add both aroma and flavour (as well as bitterness, but at a lower rate than hops added early). The boil fulfils several important functions. Apart from being an opportunity to add the flavour and aroma contribution of the hops to the wort, the boil stops enzyme action, coagulates some proteins, sterilizes the wort, and adds a degree of Maillard effect.

Once the boil is completed, the whirlpool process in step five commences. This process relies upon the 'tea leaf paradox'. The 'tea leaf paradox' refers to the fact that, while one may expect that the spiral centrifuge caused by stirring a cup of tea would result in the tea leaves gathering on the sides of the cup, they instead gather in the centre and bottom of the cup due to friction causing the water to slow down there. In the context of the whirlpool process, this means that the spiral centrifuge in the wort helps separate hop substance and sediment from the grains (known as 'trub') from the wort.

The whirlpool also represents an opportunity to add additional hops. Hops added at this stage contribute limited bitterness but significant aroma and flavour. Beers styles such as American pale ales (APAs), IPAs, and Pacific Ales commonly rely on very large amounts of hops added in the whirlpool.

Step six is to cool the wort. This needs to be done quickly since the hops continue to impart bitterness for as long as the wort is warm. The wort is then transferred to a 'fermentation vessel'.

Step seven involves aerating the wort, thereby creating a more hospitable environment for the yeast which is added ('pitched') as step eight. In step nine, fermentation occurs. Fermentation involves the yeast eating the sugars and thereby producing alcohol and carbon dioxide (CO_2). But the yeast does a lot more than that during fermentation. Yeast metabolites add to the flavour and aroma of the finished beer.

It is during the fermentation that the wort is turned into beer. So, from that point of view, fermentation is the last step in producing beer. However, while some beer styles are served – and taste their best – as soon as possible after fermentation is complete, most beers go through a maturation and clarifying process either before (such as 'lagering') or after (cask beers) packaging.

A key consideration during fermentation, and also during lagering, is the temperature. Where beer is fermented at a lower temperature than the yeast can handle,

[35] Some beer styles omit this step. Such beers are commonly referred to as 'raw ale'. See Lars Marius Garshol, 'Raw Ale', *Larsblog* (Blog Post, 5 June 2015) www.garshol.priv.no/blog/331.html.

fermentation slows down and eventually stops. And where fermentation takes place at a higher temperature than suits the yeast strain in question, off-flavours ranging from sour to grassy may be created. Too high a fermentation temperature may also result in the production of fusel alcohols (alcohols with more than two carbons), which can make the beer taste 'harsh', 'alcoholic', and 'hot'. This is perhaps the most common indicator of too high a fermentation temperature and is different to the 'softer' alcohol flavour that may be appropriate in some styles such as a Belgian Golden Strong Ale or a Baltic Porter.

The alcohol strength of beer is typically expressed as alcohol by volume (ABV). This may be measured with sophisticated instruments. But by measuring the density of the wort before fermentation commences (so-called original gravity (OG)) and comparing that to the density of the beer after fermentation (so-called final gravity (FG)), brewers can also calculate the alcohol level of the beer. An alternative to the OG–FG system is to focus on the percentage by weight of sucrose in the water measured in degrees Plato (°P).

Before packaging, the beer may also – depending on style and brewer – be either sterile-filtered or pasteurized. And here we get to a frequently overlooked fact, as noted by Bamforth, that it is the bottle that is the most expensive component of a bottle of beer![36]

1.3.1 *Designing Beer Recipes*

The discussion of the ingredients used in beer, not least when combined with that of the brewing process, highlights that possible variations in the design of beer recipes are almost endless. The combination of the choice of malts and how they are mashed, the amount and type of hops and when they are added, the choice of yeast strain and the temperature of the fermentation all open up radically different result. Looking at hops, for example, a paper from 2021 notes: 'There are more than 250 catalogued varieties of hops, and among the main attributes that differ from each other are alpha-acids, beta-acids, and essential oils. Those components give the beer a unique combination of characteristics and may even influence its category.'[37] To this may be added that new types of malts, hops, and yeasts are constantly developed.

In fact, when it comes to designing beer recipes, the main limitation seems to be our imagination. And with increasing use of generative artificial intelligence (GenAI), this is perhaps also becoming less of a limitation. Several breweries have now turned to GenAI to come up with new beers. In part, this is no doubt a gimmick. However, it does open up the fast creation of lots of new recipes that it

[36] Bamforth (n 18) 101.

[37] Pedro Castro, Eduardo Luz, and Gladston Moreira, 'Dataset for Hop Varieties Classification' (2021) 38 *Data in Brief* 107312.

could take a skilled brewer some time to come up with. Importantly for what we cover in this book, the use of GenAI to design beers also opens up some legal issues. But before briefly looking at those legal issues, it is worth saying a few words about the key question of how good GenAI is at generating beer recipes.

We tested this by asking GenAI to 'write a recipe for brewing a 40-litre batch of Irish red ale meeting the BJCP [Beer Judge Certification Program] guidelines'.[38] 'Irish red ale' is a beer style best known due to the famous 'Kilkenny Irish Beer', and the BJCP guidelines are – as discussed in more detail below – beer style guides used by judges in brewing competitions.

To start with the positive, all the recipes generated would represent a good starting point for brewing an Irish red ale. However, all were associated with issues ranging from serious to minor flaws that an experienced brewer could easily work around.

One of the recipes generated by GenAI misrepresented vital statistics from the BJCP guidelines. While the acceptable colour of an Irish red ale ranges from 9 to 14 SRM under the current BJCP guidelines, the GenAI recipe claimed that the acceptable colour range per the BJCP guidelines is 10–18 SRM. Here, GenAI was simply incorrect. Further, while the acceptable range of alcohol for an Irish red ale under the current BJCP guidelines is 3.8–5.0 per cent ABV, one of the GenAI recipes made clear that the resulting beer would be expected to be in the range of 5.4–6.1 per cent ABV. Thus, the recipe put forward did not meet the criteria for complying with the BJCP guidelines as requested in the instructions.

Turning to smaller, yet relevant, concerns, it may also be noted that one recipe was based on using 40 litres of water. But due to the loss of water, through evaporation during the boil for example, using 40 litres of water as the starting point will not produce a 40-litre batch as requested in the instructions provided.

So, what can we learn from the above? Well, most obviously we can see that GenAI can be factually incorrect. That alone should be enough to warn brewers not to rely on GenAI as the only source. Second, the experiment highlighted GenAI's inability to comply with the instructions. Third, as could be expected, GenAI makes obvious mistakes due to failing to understand context – important in legal writing.

It is easy to be impressed by GenAI and to assume that perfection is just around the corner. But when it comes to AI, the step between impressively close to perfect and actual perfection is large indeed. To see that this is so, just do some research as to how many times we have been told that we are 'two to three years' away from fully self-driving cars.

Leaving aside these technical brewing issues, brewers tempted to use GenAI may also wish to consider the legal issues involved, even though most of the legal issues may not directly affect the brewer using such a tool.

[38] This test was first discussed in Dan Svantesson, 'What Beer Brewing Can Teach Law Students about ChatGPT', *Bond University* (Blog Post, 2 February 2023) https://bond.edu.au/blog/what-beer-brewing-can-teach-law-students-about-chatgpt.

To 'work its magic', GenAI needs to be trained on large volumes of data. How that data is acquired is often a closely guarded secret, but one thing is clear – the quality of the data impacts the quality of the output. This means that providers of GenAI have an interest in acquiring high-quality datasets that may be protected in various ways – for example, sitting behind a paywall, and protected by terms-of-use agreements. Furthermore, copyright protection – a topic we address in Chapter 5 – must obviously also be considered in this context. This is true both in the context of how training data is acquired, and in relation to the output generated by GenAI, such as a beer recipe. At the time of writing, one relevant matter before the court is how the location of training is defined.[39] Another is whether an AI model could qualify as an infringing copy of its training data.[40] All this will clearly impact the future use of GenAI in the design of beer recipes.

Before concluding this section, one additional legal issue ought to be noted. Where a brewer uses GenAI to generate a beer recipe and the resulting beer turns out to be harmful to consume, complex liability issues may arise. However, we will not go into them in detail here.

1.4 A VERY BRIEF HISTORY OF BEER AND BREWING

The making and consumption of beer has a long history. A history we are here planning to summarize in less than two pages. Unrealistic? Yes, but the aim is just to provide a bit of a context. The discussions throughout the rest of the book talk more about the history of beer and law. Some chapters do so from the perspective of a selection of areas of law, and others – the country chapters – do so from a broader persecutive. Here we merely wish to say a few words about the older history of beer and beer drinking.

The birth of beer is placed around 4000 BCE and it is generally the Mesopotamians that get credited with the honour of being the true beer pioneers.[41] This claim may no doubt build on a Mesopotamian hymn to Ninkasi – the Sumerian goddess of brewing – dating back to at least 1800 BC that is regarded as the world's earliest recorded 'beer recipe'. It is comprehensive in its details and covers both the malting process, how the wort is inoculated with both honey and wine to start the fermentation, and filtering of the finished product.[42]

Recent research suggests that rice was the first cereal used to produce beer (although it was what we may now term a fruit beer). McGovern points to 'a complex beverage consisting of a grape and hawthorn-fruit wine, honey mead, and rice beer' dating back 9,000 years to the village of Jiahu in the Henan province

[39] *Getty Images (US) Inc & Ors v Stability AI Ltd* [2023] EWHC 3090.

[40] Ibid.

[41] Bamforth (n 18) 26.

[42] Patrick E McGovern, *Uncorking the Past: The Quest for Wine, Beer, and Other Alcoholic Beverages* (University of California Press, 1st ed, 2009) 64. See also Bamforth (n 18) 27–8.

of present-day China.[43] Then again, there are even more recent findings pointing to beer brewing in a cave in present-day Israel some 13,000 years ago, making beer – even if a very different beer to what we drink today – the oldest recorded man-made alcohol in the world.[44] But then again that may depend on how we define 'man-made', since there is also circumstantial evidence for the production of mead, fermented honey, in Border Cave (now in South Africa) as early as 40,000 years ago.[45] Perhaps the conclusion is that we are unlikely to ever know who brewed the first beer and where.

What we do know is that the understanding of, and appreciation for, beer and brewing does not have a single source from which it spread to the rest of the world. Rather, the discovery of alcohol in general and beer in particular happened as independent discoveries at different times and locations.[46] Regardless of who is currently credited as the first documented inventor of beer, other peoples of other times were also equally inventors of beer, only a bit later, and at a different location.

To give a proper account of the history of beer we actually have to take a step back to a time prior to the production of beer and focus on a specific key component of beer – namely alcohol. And to do that properly, we have to go back approximately 10 million years. Dunbar has highlighted that, back then, 'ancestors of the African apes (the gorillas, chimpanzees and humans) evolved a pair of enzymes that allowed them to convert alcohol back into useable sugars'.[47] This allowed our distant ancestors to consumer fermenting fruits from the forest floor, and this obviously provides an additional food source, giving an evolutionary advantage. Incidentally, the fruit in question is of about the same alcohol strength as beer (around 4 per cent ABV).

This thought is mindboggling. But it merely represents the start of alcohol consumption of our more direct predecessors. The history of alcohol is much, much older than that; it has been observed: 'Some four billion years ago, primitive single-celled microbes are hypothesized to have dined on simple sugars in the primordial soup and excreted ethanol and carbon dioxide. A kind of carbonated alcoholic beverage would thus have been available right from the beginning.'[48]

43 McGovern (n 42) 41.

44 Melissa De Witte, 'An Ancient Thirst for Beer May Have Inspired Agriculture, Stanford Archaeologists Say', *Stanford Report* (Web Page, 12 September 2018) https://news.stanford.edu/stories/2018/09/crafting-beer-lead-cereal-cultivation#:~:text=readArts%20%26%20Humanities-,An%20ancient%20thirst%20for%20beer%20may%20have%20inspired%20agriculture%2C%20Stanford,underlying%20motivation%20to%20cultivate%20cereals; Li Liu et al, 'Fermented Beverage and Food Storage in 13,000 y-old Stone Mortars at Raqefet Cave, Israel: Investigating Natufian Ritual Feasting' (2018) 21 *Journal of Archaeological Science* 783.

45 Neil Rusch, 'Controlled Fermentation, Honey, Bees and Alcohol: Archaeological and Ethnohistorical Evidence from Southern Africa' (2020) 33(1) *South African Humanities* 1.

46 Bamforth (n 18) 25.

47 Robin Dunbar, 'The Social Function of Alcohol from an Evolutionary Perspective' in Riadh Abed and Paul St John-Smith (eds), *Evolutionary Psychiatry Current Perspectives on Mental Health* (Cambridge University Press, 2022) 203.

48 McGovern (n 42) 13.

It is generally accepted that the reason humans started to settle down in year-round settlements in the Neolithic period was tied in part to the domestication of wild barley. This has been seen as the start of 'civilization'. The question then is what was the domesticated barley used for? After all, there is evidence that humans were both brewing beer and baking bread (around 13,000 years ago) before becoming farmers. Many scholars have suggested that barley bread was the driving force for this Neolithic revolution. However, since the 1950s a debate has been ongoing over whether perhaps rather than a hunger for bread, it was a thirst for beer that was the reason humans stopped being hunter-gatherers and settled down, creating so-called civilization. The 1953 symposium 'Did Man Once Live by Beer Alone?' gives a fascinating insight into the debate that continues today.[49]

Intuitively, we may think that overcoming hunger takes priority over any desire to become intoxicated. This, of course, speaks in favour of bread as the driving force. However, recent scholarship has pointed out that 'high labour inputs, low yield and easily ruined crops of early cultivation would have made cereals unsuitable for a sustenance diet, while the social, cultural and ritual importance of beer "was likely a major motivating factor for cultivating and domesticating cereals in the Near East"'.[50] Put simply, while early farming could not produce enough barley to be a reliable main source of food, it could produce enough to be a reliable source of beer. The debate will no doubt go on.

So, to conclude this very brief history of beer and brewing, it is possible that our species would not have become dominant had we not been able to consume alcohol, and it is possible that our thirst for beer was a key driving force in one of humanity's most important 'civilizing' developments – the creation of permanent settlements. Cheers to that!

1.5 BEER AS A PRODUCT

If you think about the word 'beer', what images comes to mind? Sparkling amber liquid in sunlight with a large frothy head of white foam? A velvety brown foam on top of black beer in front of a fire? Or perhaps drunk teenagers surrounded by squashed-up beer cans throwing up in a park? Beer as a product can evoke many and varied responses.

Perhaps the first thing we need to recognize when discussing beer as a product is that it naturally contains alcohol and that therefore it has been treated differently to many other products throughout history. The alcohol aspect of beer has sometimes

49 Robert J Braidwood et al, 'Symposium: Did Man Once Live by Beer Alone?' (1953) 55(4) *American Anthropologist* 515.

50 Ted Child, 'What Came First: The Beer or the Bread?', *The Growler* (Blog Post, 30 June 2023) https://bc.thegrowler.ca/history/what-came-first-the-beer-or-the-bread/. See also Jennie Cohen, 'Did Beer Spur the Rise of Agriculture and Politics?', *History* (Web Page, 23 August 2018) www.history.com/news/did-beer-spur-the-rise-of-agriculture-and-politics.

placed it alongside magic and mystery, and at other times – as mentioned – resulted in it being seen as such a harmful product that it must be banned. But measured in volume of consumption throughout history, it seems reasonable to suggest that there are reasons other than alcohol's effect as such that have prompted the consumption. Much of the beer that has been consumed throughout history has been relatively low in alcohol and the consumption has been driven by the fact that beer was the safest accessible drink. Thus, while alcohol is a natural aspect of beer, the desire to get drunk has only ever been one – arguably subordinate – reason why beer has been the preferred drink. And today, the production of low- or no-alcohol beers is a booming market. We discuss this further throughout the book.

1.5.1 *Beer Styles and Classifications*

Categorizing beers into styles is not as easy as it may sound. First, most things in brewing are matters of degree rather than binary. Second, the style landscape is not set in stone; rather it is constantly evolving as new styles are created and become popular, and other styles fall out of favour. For example, the current Beer Judge Certification Program '2021 Beer Style Guidelines'[51] used to assess beers in most amateur brewing competitions contains more than 130 different styles delineated by reference to factors such as alcohol strength, colour, fermentation profile, region of origin, style family, era, clarity, mouthfeel, body, bitterness, aroma, and flavour. The Brewers Association's '2023 Beer Style Guidelines' – used in many competitions for commercial brewers – are even more comprehensive, delineating over 160 beer styles.[52]

Nevertheless, the style distinction that most beer drinkers have heard of – although may not fully have understood – is between lagers and ales. It is often noted that fundamentally the difference between ales and lagers is that, while ales rely on top-fermenting yeast, lagers use bottom-fermenting yeast. This is correct in that, when it comes to bottom-fermentation the yeast tends to sink to the bottom of the brewing vessel at the end of fermentation while the yeast in top-fermentation tends rise to the top of the fermentation vessel after fermentation. For anyone who is careful about terminology (as lawyers tend to be), the terms 'bottom-fermentation' and 'top-fermentation' are highly misleading. As has been pointed out, if you '[o]-bserve an active fermentation for any length of time . . . you immediately notice that yeast activity is distributed throughout the liquid'.[53] In other words, beer

[51] Gordon Strong and Kristen England, '2021 Beer Style Guidelines', *Beer Judge Certification Program* (Web Page) www.bjcp.org/download/2021_Guidelines_Beer.pdf.

[52] Brewers Association, '2023 Beer Style Guidelines', *Brewers Association* (Web Page, 18 May 2023) https://cdn.brewersassociation.org/wp-content/uploads/2023/07/10124402/2023_BA_Beer_Style_Guidelines-updated.pdf.

[53] Dave Carpenter, 'What Is the Difference between Ale and Lager?', *Craft Beer & Brewing* (Web Page, 18 May 2017) https://beerandbrewing.com/what-is-the-difference-between-ale-and-lager/.

fermentation – whether for ales or lagers – takes place both at the top and at the bottom, and indeed, in between the top and the bottom. The better view is that we need, at least, a two-factor test to distinguish ales from lagers; first we ask what type of yeast was used, and second we ask at what temperature the fermentation took place.

As discussed above, ales are fermented using yeast strains of *Saccharomyces cerevisiae*. Lagers are fermented using yeast strains of *Saccharomyces pastorianus*. Ales are fermented warm (generally 16–24°C) which results in an increased creation of by-products, including esters and phenols, affecting both flavour and aroma – a desirable result in an ale but typically a fault in a lager. Lagers are fermented cold (generally 7–13°C), which suppresses many of the by-products of yeast fermentation. Interestingly, there is a link to the law here in that Duke Albrecht V of Bavaria, via a 1553 decree, prohibited summer brewing, causing brewers to unknowingly select cold-tolerant yeasts, driving the evolution of lager yeasts.[54]

If you either ferment warm with yeast strains of *Saccharomyces pastorianus*, or cold with yeast strains of *Saccharomyces cerevisiae*, you get a 'hybrid beer'. One of the most well-known examples of such a hybrid is the style now referred to as 'California Common' made famous by San Francisco's 'Anchor Steam beer'. It is a hybrid beer fermented with a lager yeast at the temperature range of an ale.

But we are not quite done with the distinction between ales and lagers. Lagers are called lagers for a reason. The origin is found in the German verb *Lagern* which means 'to store'. Lagering is a form of beer maturation, at or near-freezing temperatures, lasting weeks or even months. It takes place after fermentation but before filtration and packaging of the beer. While any traditional lager is lagered, ales are typically not. But also in this context, we can find interesting and much-loved hybrids. For example, Cologne's famous Kölsch beer is fermented with an ale yeast but is then lagered.

To conclude, arguably the best approach to distinguishing between ales and lagers is to adopt a three-factor test focused on:

1. Type of yeast strain;
2. Fermentation temperature; and
3. Lagering.

Looking beyond the lager vs ale distinction, the beer style landscape is – as demonstrated above – rich indeed. So, what if anything does law have to do with beer styles? Well, the answer is that law may impact beer styles in many different ways. Perhaps most obviously, where a brewery claims that its beer is of a particular style, the claim may be held to be misleading if the beer does not correspond with that style; such cases are, however, seemingly rare. But from a legal point of view, these issues may be particularly serious where matters such as alcohol level or the presence of potential allergens are misrepresented. It is also likely that a consumer

[54] Ibid.

buying a can of 'Imperial Stout' would feel deceived if the can contains a light lager. We discuss issues such as these throughout the book.

Another aspect where the law impacts beer styles is in relation to so-called geographical indication (GI). Such issues are discussed further in Chapter 5. Relatedly, but more generally, domestic laws may specify that to be allowed to be marketed as a specific beer style, certain conditions, for example as to percentages of ingredients need to be met. Some such situations are discussed throughout this book.

1.5.2 *Mass-Market Beer vs Craft Beer*

Writing in 2008, Professor Bamforth claimed that, for beer, '[t]here is no concept of vintage'[55] and argued that 'Beers might fairly be marketed on the basis of hop "varietal" just as much as is a wine on a grape varietal. Invariably they aren't'.[56] These are interesting observations, and ones that doubtless hold true for the mainstream mass-market beers. Such beers are primarily sold by brand. However, if we turn to the craft beer sector, the packaging and other promotional materials often emphasize the types of hops used, just as grape varietals are highlighted in the sale of wines.

More broadly, it is interesting to consider just how different the craft brewing sector is to the 'normal' mass-market brewing industry. In fact, in most regards, the craft brewing sector is more similar to the wine industry than it is to the beer industry.[57] This is illustrated, in a somewhat oversimplified manner, in Table 1.1.

While the producers of both wine and craft beer commonly emphasize – and indeed take pride in – the variations from batch to batch (we can stick with the term 'vintage'), consistency is the guiding principle for mass-market beer producers. Each batch of the beer needs to taste the same, smell the same, and look the same. In relation to such beers, the consumer knows what they will get, and successful producers ensure that they deliver just that.

The 'vintage focus' of the craft beer industry is partly driven by the need to constantly produce something new that will excite the consumers. It is also a tool to create scarcity and exclusivity. Consumers feel they must buy the newly released oak lagered banana and chocolate sour, or whatever the new beer may be, because it is part of a limited release and if they do not have it now, they will miss out. But there is also a more pragmatic reason for the craft beer industry's vintage focus – consistency in beer brewing is expensive and hard to achieve. Thus, the vintage focus is to no small degree a result of the brewers' inability to produce beer with the

55 Bamforth (n 18) 190.

56 Ibid 97.

57 For a fascinating and entertaining account of the differences and similarities between beer and wine, see Bamforth (n 18).

TABLE 1.1 *Standard beer, craft beer, and wine: a comparison*

	Standard beer	Craft beer	Wine
Focus on consistency	X		
Vintage variations		X	X
Exclusivity		X	X
Low price	X		
Terroir		X	X
Ceremony of tasting		X	X
A topic of discussion		X	X

consistency of the mass-market breweries. Doing so requires the tools and skill to adjust the process and recipe based on differences between different batches of ingredients. For example, even assuming that a small brewer manages to ensure a consistent acquisition of the hops it uses (which may be a great challenge in itself), important characteristics of the hops may vary from harvest to harvest. Consequently, adding 8 grams of Saaz hops per litre for a 60-minute boil may create a different level of bitterness from one time to another unless the hops come from the same harvest (and even then, the result may vary based on how old the hops are at the time they are used).

The focus on exclusivity, scarcity, and vintage variations also links into the product pricing. There are several reasons that craft beer is more expensive than mass-market beers. Most importantly, it is more cost-effective to brew larger batches and the mass-producers' efficiencies, for example in packaging and distribution, also allow them to sell at lower prices. But many craft beer enthusiasts might be sceptical of craft beers sold at a low price. Perhaps having paid a higher price creates an expectation of the product being superior and more interesting.

The concept of terroir is hotly debated in wine circles. At the same time, in most countries, it is nearly impossible to imagine drinkers of the standard beers debating terroir in relation to the products they consume.[58] That is not to suggest that it is wrong to discuss terroir in relation to beer – all the ingredients in beer may be discussed from that perspective. But we just do not do that for standard beers. Also in this context, craft beer is then more similar to wine than it is to the mass-market beers. Craft beers and wine are often the topic of conversation while they are being consumed, but that seems relatively pointless if you drink the same mass-produced beer all the time – successfully produced, it will taste exactly the same each time.

58 A possible exception here is the beer-crazy country Czechia, where it is quite common to hear discussions about which pub serves the best pilsner (referring to *Pilsner Urquell* – the only beer referred to as pilsner in its country of origin). While all pilsner is brewed in the same place and should taste the same everywhere, factors such as the cleanliness of the beer lines and the skill of the person pouring the beer impact its taste. In a sense, this is then terroir-style thinking applying to a mass-market beer.

For the same reason, beer tastings have become popular in relation to the craft beer scene but remains rare for the mass-market beers.

The law has shaped the craft brew scene in each country to a large degree. Most obviously, tax laws strongly impact the viability of a craft brew scene. However, that is not all. Countries adhering to strict 'purity requirements' may be leaving less scope for creativity and may, as a result, stifle innovation. More broadly, it has been noted that:

> Interestingly, in countries with strong brewing industries, the craft beer market is developing slowly ... The production of conventional beers (and the number of breweries) and craft beers is not proportional and the number of microbreweries is not as important as their size because it directly influences production. Czech Republic with more than 410 craft breweries in 2019 and Ireland with 75 craft breweries had a market share of 2% in 2019 ... and 2.8% in 2017 ... respectively. On the other hand, in countries such as Belgium, large beer companies tend to absorb craft breweries and the products become just another variety in the catalogue ... This affects interest in craft beers and their research, as consumers believe they are industrially produced. In China, craft beer production is limited because it is difficult to acquire quality local ingredients, so imports significantly increase production costs ... In addition, since there are no laws designed specifically for craft breweries, microbrewers must follow the stringent regulations for industrial producers ... Similarly, Mexican government measures such as the application of a 26.5% special tax on the production and sale of beer regardless of the size of the brewery blocked the growing production of craft beer.[59]

As is made clear in the above, craft beer has a certain attractiveness and typically sells at a considerably higher price than does its mass-market sibling. This clearly makes it attractive to portray a product as a craft beer. But before leaving the topic of the difference between mass-market beer and craft beer, it is interesting to pause to consider what exactly we mean by 'craft beer'.

In a generic – non-legal – sense it may perhaps be said that there are three key characteristics associated with those brewing craft beer: small-scale, independent, and 'craftsmanship'. But craft breweries are often also associated with other characteristics such as a local engagement, local distribution, local taproom, the use of local ingredients, unique batches, seasonal ranges, an aim for distinctiveness, and an innovative spirit.

On some markets, 'genuine' craft breweries are certified by some organization such as an industry association. For example, in 2017 the Brewers Association launched 'The independent craft brewer seal' in the US.[60] To be classed as an American craft brewery and be granted this seal, three requirements must be met:

[59] Vicente Amirpasha Tirado-Kulieva et al, 'A Comprehensive Review of the Benefits of Drinking Craft Beer: Role of Phenolic Content in Health and Possible Potential of the Alcoholic Fraction' (2023) 6 *Current Research in Food Science* 100477.

[60] Craft Beer, 'Seek the Seal™', *CraftBeer.com* (Web Page) www.craftbeer.com/breweries/independent-craft-brewer-seal.

Small

Annual production of 6 million barrels[61] of beer or less (approximately 3 percent of U.S. annual sales). Beer production is attributed to a brewer according to rules of alternating proprietorships.

Independent

Less than 25 percent of the craft brewery is owned or controlled (or equivalent economic interest) by a beverage alcohol industry member that is not itself a craft brewer.

Brewer

Has a TTB Brewer's Notice[[62]] and makes beer.

The ability to issue such 'seals of approval' provides great power, and in some markets, competing – or at least overlapping – bodies have been formed. That was, for example, the case in Australia some years ago when there were two national bodies aiming to represent Australia's craft brewers, and it was noted that there was a risk of a situation similar to the comical scene in Monty Python's classic 'Life of Brian' with competing factions being more focused on each other than on the common enemy, the Roman occupiers.[63]

At any rate, we will have reason to return to the matter of what amounts to a 'craft beer' on several occasions throughout the book.

1.6 WHAT DOES THE LAW RECOGNIZE AS BEER?

Above, we discussed matters such as beer styles, beer ingredients, and the brewing process. But there is a fundamental issue we have avoided: How do you know that what you are drinking is a 'beer'? The answer to this question is actually less straightforward than most beer drinkers might have imagined. The answer depends on both time and place – and most importantly for our book, it depends on the law. Beer laws – like all laws – vary depending on place, as each country makes its own laws. Indeed, laws may vary on a regional basis within some countries, as, for example, was the case in Germany.

Further, beer laws, like other laws, have varied over time and something recognized as 'beer' at one point in time might not qualify as beer in another time with a different regulatory framework. We may here think of the situation for brewers before and after the introduction of the German *Reinheitsgebot*.

[61] One barrel is 117.347844 litres to be exact.

[62] Office of Communications, 'Brewer's Notice', *Alcohol and Tobacco Tax and Trade Bureau US Department* (Web Page, 26 January 2020) www.ttb.gov/beer/ttb-beer-brewers-notice.

[63] Crafty Pint, 'Take Two', *The Crafty Pint* (Web Page, 16 November 2011) https://craftypint.com/news/272/take-two.

But while the impact time and location might have on the definition of what is classed as 'beer' might have been predictable, it should also be noted that what counts as beer may depend on context. For example, the law may define beer in a particular way for tax purposes, but in a different way in the context of food standards. That is perhaps not as strange as it may first sound. As we elaborate on below, tax laws might be targeting the consumption of alcohol, which may explain why, for example, beer needs to contain more than 1.15 per cent of alcohol by volume to be classed under Australia's excise law.[64] At the same time, food standards laws aim to meet other objectives, which in turn explains why the Australia New Zealand Food Standards Code will not recognize a product as beer unless it is 'characterised by the presence of hops or preparations of hops'.[65] This means that we may have a product that is commonly thought of as beer – such as a low- or no-alcohol beer – that is beer under one legal definition but not another. Particularly in the case of exports, where the producer may be unfamiliar with the law of the receiving country, these definitional differences may cause a considerable headache.

Looking at some of the countries included in our study, we find a range of definitions of beer, the most famous being the already discussed German *Reinheitsgebot* and its focus on beer being made only using barley malt, hops, and water (and yeast). The Swedish Alkohollag (2010:1622) (Alcohol law) defines beer as:

> Beer refers to a beverage produced by fermentation with dried or roasted malt as the main extract-providing substance.
>
> Beer with an alcohol content that exceeds 2.25 but not 3.5% by volume is called folköl [people's beer] and beer with an alcohol content that exceeds 3.5% by volume is called starköl [strong beer].[66]

Thus, while beer with an alcohol content that is lower than 2.25 per cent by volume is commonly sold as lättöl [light beer], in legal terms it is not really beer. Instead, the Alkohollag states that 'Drinks that are alcohol-free or that have an alcohol content of no more than 2.25% by volume are called lättdryck [light drink]'.[67]

Under Czech law, namely Art. 16(1) of the Decree of the Ministry of Agriculture No. 248/2018, beer is defined as:

> an alcoholic beverage produced by the fermentation of wort prepared from malt, water, untreated hops, treated hops or hop products which contains, in addition to

[64] *Excise Tariff Act 1921* (Cth).

[65] *Australia New Zealand Food Standards Code* s 1.1.2–3.

[66] In the original Swedish: 'Med öl avses en dryck som framställts genom jäsning med torkat eller rostat malt som huvudsakligt extraktgivande ämne. Öl med en alkoholhalt som överstiger 2,25 men inte 3,5 volymprocent benämns folköl och öl med en alkoholhalt som överstiger 3,5 volymprocent benämns starköl.'

[67] In the original Swedish: 'Dryck som är alkoholfri eller som har en alkoholhalt om högst 2,25 volymprocent benämns lättdryck.'

> the ethanol and carbon dioxide produced by the fermentation process, a certain quantity of unfermented extract; malt may be substituted for up to one-third by weight of the total extract of the original wort by an extract of, in particular, sugar, cereal starch, unmalted cereals or rice; in the case of flavoured beers, the alcoholic strength may be increased by the addition of spirits or other alcoholic beverages.

It is noteworthy that this rather detailed definition does not set any lower level of alcohol in the beer as long as it contains ethanol. It is also interesting to note the focus on malt, and the associated restriction of adjuncts, such as sugar, replacing malt.

Under Canadian law, an even more detailed definition is provided of 'beer':

> (1) Beer
> (a) shall be the product of the alcoholic fermentation by yeast, or a mixture of yeast and other micro-organisms, an infusion of barley or wheat malt and hops or hop extract in potable water;
> (b) shall contain at most 4% of residual sugars; and
> (c) may have added to it during the course of manufacture any of the following ingredients:
> (i) cereal grain,
> (ii) honey, maple syrup, fruit, fruit juice or any other source of carbohydrates,
> (iii) herbs and spices,
> (iv) salt,
> (v) flavouring preparations,
> (vi) pre-isomerized hop extract,
> (vii) reduced isomerized hop extract, and
> (viii) food additives to which a marketing authorization applies and that are set out in the Lists of Permitted Food Additives published on the Health Canada website.[68]

There are several interesting features of this definition. First of all, it gives barley and wheat malt a central position and beers brewed exclusively with other grains would not seem to qualify as beer. It is also interesting to note that the definition specifically acknowledges the practice of fermenting with a mixture of yeast and other micro-organisms. Further, a great deal of attention is directed at the hops, with specific definition provided of 'hop extract',[69] 'pre-isomerized hop extract',[70] and 'reduced isomerized hop extract'.[71]

Against the background described above, the reality is that it is not always easy to know whether you are truly drinking beer! But then again, as long as it tastes good, perhaps it does not generally matter whether the law regards it as a true 'beer' or not?

[68] *Food and Drug Regulations* CRC, c 870, B.02.130.
[69] Ibid B.02.133.
[70] Ibid B.02.134.
[71] Ibid B.02.135.

1.7 A FEW WORDS ABOUT THIS BOOK

Hopefully you have now got a feel for what this book seeks to achieve. But just to be (overly) clear, there are a few things we want to emphasize.

This book is an introduction to beer law. It does not aim to be comprehensive in any sense. The book draws attention to and explains key issues in the intersection of law and beer. The aim has been to write something accessible – and hopefully entertaining – that still is informative and meets the standards of academic works. Where possible, we have sought to use interesting 'stories' from the world of beer law to guide the reader through the often quite complex legal issues that arise.

In the book, we predominantly draw on examples and illustrations from a small number of different jurisdictions: Belgium, the Czech Republic, Germany, the Nordic countries,[72] North America,[73] and the United Kingdom and Ireland. This selection is admittedly somewhat arbitrary, and it obviously fails to capture the wide diversity of beer cultures from around the world. However, while doubtless there are many other jurisdictions that could usefully have been included in the book, we hope that the reader will agree that all the jurisdictions included add value to the stories we seek to tell. They are all 'beer countries' and have all contributed to shaping the world of beer and beer law. The Czechs drink more beer per capita than any other country. Germany has its world-famous *Reinheitsgebot*. Beer culture in Belgium is included in UNESCO's 'Intangible Cultural Heritage of Humanity'. North America revolutionized the beer world by driving the craft brew movement. The United Kingdom and Ireland, pub culture and Guiness – no need to say more. And then there are the Nordic countries – Carlsberg, Viking drinking habits, sobriety movements, and an Icelandic ban on beer lasting to 1989.

So, which of these 'beer countries' is the most beer-focused? Which is the standout beer country? Well, there are of course different ways to measure that. But one way to look at it is through the lens of the percentage of beer consumed, measured in litres of pure alcohol, compared to other alcoholic beverages. According to a 2024 WHO report, the situation is as shown in Table 1.2.[74]

Looking at the book's structure, we have sought to blend the 'heavier' beer law chapters with 'lighter' chapters giving insights into the beer culture of the noted jurisdictions. Consequently, each chapter addressing topics such as health law and beer, tax law and beer, and so on, is followed by a country-specific chapter that partly expands on the theme of the chapter that precedes it and partly gives a more general insight into the country's beer culture and broader beer law issues.

72 Specifically, Sweden, Denmark, Norway, Finland, and Iceland.

73 Including Canada, Mexico, and the United States of America.

74 World Health Organization, *Global Status Report on Alcohol and Health and Treatment of Substance Use Disorders* (Global Report, 25 June 2024).

TABLE 1.2 *Consumption of alcoholic beverages by country*

Country	Beer	Wine	Spirits	Other
Mexico	85.3	3.8	10.5	0.4
Iceland	56.2	27.6	16.2	<0.1
Czechia	52.7	21.8	25.4	<0.1
Germany	50.5	29.9	19.6	<0.1
Belgium	47.6	37.0	12.0	3.4
Finland	47.2	20.3	16.8	15.7
Ireland	45.4	26.4	20.6	7.6
United States of America	44.9	18.2	36.9	<0.1
Canada	44.3	25.7	26.0	4.0
Norway	43.8	36.6	16.5	3.0
Denmark	37.2	44.9	17.9	<0.1
Sweden	37.0	47.2	14.0	1.8
United Kingdom of Great Britain and Northern Ireland	35.4	34.6	23.6	6.4

We sincerely hope that the book can provide value for as many readers as possible, from brewers with no legal background and beer drinkers more widely, to legal scholars and lawyers practising specifically in beer law. Perhaps the book may even make you look differently, and with a deeper level of appreciation, at the fascinating, and both technically and legally complex, product that is beer. If so, we will be very pleased.

2

Germany

Purity Laws, Beer Gardens, and Beer Wars

2.1 INTRODUCTION

Germany has an eventful and chequered past. Geographically located in the centre of Europe, many wars, political decisions, and transformations that have significantly impacted European history took place on German soil – but that impact is not necessarily reflected in perceptions abroad. If you ask any person outside Germany what they associate with Germany, there is a good chance that the first thing they will mention is Oktoberfest. The typical Bavarian costume with lederhosen or *dirndl* is known almost everywhere and often viewed as 'typically German'.

Beer Consumption in Germany

According to Statista's per capita volume sales by country in 2023, beer consumption in Germany is 89 litres per person per year. This means Germans are the third-biggest beer drinkers globally, although consumption is decreasing year by year.

Oktoberfest originated as a horse race organized by the Munich militia to celebrate the wedding of the Bavarian crown prince on 17 October 1810.[1] The event was so popular that the Bavarian king authorized its repetition in 1811. The 'Theresienwiese', where the festival has been held ever since, is named after the crown prince's bride, Therese. Oktoberfest is now known far beyond the country's

[1] For further information on the history of the Oktoberfest, see Ursula Eymold, 'Oktoberfest', *Historical Dictionary of Bavaria* (Web Page, 5 June 2013) www.historisches-lexikon-bayerns.de/Lexikon/Oktoberfest#:~:text=Origin%20of%20the%20Oktoberfest%20is%20a%20festival%20organised%20in%1792%2D1854.

borders; in 2023, for example, 7.2 million guests attended, consuming around 6.5 million litres of beer.[2]

Oktoberfest highlights the cultural significance that beer has always had in German culture. German university towns boast the highest density of pubs in the country. For Germans, the term 'pub' conjures up images of a smoky room – in a half-timbered house or cellar vault – where tired workers enjoy well-earned after-work beer, students savour cool post-lecture wheat beer, and plans are made in a cosy get-together.

It is no coincidence that Johann Wolfgang von Goethe uses these images in his famous drama *Faust*. In the Leipzig pub Auerbachs Keller, which Goethe himself knew from his student days in Leipzig, Faust and Mephisto sit together with four students to drink, sing and celebrate.

> Mephisto:
> Before all else, I bring thee hither
> Where boon companions meet together,
> To let thee see how smooth life runs away.
> Here, for the folk, each day's a holiday.[3]

Even before Goethe, beer culture in German-speaking countries was reflected in literature. In his *Germania*, the Roman historian Tacitus wrote about the Germanic tribes: 'Their drink is a liquid brewed from barley or wheat, very similar to wine.'[4] (In fact, many other types of grain were also used for brewing.) Herbal beers were very common until the late Middle Ages. A mixture of herbs ('grut' or 'gruit') was used to flavour the beer, which, in Germany, consisted mainly of marsh porter and wild gale. Juniper, aniseed, fennel, rosemary, and caraway often dominate the flavours of grut beer.

For a long time, the sale of grut was monopolized by the church and the state, making it a forerunner of the modern beer tax. In addition to several words from medieval brewing, family names can also be traced back to 'grut' – such as the name of the large German scientific publishing house De Gruyter. As grut's composition was not initially regulated, it sometimes contained poisonous herbs that could cause hallucinations and illness.

We return to that topic in Chapter 3 addressing health law and beer. In any case, due to its longer shelf life, better exportability, and greater food safety,

2 L Graefe, 'Ausgeschenkte Menge Bier auf dem Oktoberfest in München von 1980 bis 2023 [Amount of beer served at the Oktoberfest in Munich from 1980 to 2023]', *Statista* (Web Page, 3 January 2024) https://de.statista.com/statistik/daten/studie/165503/umfrage/ausgeschenkte-menge-bier-auf-dem-oktoberfest-seit-1980/.

3 Johann Wolfgang von Goethe, 'The Project Gutenberg eBook of Faust [part 1]. Translated into English in the Original Metres', *Gutenberg* (Web Page, 4 January 2005) www.gutenberg.org/cache/epub/14591/pg14591-images.html#V.

4 Cornelius Tacitus, *Germany and Its Tribes*, tr Alfred John Church, William Jackson Brodribb and Lisa Cerrato (Perseus Books, 1942).

hop beer became increasingly established in the sixteenth century, a trend that had already been recognized by the Hanseatic cities and monastery breweries.

2.2 BEER AS A HISTORICAL FOODSTUFF: BEER SOUP AND 'LIQUID BREAD'

Beer was probably popular in monastery breweries for two reasons: it was permitted during Lent ('*liquida non frangunt ieunum*' – liquids do not break the fast) and its high energy content made it a nutritious – and tasty – drink to accompany otherwise meagre meals. Legend has it that every monk was allowed to drink up to 5 litres of beer a day. Medieval beer had a much lower alcohol content than most modern beer, which is why a person drinking up to 400 litres per year was not unusual.[5]

For various reasons, beer was a staple food in the Middle Ages. This historical fact – and perhaps the similar ingredients – is the basis for the slang phrase 'liquid bread', which is still used today. Various proverbs also allude to beer's nutrition, such as 'three beers are also a meal'. Three half-litres of beer contain around 600 kilocalories, which is equivalent to a lunch.

Beer production also used low-grade grain that was no longer suitable for bread production, which made it a welcome addition during famines or poor harvests. Until the nineteenth century, beer soup – a sweet or savoury dish made from bread, beer, butter, and spices – was also a widespread breakfast. The preparation of beer soup varied between regions and its flavour changed depending on the type of beer used.

In addition to its high energy and low alcohol content, beer was largely germ-free thanks to the boiling process – in stark contrast to medieval drinking water (which we will discuss further in Chapter 3). For these reasons, beer was also served to children and consumed during working hours. Non-alcoholic 'medicinal beer' was given to women who had recently given birth. The myth of the beneficial effects of 'mother beer' was spread through the advertising of very malty beer varieties such as 'Braunschweiger Mumme'.

The popularity of beer in the Middle Ages was particularly interesting to governments. As early as the Holy Roman Empire, a consumption tax was levied

[5] By way of comparison, in 2022 it was only around 92 litres/capita. See 'Deutsche Brauwirtschaft in Zahlen [German Brewing Industry in Figures]', *Deutscher Brauer-Bund* (Web Page, 10 April 2024) https://brauer-bund.de/wp-content/uploads/2024/04/STATIST-2023.pdf. For beer consumption per capita in Germany in the years 1950 to 2022 (in litres), see Statista Research Department, 'Bierverbrauch pro Kopf in Deutschland in den Jahren 1950 bis 2023 [Beer consumption per capita in Germany from 1950 to 2023]', *Statista* (Web Page, 26 June 2024) https://de.statista.com/statistik/daten/studie/4628/umfrage/entwicklung-des-bierverbrauchs-pro-kopf-in-deutschland-seit-2000/.

('beer money') and the right to serve beer commercially was granted for a fee (*Krugrecht*). The German surname 'Krüger' is derived from the *Krugrecht*. To this day, the German state levies taxes on beer in accordance with the Beer Tax Act.

2.3 BEER AS A GERMAN CULTURAL ASSET: FOLK SONGS, BEER GARDENS, AND BEER HIKES

Over the centuries, an entire culture has developed in Germany around beer brewing, beer drinking, and the commercial serving of beer. This is also reflected in the diversity of beer types.

In Germany, for example, there are twenty-five different beer styles and 5,000–6,000 different types of beer. If we look at the beer styles in the Beer Judge Certification Program '2021 Beer Style Guidelines',[6] the international impact of the German brewing tradition is clear (Figure 2.1). German styles are found in several categories, such as Berliner Weisse in the category of 'European Sour Ale' and Lichtenhainer in 'Historical Beer'. In fact, some categories such as 'Pale Malty European Lager', 'Pale Bitter European Beer', and 'Amber Malty European Lager' *only* contain German beer styles. ('German Wheat Beer' has its own category.)

Beer culture is not limited to the Oktoberfest. Many breweries offer tours that explain the production process, showcase the production facilities, and offer product tasting – probably the most appealing aspect for most guests!

In Bavaria and many other federal states, there are beer hiking trails that lead past breweries and pubs and offer beer tastings. Tours with a handcart and crates of beer are also typical, especially on Father's Day and Ascension Day. Like many 'traditions', the classic Father's Day tour was created by breweries to increase beer sales.[7] Parallels can be drawn with Valentine's Day, which was leveraged by the flower industry to increase sales. The same applies to German Beer Day, which has been celebrated by the German Brewers' Association every year since 23 April 1994 – the day the Bavarian Purity Law came into force in 1516 (see Section 2.4). Many folk songs have also been written about beer and beer consumption.

Another expression of German beer culture is the 'beer garden'. Historically, it arose from the restrictive Bavarian trade law (*Krugrecht*) and the storage of beer in cellars. Because beer could not be served in an unlicensed pub, some brewers

6 Gordon Strong and Kristen England, '2021 Beer Style Guidelines', *Beer Judge Certification Program* (Web Page) www.bjcp.org/download/2021_Guidelines_Beer.pdf.

7 Cf Lars von Törne, 'Tradition des Vatertags: Als die Söhne saufen lernten [Father's Day Tradition: When the Sons Learned to Drink]', *Tagesspiegel* (Web Page, 14 May 2015) www.tagesspiegel.de/berlin/als-die-sohne-saufen-lernten-3627148.html.

FIGURE 2.1 Photos from the German brewery town of Einbeck, famously the birthplace of the 'bock' style of beer.

FIGURE 2.1 (*cont.*)

sold their beer directly from the warehouse to the public. The customers then drank their beer in a shady spot and brought their own food. Even today, you can bring your own food to traditional beer gardens – but there are also many catered beer gardens that serve food and prohibit guests from bringing their own. Especially in Bavaria, though, many traditional beer gardens still offer small snacks (including the famous Weißwurst breakfast) and allow you to bring your own food.

Since April 1999, these traditional Bavarian beer gardens have been indirectly defined in the Bavarian Beer Garden Ordinance. According to the legislation, a Bavarian beer garden is a traditional pub with a garden, where guests are not obligated to purchase any food.[8]

[8] Compare the justification of the Beer Garden Ordinance. See 'Bayerische Biergartenverordnung [Bavarian Beer Garden Ordinance]' (Web Page, 20 April 1999) 4–5 www.staedtebauliche-laermfibel.de/pdf/Biergarten-VO.pdf.

The ordinance was preceded by years of legal disputes and a revolution. In 1995, the Bavarian Administrative Court ordered a local beer garden to close early from 9:30 p.m. to protect residents from noise. On 12 May 1995, 25,000 Munich residents demonstrated against the decision, aiming to 'preserve the beer garden culture'. The protests were taken up by the Munich media as a 'beer garden revolution' and the Bavarian state government issued the first Bavarian Beer Garden Ordinance, which was declared null and void by the Federal Administrative Court in 1999 because it failed to consider residents' interests. This led to the new version of the ordinance in April 1999 and the restriction of its scope to traditional beer gardens. This event also illustrates the power and influence of the beer and brewery lobby on politics and society.

2.4 THE GERMAN PURITY LAW: ADVERTISING MEASURE, FOOD LAW, OR TAX MEASURE?

We have already mentioned the German Purity Law and will return to it many times throughout this book, so let us explore it in more detail.

2.4.1 *The Term 'Purity Law'*

There are many possible reasons for the popularity of the German Purity Law. One could be its use in advertising by the brewing industry. From at least the 1950s onwards, the term 'purity law' (*Reinheitsgebot*) was used in Germany to distinguish German beverages from foreign beers; in the course of the so-called 'sweet beer war' of 1958, it also became better known outside Bavaria.[9] The sweet beer war was a national dispute over the question of whether malt beer could be labelled and marketed as beer or whether it had to be called a malt beverage. This dispute can also be seen as the starting point of the decades-long conflict with the European Commission ('European Beer War'), which centred on the compatibility of the purity law with EU law.

Before that, the term was less common; it was first used in an official context in 1909 by the Reichstag's Petition Commission. The term *Reinheitsgebot* was preceded by *Surrogatsverbot* (ban on replacing extract of malt with extract of sugar), but

[9] Compare on the sweet beer war. See Bundesgerichtshof [The Federal Court of Justice], 2 StR 80/57, 1958. See Martin Rath, 'Im Wendekreis des Malzbiers [In the Tropic of Malt Beer]', *Legal Tribune Online* (Web Page, 27 October 2019) www.lto.de/recht/feuilleton/f/bier-alkohol-malzbier-brauereiwirtschaft-bayern-bayoblg-drogen. On the purpose and use for demarcation and as 'fighting vocabulary', see Jurgen Kniep, 'Im Interesse des Renommees und der Exportfähigkeit unseres heimischen Braugewerbes [In the Interest of the Reputation and Export Capability of our Domestic Brewing Industry]' (2016) 67(2) *Schwäbische Heimat* 157.

the latter's first use is unclear; in the Middle Ages and early modern times, there was no separate word for 'prohibitions' and 'bans on brewing'.[10]

Today, the term 'purity law' typically refers to the Bavarian Purity Law 1516, which stipulated that only barley, hops, and water could be used in the brewing process. In its various forms, the Purity Law almost always refers to bottom-fermented beers – other additives are permitted in top-fermented beers.

2.4.2 *Historical Dimensions of the Purity Law*

Before 1516, various forms of prohibitions and bans existed in the form of brewing regulations at the municipal level – which, in some cases, contained purity laws. This began as early as 1156, when the city of Augsburg standardized a penalty for brewers who used bad beer. In Nuremberg, between 1302 and 1305, only barley was allowed to be used for brewing. Other purity laws existed in Weimar (1348), Landshut (1409), Weißensee (1434), Regensburg (1447), Munich (1453–1487) and Landshut again (1486). Also worth mentioning is a purity law from London (1484) and one for Thuringian bratwurst (1432).

The Purity Law 1516 covered the entire Duchy of Bavaria, and, in material terms, was similar to its predecessors. These regulations can be categorized as food law, especially as mechanisms for quality control ('beer inspection') were regulated separately or in police regulations.[11] One of the reasons given for the Purity Laws is the victory of hopped beer in southern Germany that may have resulted in installing the Purity Law as effecting easier taxation if only hops could be used.[12]

The history of the Purity Law picks up speed again with the first German nation-state, the German Empire of 1871. It was first laid down at an imperial level – albeit under a different name – in the amended Brewing Tax Act 1906. Even before that time, the legislative competence for beer taxation in accordance with Art. 35, paragraph 1 of the Reich Constitution of 16 April 1871 lay solely with the Reich, and in the Beer Tax Act of 31 May 1872 other substances were also permitted in brewing. However, the southern German imperial territories of Bavaria, Baden, and Württemberg, which had their own absolute purity law, were excluded from its scope (Figure 2.2).

The German kingdoms probably wanted this 'right of reservation', which they secured in 1870 before joining the empire, because of how much state revenue the

[10] Klaus Rupprecht, 'Reinheitsgebot, 1516 [Purity Law, 1516]', *Historisches Lexikon Bayerns* (Web Page, 28 July 2016) www.historisches-lexikon-bayerns.de/Lexikon/Reinheitsgebot,_1516#Begriff.

[11] Rupprecht (n 10).

[12] Richard W Unger, *Beer in the Middle Ages and the Renaissance* (University of Pennsylvania Press, 2004) 109.

FIGURE 2.2 Weizen Doppelbock: a unique German style.

beer tax generated (rather than because purity laws helped maintain food quality).[13] This conclusion is supported by the tax legislation in Württemberg; in 1827, malt substitutes were permitted, which was only criticized when sales of Württemberg beer collapsed.[14] As such, the purpose of purity laws changed during this period from food regulation to fiscal support.[15]

Even today, the Purity Law, from the state's point of view, serves more of a fiscal purpose, and, from the brewing industry's point of view, a marketing one. These

[13] Cf Kniep (n 9) 158.

[14] Ibid.

[15] The 'reserved' absolute purity law continued to apply after the end of the German Reich in the Beer Tax Act 1918, the Beer Tax Act 1952 in the Federal Republic of Germany, and the implementing regulation of the Provisional Beer Act.

purposes are supported by the fact that beer brewed in accordance with the Purity Law is protected at the European level as a traditional foodstuff.[16]

2.4.3 *The European Beer War: The Purity Law under Attack*

The 'European beer war'[17] or 'European beer dispute' took place from 1958 to 1987 between the Commission of the European Communities and the West German Federal Government. The Federal Government attempted to justify the German Purity Law giving various reasons (above all, health and consumer protection),[18] presumably to protect domestic breweries from European competition.[19] The Commission believed that the Purity Law, as a 'measure having equivalent effect to quantitative restrictions on imports', would violate the principles of the 'Cassis de Dijon' judgment,[20] and initiated infringement proceedings against the Federal Republic of Germany.

The European Court of Justice (ECJ) lifted the bans inherent in the Purity Law for foreign breweries, which meant that domestic German breweries were still subject to the Purity Law.[21] The 'Dassonville' and Cassis de Dijon judgments, which were hotly debated at the time, are now widely recognized – the same conclusion would be reached today.[22]

As a result of the ECJ judgment, the constitutionality of the application of the Purity Law to domestic breweries only was in question, but the Federal Administrative Court assessed this question (in particular, its compatibility with Arts. 3 and 12 of the German Constitution) in 2005 and concluded that the relevant provisions of German beer law are constitutional due to the possibility of

[16] *Regulation (EC) No 1333/2008 of the European Parliament and of the Council of 16 December 2008 on Food Additives* [2008] OJ L 354/16, art 20 and annex IV.

[17] Not to be confused with the 'sweet beer war' on the national level in 1958, where the question was if malt beer could be called 'beer'.

[18] As to the Argumentation of the Federal Government, see Doris König, 'Das Problem der Inländerdiskriminierung – Abschied von Reinheitsgebot, Nachtbackverbot und Meisterprüfung? [The Problem of Discrimination against Nationals – Farewell to the Purity Law, the Ban on Night Baking and the Master Craftsman's Examination]' (1993) 118(4) *Archiv des öffentlichen Rechts* 591, 603–5; Michael Schweitzer and Rudolf Streinz, 'Reinheitsgebot fur Bier und freier Warenverkehr' (1984) *Recht der internationalen Wirtschaft* 41. Today, the Purity Law can only be found in § 9 VorlBierG.

[19] According to § 9 VorlBierG, the distribution of differently brewed beer under this designation was prohibited, as well as the import of beer with additives that were permitted in the country of origin but prohibited in the Federal Republic of Germany. See *Commission of the European Communities v Federal Republic of Germany* (C-178/84) [1987] ECJ 1227.

[20] *Rewe-Zentral AG v Federal Monopoly Administration for Spirits* (C-120/78) [1979] ECJ 649.

[21] König deals in detail with this problem and the solutions offered by Community and constitutional law.

[22] A different view was taken by Schweitzer and Streinz (n 21), who considered a justification by art 36 of the EEC Treaty (health protection) possible, taking into account the 'Nisin' judgment of the European Court of Justice.

exceptions.[23] For example, section 9(7) VorlBierG allows for an exception upon application for beer that is destined for export, meant to be used for scientific experiments or 'beer specialities' that include additional ingredients solely for the sake of taste. There has not yet been a case in which a beer did not fall under the exceptions and a complaint was successfully lodged. Accordingly, the Purity Law still applies in this form today.

[23] Federal Administrative Court, 24 February 2005 – 3 C 5/04, NJW 2005, 1736.

3

Healthy Laws for Unhealthy Beers?

3.1 INTRODUCTION

It has been noted that 'alcohol is a risk factor for more than 200 health problems, yet it is the most widely consumed psychoactive substance globally',[1] and that beer is the most consumed alcoholic beverage in the world.[2] Why is that? Why do people keep drinking alcoholic beverages despite the risks?

Answering that question may take us too far afield from beer law. However, it does bring us to another, related question: why does the law allow people to keep consuming alcoholic beverages such as beer despite the risks and societal costs? This contradiction between use and risk is something that lawmakers must always keep in mind, and clearly shapes how the law regulates beer production, sale, and consumption.

There are two distinct sides to the health and safety debate around beer – the ascendant side has varied throughout history. Most modern discussions focus on beer's potential for harm. Consequently, this chapter centres on how the law has sought to regulate the negative health impacts of beer consumption.

But, earlier in history, beer was viewed very differently. It has been seen as a cure for a range of illnesses and has been an important source of nutrition. Unsurprisingly, this view shaped how the law approached beer and beer consumption, which we discuss below.

Broadly speaking, the change in messaging from 'beer is good for your health' to 'beer is bad for your health' has nothing to do with beer – the beer has remained the same. In part, it stems from advances in health science. We now know that certain

1 Nancy López-Olmedo et al, 'Warning Labels on Alcoholic Beverage Containers: A Pilot Randomized Experiment among Young Adults in Mexico' (2023) 23(1) *BMC Public Health* 1156, 2.

2 WHO, *Global Status Report on Alcohol and Health and Treatment of Substance Use Disorders*, WHO Doc CC BY-NC-SA 3.0 IGO (25 June 2024) 66 (*WHO Report on Alcohol and Health and Treatment of Substance Use Disorders*).

things – such as sugar, alcohol, processed red meat, asbestos, and tobacco – are bad for us. Arguably, though, an even stronger reason for the change in messaging is the increase in available alternatives.

Beer – a comparatively nutritious product that has been sterilized through the boiling of the wort, and that contains natural antiseptics from hops, a richness of B vitamins from yeast, antimicrobial properties from alcohol, and low pH – is clearly a much safer alternative than dirty water. But, compared to clean water, especially in an era of widespread obesity and alcoholism, beer ends up looking less beneficial. How beer is perceived clearly depends on the time and place.

To take a somewhat silly example. While a doctor in a modern, developed country with plenty of alternatives might not recommend drinking beer, that same doctor, if stranded on a deserted island with a choice between drinking salty ocean water or beer, would presumably recommend the beer. So, our first key observation is that judging whether beer is 'good' or 'bad' from a health perspective should be approached from a comparative point of view. This, in turn, must affect how the law approaches beer.

In this chapter, we will highlight the health benefits and health issues associated with beer and explore how the law has sought to address both. We start with examples where the law has looked favourably on beer. This discussion is predominantly approached from the perspective of individual health – that is, what would a doctor say?

However, it is also important to consider beer law from a public health perspective. We are delighted to include an insightful discussion by Dr Michal Koščík of Masaryk University (in the Czech Republic) on this topic. We then approach areas of law that aim to limit or prevent the production, distribution and/or consumption of beer, followed by a few observations about how beer-related health data are collected and used. Finally, we conclude by expressing some thoughts about beer, law, health, and the future.

3.2 HEALTHY BEER AND THE LAW

Beer and other alcoholic beverages have been linked to a wide range of health benefits throughout history. For example, as noted by renowned beer writer Professor Charles Bamforth (to whom we refer frequently in this book), hops have been said to 'work wonders for constipation, overcome premature ejaculation, and ease anxiety'.[3] Milk stout has been credited with promoting lactation in new mothers. And beer has been linked to many other health benefits, such as better sleep quality, improved self-confidence, and less dandruff. According to the Finnish national epic *Kalevala*, the 'ancient beer of Kalew' could make the feeble hardy, dry

[3] Charles W Bamforth, *Grape vs Grain: A Historical, Technological, and Social Comparison of Wine and Beer* (Cambridge University Press, 2008) 95.

the tears of women, cheer the broken-hearted, make the aged young, embolden the timid, and fill the mind with wisdom.[4] Plato also expressed the view that people older than forty could drink freely to relieve the desiccation of old age.[5]

We would do well to approach many of these claims with scepticism. Nevertheless, beer – like other alcoholic drinks – clearly has benefits for both individuals and society. McGovern, for example, explains that humans drink globally because of alcohol's hydrating and nutritional properties. He also points out that moderate consumption of alcohol lowers cardiovascular and cancer risks, ensuring people live longer and reproduce more, which was 'crucially important in antiquity, when life spans were generally short'.[6] Beer contains a unique set of nutritional components, such as antioxidants, phosphorus, calcium, potassium, manganese, fluoride, and silicon.[7]

Other sources have emphasized the social and mental health benefits of beer-drinking. Some researchers have, for example, demonstrated that:

> Social drinkers have more friends on whom they can depend for emotional and other support, and feel more engaged with, and trusting of, their local community. Alcohol is known to trigger the endorphin system, and the social consumption of alcohol may thus have the same effect as the many other social activities such as laughter, singing and dancing that we use as a means of servicing and reinforcing social bonds.[8]

However, there are also clear indications that alcohol can harm our health even in small quantities.

Before leaving the topic of beer's argued and real positive impacts on health, we must make two observations: firstly, the pursuit of better beer has had a tremendous impact on innovations that support good health. Advances by pioneering brewers and beer industry workers have informed all other fermentation industries, the pharmaceutical industry, and biotechnology producers.[9] This contribution cannot be ignored when assessing the societal health impact of beer.

Secondly, not all beers are the same from a health perspective. Beers obviously vary in alcohol content. But that is only one variable. Some beers contain, for example, fewer calories. Another health factor is yeast; Bamforth has suggested that

4 Ibid 39.

5 Ibid 19.

6 Patrick E McGovern, *Uncorking the Past: The Quest for Wine, Beer, and Other Alcoholic Beverages* (University of California Press, 1st ed, 2009) 17.

7 Allison Krupp, 'Could This Popular, Bitter Drink Have Healing Powers?', *healthline* (Web Page, 3 April 2020) www.healthline.com/health/food-nutrition/medicinal-beers#medicinal-beer-origins.

8 RIM Dunbar et al, 'Functional Benefits of (Modest) Alcohol Consumption' (2017) 3(2) *Adaptive Human Behavior and Physiology* 118, 118.

9 Bamforth (n 3) 2.

the German *hefeweizen* is arguably the healthiest beer because it is loaded with yeast and thus rich in vitamins.[10]

With all this in mind, we can now consider how the law has facilitated – and, indeed, promoted – beer-drinking.

3.2.1 *Healthy Beer and the Law of the Past*

Throughout history, the laws of many countries have prescribed beer allocations, for example to soldiers and sailors. We give some illustrations of this in the next chapter addressing the Nordic countries. Clearly, any such laws may be viewed as the law expressing a positive attitude towards beer. After all, the rulers' interest was to keep soldiers and sailors healthy and strong, and the beer allocation must be seen in that light.

But the law has also endorsed beer in other ways. Consider the English Beerhouse Act 1830 (which we will discuss more than once in this book).[11] One of the aims of the Beerhouse Act was to increase competition in the brewing and sale of beer to lower its price, which would help make it preferable to more alcoholic drinks, especially gin. US president Thomas Jefferson expressed a similar sentiment in 1815, writing that he wished to see beer 'become common instead of the whiskey which kills one third of our citizens and ruins their families'.[12]

These are only a small sample of laws that, one way or another, endorse beer-drinking – but they clearly demonstrate that, throughout history, the law has endorsed beer.

3.2.2 *Healthy Beer and the Law Today*

Modern examples of laws that endorse beer-drinking do not exist (at least, not in the countries we focus on in this book). That shows a radical change in how the law relates to health and beer. So why have lawmakers not banned beer? Beer production remains legal. The law even tolerates home brewing. The sale of beer is regulated, but not prohibited. The consumption of beer is allowed, albeit with many restrictions.

Many other products that have been found to be harmful to the human body have been made illegal. The fact that modern lawmakers have not prohibited beer shows that the law accepts beer, and it would be a brave (or, perhaps more accurately, foolish) politician who would suggest making beer illegal now. This – the fact that the law accepts beer – is important to remember as we turn to how the law regulates beer for health reasons.

[10] Ibid 149.

[11] An Act to permit the general Sale of Beer and Cyder by Retail in England 11 Geo. 4 & 1 Will. 4. c. 64.

[12] Bamforth (n 3) 50.

3.3 PUBLIC HEALTH PERSPECTIVES ON BEER LAW, BY MICHAL KOŠČÍK

Health is a highly individual matter, which might lead to the conclusion that choices regarding healthy or unhealthy behaviour should be personal. From a pub customer's perspective, it is entirely their choice whether they enjoy a few more beers tonight or avoid a hangover tomorrow. However, the perspective of people who have noisy neighbours, have been harassed by drunken pub-goers, or have witnessed car accidents caused by drunk drivers might be different.

It is easy to see that individual drinking habits directly affect other people's health and well-being. These effects can be addressed by the law, which offers various tools to provide compensation to victims and to punish unruly drinkers. However, law enforcement is only efficient to a certain degree and tends to focus more on dealing with the consequences of incidents rather than their prevention. The most obvious problem with a legal solution is that it does not change the health outcome. If you are hit by a car, you may be compensated with money and the driver may be punished, but your health will still be adversely affected.

Drinking directly affects families and neighbourhoods – and can also impact society. Societal effects are often not immediately obvious, but it is important to analyse them and address them with regulation and health policy. Beer availability and drinking habits influence the health and well-being of a population, including its non-drinking portion. Below, we offer two important perspectives on beer. The first is on beer as food, because no population can survive without it. The second covers beer as a drug that affects people's behaviour.[13]

3.3.1 *Beer as a Food*

Beer provides nutrition and may be approached as a food product. That is the point of departure here.

3.3.1.1 Beer as Food Staple in the Past and Now

Beer is a product of fermentation, a technique used for preserving food since the earliest civilizations. Historically, beer played an important role in preserving parts of the harvest for later use. It could also be produced from grains unsuitable for other forms of consumption and was used to salvage dry bakery leftovers by mixing them into the malt.[14] Beer is an ancient 'energy drink' that enabled the storage and transport of energy from fields to large infrastructural or industrial projects.

[13] Apart from these two perspectives, it could be possible to analyse beer from other public health perspectives – for example, as an environmental factor (impact of beer industry on pollution) or beer as a factor of socio-economic health determinants.

[14] Alan Dychmenko, Milan Gersl, and Tomáš Gregor, 'Brewing Beer Using Bakery Leftovers as a Substitute for Malt' *Research Gate* (Web Page, February 2023) www.researchgate.net/publication/372678095_Brewing_beer_using_bakery_leftovers_as_a_substitute_for_malt.

While concluding that societies could not survive or evolve without beer would be incorrect, we cannot overlook the role of beer in the diet of workers involved in projects that advanced civilizations. Examples range from the builders of the Egyptian pyramids to workers during the Industrial Revolution, who laid the groundwork for the current globalized world.[15] The beer industry was regulated and encouraged by rulers and governments of most European countries as part of their food and economic policy.

Beer is mainly made of water and can contribute to the fluid intake necessary for survival.[16] A popular myth persists that, in medieval Europe, beer was safer to drink than water. There is some scientific evidence from eighteenth-century England suggesting that citizens of towns with better access to beer had lower mortality from waterborne illnesses.[17] However, this was likely not the case in most places throughout history. Populations cannot survive long term without access to fresh water, and even in medieval times, efforts were made to protect the quality of water sources (Figure 3.1). Even if we accept that, in certain places at certain times, it was safer to drink beer than water, it would be incorrect to conclude that drinking beer instead of water consistently protected populations from waterborne illnesses.

Historically, drinking beer was not a lifestyle choice but a means of sustenance, especially for workers in labour-intensive professions. Consequently, beer became a dietary staple in many places. Even today, the caloric importance of beer cannot be underestimated. Global beer production reached 188 billion litres in 2023[18] – enough energy to sustain roughly 70 million active adults for a year.

That production volume could be viewed as either an important source of energy for some populations or an inefficient use of resources that could be better directed towards healthier food. In modern developed countries, there are few rational reasons to treat beer as an essential food staple, because cheaper and healthier alternatives are almost always available. Drinking beer has become a lifestyle choice – one with measurable impacts on both individuals and society.

3.3.1.2 Alcohol-Related Health Risks and Benefits of Drinking Beer

In the twenty-first century, 70 per cent of premature deaths worldwide are caused by non-communicable (chronic) diseases.[19] While it would be incorrect to attribute these deaths to beer alone, there is compelling evidence that drinking beer regularly

[15] The answer to the question of whether either beer or work at such projects was actually beneficial to workers is rather complex.

[16] Here one must be mindful of the diuretic effect of beer, so completely replacing water with beer is not sustainable.

[17] Francisca M Antman and James M Flynn, 'When Beer Is Safer than Water: Beer Availability and Mortality from Waterborne Illnesses' (2024) 171 *Journal of Development Economics*, 103343.

[18] BarthHaas, *BarthHaas Report 2023/2024* (Report, July 2024).

[19] WHO, *Global Status Report on Alcohol and Health 2018*, WHO Doc CC BY-NCSA 3.0 IGO (2018) (*Global Status Report on Alcohol and Health 2018*).

FIGURE 3.1 Tallinn (Estonia): medieval well.

leads to bad health outcomes. The most obvious reason is that beer contains alcohol, which has well-documented negative effects on human health.

The alcohol we drink, ethanol, is classified by the International Agency for Research on Cancer (IARC) as a Group 1 carcinogen. Its consumption increases the risk of developing almost every non-communicable disease, including cancer, diabetes, hypertension, dementia, and depression. Men are disproportionately affected; the World Health Organization (WHO) estimates that, of the 2.6 million deaths per year that are directly attributable to alcohol, men comprise approximately 2 million (77 per cent).[20]

This is not a book about alcohol in general, so it is important to look at beer specifically. We know beer is the most popular alcoholic beverage worldwide – approximately a third of globally consumed alcohol is consumed in beer.[21] Many researchers have explored how beer compares to other alcoholic beverages. The

[20] Ibid.
[21] Ibid.

inconvenient truth? Beer cannot be considered a less dangerous alternative to spirits. In fact, certain risks are even amplified by drinking beer. A US study found that beer is more likely to be consumed by underage drinkers than any other alcohol and is often associated with binge drinking.[22] It is also more common to drink spirits in combination with beer than wine.[23]

There are studies that demonstrate positive effects of moderate beer-drinking on human health. For example, de Gaetano et al. concluded that the so-called French paradox (the theory that moderate wine-drinking has cardioprotective effects) also applies to moderate beer consumption. Their consensus was that moderate alcohol consumption protects against total mortality, both in healthy adults and in cardiovascular patients.[24]

In 2021, a Spanish research group similarly found that moderate drinking decreases the risk of overall mortality, diabetes, osteoporosis, and cardiovascular disease.[25] These studies have not, however, been accepted without controversy.[26] The WHO currently holds that any alcohol consumption negatively affects health,[27] a position that has been criticized for being too dogmatic. The editorial of *Lancet Rheumatology*, for example, pointed out that peer-reviewed studies[28] observed the possibility of alcohol protecting against rheumatoid arthritis.[29]

3.3.1.3 Obesity-Related Risks of Drinking Beer

The WHO has identified a global obesity pandemic.[30] The European Commission estimates that 53 per cent of the EU population is overweight or obese, and the US

22 John D Rogers and Thomas K Greenfield, 'Beer Drinking Accounts for Most of the Hazardous Alcohol Consumption Reported in the United States' (2015) 60(6) *Journal of Studies on Alcohol* 732.

23 Ibid.

24 G de Gaetano et al, 'Effects of Moderate Beer Consumption on Health and Disease: A Consensus Document. Nutrition, Metabolism and Cardiovascular Diseases' (2016) 26(6) *Nutrition, Metabolism, and Cardiovascular Diseases* 443.

25 Ascensión Marcos et al, 'Moderate Consumption of Beer and Its Effects on Cardiovascular and Metabolic Health: An Updated Review of Recent Scientific Evidence' (2021) 13(3) *Nutrients* 879.

26 It is important to note that co-authors of both papers declared a conflict of interest due to funding from the beer or wine industry.

27 World Health Organization, 'No Level of Alcohol Consumption Is Safe for Our Health' (News Release, 4 January 2023) www.who.int/azerbaijan/news/item/04-01-2023-no-level-of-alcohol-consumption-is-safe-for-our-health.

28 Zhichao Jin et al, 'Alcohol Consumption as a Preventive Factor for Developing Rheumatoid Arthritis: A Dose-Response Meta-analysis of Prospective Studies' (2014) 73(11) *Annals of the Rheumatic Diseases* 1962.

29 The Lancet Rheumatology, 'Alcohol and Health: All, None, or Somewhere In-Between?' (2023) 5(4) *The Lancet Rheumatology* e167.

30 World Health Organization, 'Controlling the Global Obesity Epidemic' (Web Page) www.who.int/activities/controlling-the-global-obesity-epidemic.

TABLE 3.1 *Comparison of caloric content of selected beers and sugary drinks*

Drink	Kilocalories per 100 millilitres
IPA (Punk IPA Brewdog)	46
Sugary energy drink (Red Bull)	45
Weissbier (Franziskaner)	43
Pilsner (Pilsner Urquell)	42
English ale (Fullers)	40
Coca Cola	39
Light beer (Bud Light)	27
Iced tea (sweetened and bottled)	25
Sports drink (Gatorade)	23
Tonic (Schweppes)	19
Alcohol-free pilsner	14

public health authority, the Centers for Disease Control and Prevention (CDC), has found the same for 74 per cent of US adults.

One of the main strategies to tackle global obesity is incentivizing consumers to replace high-calorie foods and drinks with lower-calorie ones. In line with this approach, over fifty countries have introduced taxes on sugar-sweetened beverages.[31] If we compare the caloric content of popular beer types with sugary drinks, we will find that most beloved beers are actually denser in calories than soft drinks (Table 3.1).

A typical serving size of beer contains more calories than a typical serving size of wine or hard liquor. Beer is also often consumed with meals and is known for increasing short-term appetite. As a result, adding beer to a meal increases the caloric intake in two ways: firstly through the calories in the beer itself, and secondly by leading someone to eat more than they otherwise would. After the meal is eaten, the alcohol in beer inhibits the burning of fat. Even in moderation, habitual drinking of alcohol with food is a risk factor for obesity.[32]

3.3.1.4 Beer as an Ultra-Processed Food

A novel approach to assessing the risks of a food is to focus not only on its micro- and macronutrients, but also on how it is made. The Nova classification, developed by Brazilian epidemiologist Carlos Augusto Monteiro, divides foods into:

1. unprocessed foods;
2. processed culinary ingredients;

[31] The Obesity Evidence Hub, 'Countries That Have Taxes on Sugar-Sweetened Beverages (SSBs)', *Obesity Evidence Hub* (Web Page, 21 March 2024) www.obesityevidencehub.org.au/collections/prevention/countries-that-have-implemented-taxes-on-sugar-sweetened-beverages-ssbs.

[32] Martin R Yeomans et al, 'Alcohol and Food Intake' (2003) 6(6) *Current Opinion in Clinical Nutrition and Metabolic Care* 639.

3. processed foods;
4. ultra-processed foods.

The adverse effects of ultra-processed foods on human health have been well documented. An umbrella review involving nearly 10 million participants showed direct associations between eating more ultra-processed foods and higher risks of all-cause mortality, cardiovascular disease, mental disorders, overweight, obesity, and type 2 diabetes.[33] Clearly, ultra-processed foods should be avoided where possible.

Beer, in its purest form, does not fall into the ultra-processed category; fermented products are categorized as processed foods (Group 3), not ultra-processed foods (Group 4). However, lower-quality beers and beers from large industrial breweries often contain highly processed ingredients such as corn syrup, propylene glycol, added sugars, and maltodextrin. The NOVA classification is an example of modern science supporting the timeless sixteenth-century *Reinheitsgebot* already mentioned many times in this book.

3.3.2 *Beer as a Drug*

Alcohol is a substance that affects human behaviour, and not always for the better. Arguably, the most harmful trait of alcohol is its potential to trigger impulsive behaviour and violence. The causal relationship between aggression and alcohol consumption is well documented.[34] Alcohol consumption also correlates with crime. According to a 2001 US study, 'alcohol was consumed prior to about half of all homicides and assaults, and nearly 40 percent of state prisoners report committing their current offense under the influence of alcohol'.[35]

There is scarce research on whether beer drinkers are more or less prone to aggression compared to drinkers of other alcoholic beverages. A study that explored the relationship between alcohol consumption and homicide rates in the US discovered that beer and spirit consumption were positively correlated with homicide rates, while wine consumption was negatively correlated with homicide rates.[36] Beer is most likely to be associated with underage drinking,[37] and it was observed that 'beer consumption by high school students was positively associated with the likelihood of getting into a physical fight'.[38]

[33] Melissa M Lane et al, 'Ultra-processed Food Exposure and Adverse Health Outcomes: Umbrella Review of Epidemiological Meta-analyses' (2024) 384 *British Medical Journal Publishing Group* e077310.

[34] Monica F Tomlinson et al, 'Recreational Drug Use and Human Aggressive Behavior: A Comprehensive Review since 2003' (2016) 27 *Aggression and Violent Behavior* 9.

[35] Susan E Martin, 'The Links between Alcohol, Crime and the Criminal Justice System: Explanations, Evidence and Interventions' (2001) 10(2) *American Journal on Addictions* 136.

[36] Sara Hockin, Meghan L Rogers, and William Alex Pridemore, 'Population-Level Alcohol Consumption and National Homicide Rates' (2017) 15(2) *European Journal of Criminology* 235.

[37] Rogers and Greenfield (n 22).

[38] Ioana Popovici, 'Alcohol Use and Crime: Findings from a Longitudinal Sample of U.S. Adolescents and Young Adults' (2012) 36(3) *Alcoholism, Clinical and Experimental Research* 532.

Another negative effect of alcohol is that it impairs thinking and muscle coordination. Almost any human activity becomes more dangerous and has worse outcomes when combined with alcohol. Examples include the effects of alcohol on car drivers, alcohol-related injuries in the workplace, and alcohol-related crimes. The extensive research on US highway accidents in 1983 also found that beer consumption was significantly and positively associated with highway fatalities, perhaps because many drivers considered it a 'soft' alcoholic beverage that would not impair their ability to drive.[39] Additionally, around 2 per cent of premature deaths worldwide are attributed to suicide – with which alcohol has a well-researched relationship.

Alcohol also leads to irresponsible behaviour when it comes to communicable (infectious) diseases. Multiple studies on communicable diseases observed that alcohol drinkers are more likely to contract communicable diseases and, when they acquire them, less likely to recover. Alcohol is especially responsible for risky sexual behaviour, contributing to the spread of HIV, viral hepatitis, and tuberculosis.[40]

Alcohol is an addictive substance. The WHO estimates there are 209 million people with alcohol dependence who are unable to quit drinking.[41] Details of the report show that the most affected population groups are adult men in Europe and the Americas. In Europe, 7.1 per cent of all adult men are addicted to alcohol and a further 6.3 per cent drink excessively. In the Americas, 7.1 per cent of all adult men are addicted to alcohol and a further 6.4 per cent of men drink excessively.[42] Coincidentally, those two regions have proportionally higher beer consumption than other regions in the world.

One of the ways to estimate alcohol's effect on society is to compare its harm with the harm caused by other drugs. This is usually done by a panel of experts measuring the harm to both individuals and society using pre-selected criteria. In studies from developed countries, alcohol usually takes the top spot in 'most harmful drug' rankings. A drug harms ranking study in Australia, for example, found alcohol to be, overall, the most harmful drug, ahead of both crystal meth and heroin.[43]

A similar study in Europe put alcohol in first place (ahead of heroin).[44] A survey of German addiction medicine experts put alcohol in fourth place, behind heroin

39 Israel Colón and Henry SG Cutter, 'The Relationship of Beer Consumption and State Alcohol and Motor Vehicle Policies to Fatal Accidents' (1983) 14(2) *Journal of Safety Research* 83.

40 Neo K Morojele et al, 'Alcohol Use and the Risk of Communicable Diseases' (2021) 13(10) *Nutrients* 3317; *WHO Report on Alcohol and Health and Treatment of Substance Use Disorders* (n 2); *Global Status Report on Alcohol and Health 2018* (n 19).

41 *WHO Report on Alcohol and Health and Treatment of Substance Use Disorders* (n 2).

42 Ibid.

43 Yvonne Bonomo et al, 'The Australian Drug Harms Ranking Study' (2019) 33(7) *Journal of Psychopharmacology (Oxford)* 759.

44 Jan Van Amsterdam et al, 'European Rating of Drug Harms' (2015) 29(6) *Journal of Psychopharmacology (Oxford)* 655.

and ahead of cocaine.[45] A multifactor analysis of the harms caused by the misuse of drugs in the UK concluded that 'overall, alcohol was the most harmful drug (overall harm score 72), with heroin (55) and crack cocaine (54) in second and third places'.[46] These surveys were based on different methodologies, but make a convincing argument that alcohol is currently one of the most harmful substances in Western culture. Its effects vastly exceed those of illicit drugs, perhaps because it is regulated more liberally.

3.3.3 *Regulatory Response to Alcohol*

We discuss some of the ways in which the law has responded to alcohol below. Here, we focus on ethical considerations and beer policy.

3.3.3.1 Ethical Considerations

Most beer is produced and consumed in countries of Western culture that emphasize individual freedom, individual responsibility, and the concept of a welfare state based on a certain degree of solidarity. This approach assumes that most people will make rational, responsible, and informed choices about their actions, leading to their own well-being and, ultimately, a prosperous society.

Enjoying beer responsibly means considering more than just the risk of a hangover, a broader waistline, or long-term health effects. Every extra beer can have direct effects on the well-being, health, and safety of a drinker's family and friends – and even people they encounter on the way home from the pub. Interestingly, beer consumption also affects society as a whole. Thinking about how one extra beer this afternoon can harm society is similar to considering whether recycling one plastic bottle will save the planet. The effect of a single event is insignificant, but the prevalence of the effect is what counts.

Widespread drinking makes society less safe and erodes social solidarity because it places a significant burden on social services. It makes individuals who live healthier lifestyles question why they should carry the cost of irresponsible choices made by others.

3.3.3.2 Beer Policy

Beer, despite its social costs, also has its benefits. Production of beer creates jobs and generates employment along the chain of distribution. There are also intangible

[45] Udo Bonnet et al, 'Ranking the Harm of Psychoactive Drugs Including Prescription Analgesics to Users and Others – A Perspective of German Addiction Medicine Experts' (2020) 11 *Frontiers in Psychiatry* 592199.

[46] David J Nutt, Leslie A King, and Lawrence D Phillips, 'Drug Harms in the UK: A Multicriteria Decision Analysis' (2010) 376 (9752) *The Lancet* 1558.

benefits, such as the enjoyment individuals get from drinking, socializing and relaxing, which are difficult to quantify but still important.

Policymakers must balance the need to protect public health and society from harm while respecting individuals' freedom to make lifestyle choices and safeguarding jobs and businesses. Many governments find themselves in absurd situations: they implement policies to reduce beer consumption while simultaneously subsidizing hop farmers, offering favourable tax treatment to pub personnel, and developing policies to protect local pubs from going out of business.

Western societies are experiencing demographic changes, with aging populations that will continue working until their late sixties. The economic perspective of a country where the majority of middle-aged people suffer from obesity and non-communicable diseases is very different from the perspective of a country *without* that burden. In some ways, public health policy is also economic policy. Ignoring public health issues connected with beer consumption brings long-term pain. But protecting jobs in the beer and hospitality industries today may lead to a future without a population healthy enough to work in other important jobs.

Getting beer policy right is tricky. Totally banning alcohol is not only unthinkable in most countries due to public opinion, but also irrational from a public health perspective. People already addicted to alcohol would turn to illegal sources or home production, creating even greater health risks (like that of methanol contamination).[47] Therefore, the most rational approach is regulation that targets populations with the highest risks of alcohol abuse. Evidence suggests that economic incentives, such as excise taxes, and preventive programmes and behavioural incentives, such as removing the visibility of alcohol from public spaces, can be effective.

These policies often face backlash. The Nanny State Index research initiative monitors, with a certain dose of irony, 'a league table of the worst places in Europe to eat, drink, smoke and vape'[48] and publishes annual reports that challenge the effectiveness of European policies on lifestyle drugs. The initiative raises a valid point: policies that limit individual freedoms but have no effect on reducing drinking prevalence should be withdrawn. On the other hand, the initiative has yet to provide convincing data on the failures of these policies.

Evidence also suggests that treating beer as a 'lesser evil' compared to drinks with higher alcoholic content is a dangerous fallacy. The social and health costs associated with beer are the same as those associated with alcohol consumed in any other form, and policy that distinguishes between alcohol types only confuses consumers. Unfortunately, most governments make this mistake by creating exceptions in favour of beer or wine. Of all alcoholic beverages, beer is the least likely to have its

[47] Ironically, illegal domestic production of beer poses little risk of methanol contamination. Due to its low price, beer is also the least likely alcoholic beverage to be smuggled from other countries. Therefore, it would be the most rational target for any potential prohibition policy.

[48] Christopher Snowdon, 'Nanny State Index', *Institute of Economic Affairs* (Web Page, 2023) https://nannystateindex.org/.

marketing regulated.[49] Data from the Global Health Observatory show us that 148 countries in the world employ excise taxes on alcohol, but the average tax share on spirits is much higher (26.5 per cent) than the average tax share on beer (17.2 per cent).[50] There is real-world evidence that 'increasing the beer tax or price of alcohol can reduce the rates of robbery, assault, and homicide'.[51] Economic studies show that excise taxes can reduce consumption, but are most efficient if they increase the price of products by at least 20 per cent.[52]

So why does the average global excise tax percentage on beer sit below that threshold? According to economists, 'where taxes are effective in changing health behaviours, the predictability of the revenue stream is reduced'.[53] In other words: governments are probably keeping excise taxes low because they fear higher tax rates would successfully reduce beer-drinking consumption and make tax revenues unpredictable. The many connections between beer and tax law are explored in more detail in Chapter 11.

To conclude, I will repeat that it is difficult to get beer policy right. We must be wary of scientism – an excessive belief that science and data can provide instructions on the only proper way of living our lives. It is important to recognize that health and life expectancy are not the only values to consider in policymaking. On the other hand, the 209 million people addicted to alcohol and the millions of victims of alcohol-related crimes and accidents demonstrate that liberal solutions based on individual choice have their limits when it comes to policy on addictive substances.

3.4 UNHEALTHY BEER AND THE LAW

Beer has been linked to a long list of health conditions ranging from cancer to 'man boobs'. When we discuss the health concerns associated with beer, we focus on concerns associated with common, current, and long-standing beer ingredients: malt, hops, yeast, and water, as well as common adjuncts such as sugar and spices like coriander.

However, brewers have not always been shy about what they throw into their beers. Some of the more 'exotic' – and no doubt harmful – adjuncts that brewers have used in their beers include oxen gall, soot, bark, mushrooms, and opium. The following is an amusing anecdote showcasing the amounts of opium sometimes added to beers in the past:

49 *WHO Report on Alcohol and Health and Treatment of Substance Use Disorders* (n 2).

50 Global Health Observatory, 'Taxes on Alcoholic Beverages', *World Health Organization* (Web Page, 2022) www.who.int/data/gho/data/themes/topics/taxes-on-alcoholic-beverages. Interestingly, there are over twenty countries, mainly from Europe, that do not impose any excise tax on wine.

51 Popovici (n 38) 532.

52 Alexandra Wright, Katherine E Smith and Mark Hellowell, 'Policy Lessons from Health Taxes: A Systematic Review of Empirical Studies' (2017) 17(1) *BMC Public Health* 583.

53 Ibid.

> Professor Andrew Ure, the well-known Scottish political economist and chemist, and far too serious to tell a tall Glaswegian story, recalled that the amount of opium added to the beer sold on one early Clyde paddle steamer was so excessive that he could have carried out post-mortems on its victims without their realising what was happening.[54]

We do not aim to address the health implications of these exotic adjuncts. However, there is one ingredient that deserves special mention in this context: grut, the variable mixture of herbs discussed in Chapter 2. Interestingly, it seems health concerns prompted legislative intervention, leading to the elimination of grut as an ingredient.

> The decline of gruit was accelerated in the sixteenth and seventeenth centuries by the increasingly prevalent belief that bog myrtle (*Myrtica gale*), one of the principal ingredients, could harm the consumer's health. Eventually, legislation was introduced that prohibited the use of gruit, and it disappeared from use in Germany in the eighteenth century. Ironically, modern chemical analysis has failed to detect any toxic components in bog myrtle ... it is possible that one of the other secret ingredients in gruit was actually poisonous![55]

3.4.1 *Unhealthy Beer and the Law of the Past*

When we speak about legislative responses to alcohol, many people will think of the prohibition in the US between 1920 and 1933. We discuss US Prohibition in Chapter 10, which addresses North America.

But the US was far from alone in adopting this extreme legislative approach. As we refer to on a few occasions throughout this book, a law enacted in 1900 outlawed the production of alcoholic beverages, including beer, in Iceland. Importing such beverages, however, was still allowed. In 1908, a referendum saw about 60 per cent of all voters favour a ban on alcohol (although it took no less than seven years to implement it). The complete 1915 ban on alcohol lasted until 1989 – albeit with exemptions, such as beer produced for the British occupation forces during World War II, and, later, beer produced for the US defence forces at the Keflavík station.

3.4.2 *Unhealthy Beer and the Law Today*

Health recommendations for beer and alcohol consumption have changed dramatically over time in the countries covered in this book. For example, a 2023 report by

54 TR Gourvish and RG Wilson, *British Brewing Industry, 1830–1980* (Cambridge University Press, 1994) 7 citing RG Wilson, 'Greene King: A Business and Family History' (1983) 58(4) *Business History Review* 639.

55 Michael Moir, 'Hops – A Millennium Review' (2000) 58(4) *Journal of the American Society of Brewing Chemists* 131, 132.

the Canadian Centre on Substance Use and Addiction (CCSA) states that zero alcohol is the only risk-free approach, that two standard drinks – each the equivalent of a 341-millilitre serving of 5-per-cent-alcohol beer – per week is deemed low-risk, and that any more than two standard drinks increases negative outcomes, including certain forms of cancer.[56] This advice is much stricter than an earlier 2011 report that allowed a maximum of ten drinks a week for women and fifteen drinks for men.

Similarly, the *Nordic Nutrition Recommendations 2023* (NNR2023) emphasizes that:

> Alcohol is not an essential nutrient, and from a nutritional point of view, energy contribution from high intake of alcoholic beverages affects diet quality negatively. Based on this and new systematic reviews, and since no threshold for safe level of alcohol consumption has currently been established for human health, the NNR2023 recommends avoiding alcohol intake. If alcohol is consumed, the intake should be very low. For children, adolescents and pregnant women abstinence from alcohol is advised.[57]

Interestingly, the NNR2023 also points to the impact alcohol consumption has on the environment (a topic we do not discuss in detail in this book).

> Consumption of alcoholic beverages contributes to negative environmental impact just as non-alcoholic beverages ... Alcoholic beverages have a climate impact associated with the energy and fuel used in manufacturing, transportation and post-use. Alcoholic beverages generated 3% of the dietary climate impact in a Swedish study ... The crops used for alcohol production, barley and wheat, may be associated with low biodiversity if produced in large-scale cropping systems with low diversity.[58]

The NNR2023 recommendations align with the WHO's views. In 2023, the WHO noted that 'no level of alcohol consumption is safe for our health'[59] and that 'alcohol use is among the leading risk factors for premature mortality and disability because of its causal relationship with multiple health conditions, which also include non-intentional injuries and suicides'.[60]

Against this background, it is unsurprising that health-focused laws today seek to affect beer consumption in various ways.

3.4.2.1 Legal Drinking Age

The legal age for purchasing and consuming alcohol is eighteen years in the majority of countries globally, and, according to a 2024 WHO report, 'in 2019, 2.3

[56] C Paradis et al, *Canada's Guidance on Alcohol and Health* (Final Report, January 2023).

[57] Nordic Council of Ministers, 'Nordic Nutrition Recommendations 2023 Alcohol' (Web Page, 2023) https://pub.norden.org/nord2023-003/alcohol-.html.

[58] Ibid.

[59] World Health Organization (n 27).

[60] Benjamin O Anderson et al, 'Health and Cancer Risks Associated with Low Levels of Alcohol Consumption' (2023) 8(1) *The Lancet Public Health* e6.

billion people lived in a country with an on-premise and/or off-premise beer minimum legal purchase age of 18 years'.[61] But the legal drinking age seems to be going up globally. The same report stated: 'Since 2012, the percentage of the world's population living in a country with a beer minimum legal purchase age higher than 18 years has almost doubled (from 312 million to 606 million).'[62]

Of the countries examined here, the eighteen-year age limit applies in Norway, Mexico, Ireland, Finland, the Czech Republic, Sweden (see, however, below), and the UK. In contrast, Belgium, Germany, and Denmark have legal drinking ages of sixteen years. Canada's is nineteen years, Iceland's is twenty years, and the US's is twenty-one years.[63] Of the countries included in our book, there is a five-year difference between the lowest drinking age and the highest. That is quite remarkable.

3.4.2.2 Limiting the Production and Sale of Alcohol

The production of alcoholic beverages such as beer is typically heavily regulated, and any beer made for commercial purposes typically requires some type of production licence. At the same time, producing beer for personal consumption – home brewing – is typically allowed. Home brewing is legal in all countries studied in this book but restrictions – such as annual tax-free production level limits – are sometimes imposed.

As might be expected, laws governing selling and serving beer normally correspond to the legal drinking age. For example, in countries where the legal age for purchasing and consuming alcohol is eighteen years, there is a corresponding legal obligation not to sell or serve beer to anyone under eighteen.. However, some countries – such as Sweden – distinguish between purchases made in licensed venues and purchases made in shops. At eighteen, a person may buy alcoholic drinks in licensed venues in Sweden, but to buy alcohol from Systembolaget (a government-owned liquor store chain), they must be twenty years or older.

Some laws also set minimum prices for alcohol. The so-called minimum unit price, also known as a floor price, can be used to mandate the minimum price a 'unit' (that is, a standard drink) of alcohol can be sold for. Ireland, Scotland, Wales, and ten of Canada's thirteen provinces all have minimum unit prices.[64] But minimum-price laws can raise complex legal issues[65] in the context of trade agreements, a topic we will get to in Chapter 9.

Relatedly, in some countries such as Finland, the law specifically prohibits volume discounts – where an alcoholic beverage is more expensive per unit when bought individually than as part of a multi-package (Figure 3.2). Another way in

[61] *WHO Report on Alcohol and Health and Treatment of Substance Use Disorders* (n 2) 69.

[62] Ibid.

[63] There is, however, some minor variation across the United States. See, for example, the laws of Wisconsin.

[64] World Health Organization, *No Place for Cheap Alcohol: The Potential Value of Minimum Pricing for Protecting Lives* (Report, 2022).

[65] Ibid 33–40.

FIGURE 3.2 Alko: Finland's alcohol monopoly stores.

which the price of beer can be regulated is through restrictions on 'happy hour' pricing. For example, in the US, after-work discounts are banned in Alaska, Indiana, Massachusetts, North Carolina, Oklahoma, Rhode Island, Utah, and Vermont.

Beer sale times can also be regulated. For example, the Swedish monopoly store Systembolaget is closed on Sundays, and in some US states (Mississippi, North Carolina, Texas, and Utah), state liquor stores are closed on Sundays. In many countries, the law also imposes restrictions on the time of day during which alcohol can be sold.

3.4.2.3 Limiting Where Beer Can Be Consumed

The law often defines certain areas where you cannot drink alcohol. Such laws may be motivated by a range of reasons, including maintaining public order, preventing alcohol-related antisocial behaviour, and stopping crime. While those reasons are broadly related to public health, others are more directly health-related – such as the rationale behind prohibiting the consumption of alcohol near schools and playgrounds.

3.4.2.4 Activity Limitations

In all countries we study in this book, laws limit what a person may do when their blood alcohol level exceeds certain limits. The most well-known example is the illegality of driving while intoxicated (a topic we return to in Chapter 13). But there are also other examples of how the law restricts what we can do if we have a few too many beers.

For example, an intoxicated person is often not allowed further alcohol. Under the UK's Licensing Act 2003,[66] it is an offence to sell or attempt to sell alcohol to a person who is drunk. And if you are in a pub, you need to keep a close eye on the drunkenness level of your friends as well – at least, if you are thinking of buying them a beer. Under the same law, it is an offence to knowingly obtain or attempt to obtain alcohol for consumption on the premises by a person who is drunk. This raises some rather interesting questions.

While ill-advised from a health perspective, it is indisputably the case that a great number of people go to pubs with the aim (to some degree) of getting drunk. As anyone who has visited a pub can attest, it is also a fact that 'drunk' people in pubs often continue drinking. So how does the law define being drunk? Regrettably, the Licensing Act does not tell us much. In some sections, it outlines rules for people who are 'drunk or disorderly'. That suggests a person can be 'drunk' without being 'disorderly' – and that it might not always be easy to determine whether a person is classed as drunk. This observation is also relevant when considering that being 'drunk and disorderly' is an offence.

In the end, perhaps, we have to conclude that – as with other illusive concepts – we know drunkenness when we see it. But perhaps that does not fully apply in relation to our own possible drunkenness. The other alternative is that 'drunk' – as has been argued in relation to 'privacy' – is a concept we can best identify when we lose it. But, for drunkenness, becoming 'un-drunk' takes us into the terrible territory of hangovers. And hindsight will not help us when trying to assess whether it is lawful to buy another round of beers for our friends.

Interestingly, Aristotle observed that different drinks caused different types of drunkenness: 'Men who have been intoxicated with wine fall down face foremost, whereas they who have drunk barley beer lie outstretched on their backs; for wine makes one top-heavy, but beer stupefies.'[67]

3.4.2.5 Advertising Restrictions

Several countries restrict beer advertising. Those restrictions often relate to where beer can be advertised or who can be targeted by advertising. In some cases, they require prior approval of ads or regulate how beer is portrayed.

In Mexico, for example, advertisements for beer and other alcoholic drinks must generally be approved in advance by the Federal Commission for Protection against Sanitary Risks (COFEPRIS). Advertisements may be rejected where they:

66 *Licensing Act 2003* (UK) s 141.
67 Bamforth (n 3) 30.

- are addressed to minors;
- promote an irresponsible consumption of alcoholic beverages;
- transmit ideas or images of success, fame, prestige, tranquillity, joy, or euphoria as a consequence of the consumption of alcoholic beverages;
- show alcohol as a triggering element of interpersonal relationships;
- attempt to create an association between the consumption of alcohol with creative, educational, sport, domestic, or professional activities or religious or civic celebrations;
- exalt the social prestige, virility, or femininity of the target audience.

Advertising restrictions can also differentiate between different levels of products. Under Finnish law, for example, the advertising of strong alcoholic beverages – that is, those containing more than 22 per cent of alcohol by volume – is prohibited by the Alcohol Act, affecting a small number of unusually strong beers. Most beers fall into the category of 'mild alcoholic beverages' and can be marketed with some restrictions. Those restrictions include:

- not depicting minors, visibly intoxicated people, or disorderly behaviour;
- not implying that alcohol enhances performance, advances social success, or improves sexual prowess.

Interestingly, Finnish law also places restrictions on the timing of beer advertising. Even if an advertisement complies with the relevant restrictions, it cannot run on television or radio between 7 a.m. and 10 p.m.

The law can also impose requirements to include health statements. For example, since 1 July 2024, alcohol marketing in Belgium must include the text: 'Alcohol abuse harms your health.'[68] Beer advertising restrictions can be found in the other countries we discuss in this book, although their focus and level of strictness varies.

3.4.2.6 Labelling Requirements

Another way in which the law seeks to address beer-related health concerns is through labelling requirements (discussed further in Chapter 7). There are two classes of labelling requirements: those specifically focused on the health risks associated with beer consumption and those focused on alerting the drinker to the volume of alcohol consumed.

A 2023 Mexican study concluded: 'Visible health warning labels could lead individuals to think about the health risks of alcohol, reducing the attractiveness

[68] Advertising Ethics Jury, 'Communication Centre Launches New Educational Message on Alcohol Advertising, in Consultation with Industry', *JEP* (Web Page, 26 February 2024) www.jep.be/fr/le-centre-de-la-communication-lance-un-nouveau-message-educatif-en-matiere-de-publicite-pour-lalcool-en-concertation-avec-le-secteur-concerne/.

of the product and decreasing the intention to purchase and consume alcohol.'[69] Labelling requirements focused on the health risks of beer consumption can be found in several countries, such as Ireland.[70]

Some countries have adopted labelling requirements that help people monitor how much alcohol they drink. Typically, this involves measuring alcohol consumption in 'standard alcoholic drinks'.[71] This system is quite rare, and of the countries included in this book, only Denmark has adopted it.[72] Internationally, there is no agreement on what amounts to a standard drink, which has resulted in calls for an 'international standard drink' (ISD) definition.[73]

3.4.2.7 The Beer Industry Responds: Light, Low, and No

So what do you do if you are not allowed to advertise your beers the way you want? The obvious answer is to create a version of the beer that falls outside the advertising limitations – for example, by making it low- or no-alcohol. This approach has resulted in famous beer brands promoting their no- or low-alcohol versions in contexts where full-strength beers could not be advertised.

While this approach could be viewed cynically, there is a genuine market for no- and low-alcohol beers, and manufacturers will naturally seek to build brand recognition across those market segments.

In addition to producing low- and no-alcohol beers, the brewing industry has also taken other steps to produce healthier beers. Light (or 'lite') beers with lower calories are now common in many countries.

3.5 BEER, LAW, HEALTH, AND DATA PRIVACY

While discussing the cross-section between beer, law, and health, a few words ought to be stated about data privacy. Information about a person's health is often viewed as particularly sensitive. So, when an entity records what beer and how much a person consumes, that can be considered a collection of sensitive information under data privacy laws such as the EU's General Data Protection Regulation (GDPR), which applies in Belgium, the Czech Republic, Denmark, Finland, Germany, and Sweden (as well as in Iceland and Norway, despite them not being members of the EU).

But when is information about our beer-drinking habits being collected, and by whom? The most obvious: the retail outlets from which we buy beer. Pubs and

[69] López-Olmedo et al (n 1).

[70] *Public Health (Alcohol) Act 2018* and *Public Health (Alcohol) (Labelling) Regulations 2023*.

[71] Global Health Observatory, 'Number of Standard Alcoholic Drinks Displayed on Containers', *World Health Organization* (Web Page) www.who.int/data/gho/indicator-metadata-registry/imr-details/3788.

[72] *WHO Report on Alcohol and Health and Treatment of Substance Use Disorders* (n 2) 238–42.

[73] Ibid 126.

retailers with loyalty programmes may end up collecting detailed data about what we buy, how much, and when.

Other entities can also obtain detailed data about our drinking habits. Many people are dedicated users of social media platforms, such as Facebook, TikTok, and Instagram, and may post images and comments about their drinking habits. There is also a growing number of social media platforms focused on beer and 'beer rating', such as Untapped[74] and the previously popular Ratebeer.[75] Those platforms are arguably best positioned to collect detailed drinking data, since users not only post about what, when, and where they drink, but may also include information about with *whom* they drink.

3.6 BEER, LAW, HEALTH, AND THE FUTURE

'Folks around here say that Jeppe drinks, but they don't say why Jeppe drinks' (*Folk siger vel i herredet at Jeppe drikker, men de siger ikke hvorfor Jeppe drikker*). This is perhaps the most famous line in Holberg's celebrated 1722 play, *Jeppe on the Hill*. The principal character, Jeppe, is a poor and oppressed peasant. He is abused by his wife and trodden down by his superiors.

The quoted line from *Jeppe on the Hill* has been the subject of much discussion and analysis. One possible interpretation is that excessive drinking, while (for good reasons) seen as a problem, may rather – or, at least, also – be viewed as a symptom and consequence of underlying problems. That could be something lawmakers regulating the consumption of beer and other alcohol products need to reflect upon.

If excessive drinking is a symptom of other problems, would society be better addressing the underlying issues rather than just regulating the consumption of alcohol? Of course, removing the option of alcohol as a coping mechanism may be helpful – but only if people do not turn to something potentially more harmful instead.

This chapter has illustrated that perceptions around the health impacts of beer have varied considerably over time. It has also demonstrated that these variations stem from the need for a comparative perspective more than from any changes in the beer itself. Beer today is, objectively speaking, approximately as healthy as it was 100, 400, or 800 years ago. Compared to the potentially dirty water in a medieval town or the gin of the 'gin craze' in England, beer is the healthy choice and, in those contexts, the law will promote its consumption. But compared to many of the drink options today – not least pure water – beer is the unhealthy choice, and so the law seeks to limit or even prevent its consumption.

[74] Untapped, 'Find Beers You'll Love' (Web Page) https://untappd.com/.

[75] Ratebeer, 'Your Guide to the World of Beer' (Web Page) was at www.ratebeer.com/. However, the site has now shut down: see www.forbes.com/sites/dontse/2025/01/22/why-ratebeer-is-shutting-down-and-the-person-trying-to-save-it/.

We have already pointed to research highlighting public health benefits associated with beer consumption. But, in most parts of the world today, the only context in which beer is promoted as healthy is 'beer spas'.

Bathing in barrels of beer is not a new idea (it likely goes back to the Middle Ages).[76] The claimed health benefits include stress relief, cleansing the skin, and releasing toxins from the body. The vitamins B6 and B12 in beer are said to encourage the growth and repair of skin cells and may even treat skin conditions like acne, psoriasis, and cellulite.[77] But it is not all good news. The alcohol in beer may have a negative impact on skin by drying it out and weakening it.[78] And perhaps this summarizes the relationship between beer and health in the best possible way: whether people drink it or bathe in it, the health and safety impact of beer will not be solely 'good' or solely 'bad', for individuals or for societies.

Claims such as the WHO's suggestion that no level of alcohol consumption is safe for us are likely correct from a purely physical perspective. They can, however, be criticized as being too simplistic, because they fail to account for the mental health dimension we discussed earlier. From a lawyer's perspective, given that beer (and alcohol more broadly) is often held accountable for indirect harms such as drink-driving accidents and domestic violence, justice requires that we also acknowledge indirect positive consequences, such as the social and mental health benefits of beer-drinking. The question quickly arises: just how indirect can the consequences be that we reasonably take into account? Is it, for example, justified to discuss the sense of happiness and belonging sparked by taking part in traditional festivities that involve beer-drinking? Perhaps that is the core reason it is so difficult to assess the health and societal impacts – negative and positive – of alcoholic beverages such as beer. Where do we draw the line of causality?

76 Nikolina Ilic, 'So, Turns Out Beer Spas Are the Newest Thing in Wellness', *Australian Men's Health* (Web Page, 18 October 2022) https://menshealth.com.au/beer-spas-are-the-newest-thing-in-wellness/.

77 Hannah Prensky, 'Beer Spa: Health Hack or Tacky Tourist Trap?', *Columbia Science Review* (Web Page, 11 July 2019) www.thecolumbiasciencereview.com/blog/beer-spa-health-hack-or-tacky-tourist-trap.

78 Ibid.

4

The Nordic Countries

From 'Lagom' to the Extreme and Back Again

4.1 INTRODUCTION

The Nordic countries[1] – Sweden Denmark, Norway, Finland, and Iceland – are perhaps best known for being cold, comparatively sparsely populated, and in many ways countries of extremes, such as between fire and ice in Iceland, and the extreme contrasts between the midnight sun of the long summer nights on the one hand, and the long dark winters with *aurora borealis* on the other.

And the Nordic countries are also countries of extremes when looked at from the perspective of beer and beer law. To see that this is so, we need only consider how recently beer was banned in Iceland.

Another example of extremes is found in the remarkable characteristics of Norwegian 'Kveik' yeast fermenting at speeds and temperatures far outside the norm. And a further example is found in the exhilarating prospect – based on the Finnish National Epos *Kalevala* – that hopped beer was already known in Finland during prehistoric times. And while on the topic of extremes, drinking, and Finland, it may be noted that the Finns appear to have a particularly rich vocabulary of drinking words, such as *Kalsarikänni* (getting drunk at home in your underwear with no intention of going out).[2]

But the Nordic countries are also characterized by a focus on 'moderation' that is perhaps best summarized in the term 'lagom', meaning 'just enough' or 'just right'. To understand that term, we need to go back in time to the tables of the longhouses in Viking-era Scandinavia.

[1] We do not discuss Greenland, Faroe Islands, and Åland here.

[2] Lars Marius Garshol, 'A Small Dictionary of Finnish Drinking Words', *Larsblog* (Blog Post, 16 August 2020) www.garshol.priv.no/blog/413.html.

Beer Consumption in the Nordic Countries

Beer consumption in the Nordic countries varies greatly, but none of them make it onto the top ten list for beer consumption per capita.

While Finns consume 70 litres per year per capita, Swedes only consume about half that (36 litres per year per capita). The other relevant figures are 53 litres for Danes and 46 litres for Norwegians. All according to Statista's per capita volume sales in the beer market worldwide, by country in 2023 (no statistics were included for Iceland). However, another source (www.globaldata.com) indicates that 'The Per capita consumption of Beer segment in Iceland reached 77.45 Litres in 2022', suggesting that Icelanders consume the most beer per capita in the Nordic countries.

At least according to folklore, the term lagom stems from the phrase *laget om* (around the team), from the Viking tradition of drinking enough when the drinking horn was passed around, without drinking so much that there is not enough for everyone. Some support for this being the proper origins of the word lagom – or at least the existence of the Nordic 'lagom' mentality as a guiding principle in Viking drinking etiquette – can be found in Hávamál. Hávamál is a combination of different poems, attributed to the Norse god Odin, presenting advice for living, proper conduct, and wisdom. In Verse 19, we can read Odin's instruction to: 'Keep not the mead cup but drink thy measure.'[3]

Given the topic of our book, we may also take note of Odin's attitude to ale. In several verses he warns of the impact ale has on a person's abilities. For example, in Verse 12, we can read: 'Less good than they say for the sons of men is the drinking oft of ale: for the more they drink, the less can they think and keep a watch o'er their wits.' This thinking, while ancient in origin, is clearly reflected in many ways in which the law regulates beer and alcohol more broadly; just think of laws against drink-driving as an example.

4.2 BEER AND DRINKING IN THE NORDIC COUNTRIES

Beer has long been an important drink in the Nordic countries, and brewing for domestic consumption has a strong tradition. It has, for example, been argued by some scholars that 'agriculture in Finland started because the migrating tribes had accustomed themselves to beer and needed cultivated grain to produce the drink'.[4]

Drinking vessels have been found with residues of a type of beer dating to the Nordic Bronze Age (1700–500 BCE).[5] One such example is the grave of a young

[3] Sæmund Edda and DL Ashliman (eds), '*Hávamál [The Words of Odin the High One]*' (Web Page) https://sites.pitt.edu/~dash/havamal.html.

[4] Jussi Rokka, 'The Oxford Companion to Beer Definition of Finland', *Craft Beer & Brewing* (Web Page) https://beerandbrewing.com/dictionary/YqQCIJCikv/.

[5] Svante Ekelin, 'The Oxford Companion to Beer Definition of Finland', *Craft Beer & Brewing* (Web Page) https://beerandbrewing.com/dictionary/AC59dSBeYm/.

women from 1370 BCE that contained a beaker with the residue of a drink that appears to be a fermented mix of berries, wheat, and honey, flavoured with bog myrtle.[6] It would perhaps be difficult to sell this as beer today, but it is clearly a mix of beer, wine, and mead.[7]

Apart from in Iceland, where there was a scarcity of grain towards the end of the Middle Ages and onwards, the drinking of beer, instead of the impure water, remained important for health reasons until well into the eighteenth century.[8] For example, the crew on a ship like the world-famous Vasa ship – that sank in the Stockholm harbour in 1628 and may be seen to this day at the Vasa Museum – was to be provided with between two and four litres of weak beer, 'ship's ale' per day depending on their rank.[9] Additional beer rations were provided to the crew just before battles to promote bravery and fighting spirit.[10] Indeed, in the case of the Vasa ship, 'Vice Admiral Henrik Fleming had purchased extra beer of good quality with his own money for this purpose'.[11] Getting drunk while in service on a ship like the Vasa, or selling beer onboard, was, however, illegal.[12]

While the issue of how to deal with drunken sailors has even made its way into popular folksongs all over the world, we may pause here and consider the fact that the common sailors on the Vasa ship were put to shame by nuns. It has been noted that nuns in the Swedish Solberga Abbey were each entitled to a ration of five litres of beer per day.[13] These beers would have been relatively weak, like the 'ship's ale', but it says something about the role beer played in the diet.

Drinking has also been an important social event in the Nordic countries throughout history and remains so today. Perhaps the fact that Vikings would not speak of celebrating Yule (Christmas) but rather say 'drink Yule' most clearly illustrates the central role of drinking in the Nordic culture.[14] However, other traditions live on today.

6 Lars Marius Garshol, 'Nordic Grog', *Larsblog* (Blog Post, 9 February 2015) www.garshol.priv.no/blog/316.html.

7 For more information about this 'Nordic Grog' see Patrick E McGovern, Gretchen R Hall, and Armen Mirzoian, 'A Biomolecular Archaeological Approach to "Nordic Grog"' (2013) 2(2) *Danish Journal of Archaeology* 112.

8 Ekelin (n 5).

9 Matilda Jarl, 'Tobaks- och alkoholkonsumtion ombord på flottans fartyg under 1600- och 1700-talen [Tobacco and Alcohol Consumption on Board Ships of the Fleet in the 17th and 18th Centuries]' (2022) 79 *Forum Navale* 170.

10 Vasa Museet, '12. In Battle', *Vasa Museet* (Web Page, 13 October 2020) www.vasamuseet.se/besok/audioguide/audioguide-enkel-svenska/textversion-enkel-svenska/12.-i-strid.

11 Vasa Museet, 'Vasa – The Machine of War', *Vasa Museet* (Web Page, 18 June 2020) www.vasamuseet.se/en/explore/vasa-history/machine-of-war.

12 Jarl (n 9) 167 and 189.

13 Ekelin (n 5).

14 Lars Marius Garshol, 'The True Meaning of Christmas', *Larsblog* (Blog Post, 15 December 2020) www.garshol.priv.no/blog/419.html.

Following drinking etiquette is important, but beer consumption is associated with fewer traditions than is the consumption of spirits. However, the word *öl* in Swedish, or Danish *øl*, is still used as a reference to special occasions. For example, originating in the days during which one would build one's own house with help from friends and neighbours, *taklagsöl* (roof truss beer or roof truss party) was a party held to thank those who helped at the stage when the roof truss was put into place. *Gravöl* or Danish *gravøl* (funeral beer or funeral wake) is another example of a tradition that remains today.

Nevertheless, the widespread drinking – both beer and spirits – led to a strong sobriety movement in the Nordic countries during the 1800s and early 1900s. That movement and the laws to which it gave rise are noted throughout the book in various contexts. Here, we will only note some odd outcomes, such as that for a period from 1922, in Sweden, strong beer (above 3.6 per cent ABV) was only available in pharmacies and required a doctor's prescription.[15] Further, the Icelandic ban on beer, introduced in 1915, lasted until as recently as 1 March 1989 (now celebrated as 'Beer Day' in Iceland). However, the idea of the government exercising tight control on the sale of alcohol – for example, the Norwegian *Vinmonopolet* – lives on in several of the Nordic countries, despite being subject to legal challenges on some occasions. For example, the Swedish governmental monopoly on the sale of alcohol was challenged before the European Court of Justice (now Court of Justice of the European Union) in 1997. However, the Court ruled that the relevant EC law 'does not preclude domestic provisions relating to the existence and operation of a national monopoly on the retail of alcoholic beverages such as those mentioned in the order for reference'.[16] Thus, the state monopoly – already envisaged by the Swedish King Karl XII in the early 1700s – lives on. The most recent debates were centred around *gårdsförsäljning* (that is, allowing small-scale producers of alcoholic beverages to sell their products for consumption off-site.[17]

4.3 BREWING AND THE BREWING MARKET IN THE NORDIC COUNTRIES

Brewing beer for household consumption has a long tradition in the Nordic countries. Indeed, brewing beer at certain times of the year – All Saints' Day and Christmas – has been a legal obligation at least in Norway. Writing about King

15 Internet Archive, 'Beer Politics through the Ages', *The Wayback Machine* (Web Page) https://web.archive.org/web/20131205205719/http:/sverigesbryggerier.se/om-oss/historia/olpolitik-genom-tiderna/.

16 *Criminal Proceedings against Harry Franzén* (C-189/95) [1997] CJEU 504.

17 Camilla Waltersson Grönvall and Zandra Milton, 'Bättre förutsättningar för besöksnäringen i fråga om småskalig produktion av alkoholdrycker [Better Conditions for the Tourism Industry in Terms of Small-Scale Production of Alcoholic Beverages]', *Government Offices of Sweden* (Web Page, 4 July 2024) www.regeringen.se/rattsliga-dokument/lagradsremiss/2024/07/battre-forutsattningar-for-besoksnaringen-i-fraga-om-smaskalig-produktion-av-alkoholdrycker/.

Håkon the Good (king from 934 to 961) in *Heimskringla*, Snorri Sturluson states that he 'made a law that the festival of Yule [Christmas] should begin at the same time as Christian people held it, and that every man, under penalty, should brew a meal of malt into ale, and therewith keep the Yule holy as long as it lasted'.[18] Building on this, the 'Gulathing law' from the twelfth century, includes the following rule:

> Yet another beer brew we are required to make, man and wife from equal amounts of malts, and to bless it Christmas night in thanks to Christ and St Mary, for a good year and peace.
>
> If this is not done, three marks must be paid to the bishop. But if someone sits three winters without doing so, or cannot pay the fees that we have added for our religion, and this can be proven, then he has forfeited every penny of his worth. The king shall have half, and the bishop the other half. But he may confess his sins and make church penance and stay in Norway. If he will not he shall leave the realm of our king.[19]

The harsh penalties are noteworthy: potential forced exile for failing to engage in homebrewing!

In Norway, commercial brewing only became common in after about 1820,[20] and the longstanding 'homebrew' tradition has resulted in widespread production of farmhouse ales, with Norwegian farmhouse ales being the most prominent today. In fact, these Norwegian farmhouse ales are associated with the remarkable and unique Norwegian 'kveik' yeast[21] fermenting at speeds and temperatures far outside the norm. While lager yeasts enjoy low temperature (around 10°C), and ale yeast ordinarily works best up to the low 20s °C, kveik yeast happily works at temperatures up to over 40°C without creating off-flavours. Kveik is now widely available to both home brewers and commercial breweries around the world.

But the Norwegian kveik yeast is not the only major yeast story to tell about the Nordic countries. In fact, despite the remarkable features of kveik, there is another yeast innovation that is the Nordic countries' biggest contribution to global beer brewing. In 1875, the founder of Carlsberg – J. C. Jacobsen – set up the highly successful[22] Carlsberg Research Laboratory. Working in that laboratory, Emil

[18] Snorri Sturluson, 'Heimskringla The Chronicle of the Kings of Norway', *Gutenberg* (Web Page, 27 November 2009) [15] www.gutenberg.org/files/598/598-h/598-h.htm#link2H_4_0072.

[19] Lars Marius Garshol, 'When Not Brewing Christmas Beer was Illegal', *Larsblog* (Blog Post, 7 December 2019) www.garshol.priv.no/blog/407.html citing Ragnar Hauge, *Lover om alkohol i Norge: fra landskapslovene til 1814 [Laws on Alcohol in Norway: From the Provincial Laws to 1814]* (Rusmiddeldirektoratet, 1998).

[20] Kjetil Jikiun, 'The Oxford Companion to Beer Definition of Norway', *Craft Beer & Brewing* (Web Page) https://beerandbrewing.com/dictionary/S6IME05aK7/.

[21] For a detailed discussion of kveik (and many other beer-related matters), see Lars Marius Garshol, 'Larsblog' (Blog Posts) www.garshol.priv.no/blog/.

[22] For example, the pH scale, which is a method for specifying the level of acidity or alkalinity of a solution on a scale from 0 to 14, was invented by S. P. L. Sørensen working in the Carlsberg

C. Hansen managed to isolate a single cell of good yeast excluding the wild yeast that made the quality of each batch uncertain. Wild yeast can cause beer to taste like baby vomit or urine, for example, and indeed can make the beer unhealthy to drink.

By propagating that single cell into a pure yeast culture (the *Saccharomyces Carlsbergensis*, now commonly referred to as *Saccharomyces pastorianus*) consistent results could be achieved on a production scale from November 1883. Importantly, as so-called beer sickness or yeast sickness (caused by wild yeast) was a widespread problem at the time, Jacobsen generously gave the pure yeast away for free to other brewers and the Carlsberg yeast remains widely used today.

Before leaving the topic of *Saccharomyces Carlsbergensis*, one more point is in order; we ought to pause to consider just how amazing yeast is (the hidden hero in the beer-making process). Carlsberg scientists have managed to extract living yeasts cells from a 133-year-old bottle of the original Carlsberg lager and used those cells to recreate the 1883 original (Figure 4.1).[23]

The other beer ingredient that deserves special attention in the Nordic context is hops. As hinted at above, there have been suggestions that the Finnish National Epos *Kalevala* and certain linguistic indicators are proof of a very early use of hops in beer in what is now Finland. Rune XX of the *Kalevala* contains a nice, clear 'beer recipe': 'Beer arises from the barley, Comes from barley, hops, and water.'[24] Indeed, it has been noted that *Kalevala* devotes 'more lines to the creation of beer than the creation of the world'.[25] At any rate, while written down much later, this may point to hopped beer already being known in Finland during prehistoric times, even though conventional wisdom considers the first reference to beer brewed with hops to stem from the Hallertau region in Bavaria in year 736.[26]

We may of course never know this for sure, but it is worth noting that hops seem to have grown wild in parts of the Nordic countries from 9000 BCE.[27] Furthermore, it has been noted that there are signs of hop cultivation in Norway from around 500

laboratory in 1909. See Carlsberg Breweries, 'The Invention of the pH Scale', *Carlsberg Group* (Web Page) www.carlsberggroup.com/pursuit-of-better/scientific-discoveries/ph-scale/.

23 Carlsberg Breweries A/S, 'Rebrewing the First Quality Beer Using Carlsberg's Original Purified Yeast', *Carlsberg Group* (Web Page) www.carlsberggroup.com/pursuit-of-better/scientific-discoveries/1883-rebrew/.

24 Rune XX as reproduced in Charles W Bamforth, *Grape vs. Grain: A Historical, Technological, and Social Comparison of Wine and Beer* (Cambridge University Press, 2008) 36.

25 Joshua J Mark, 'Beer in the Ancient World', *World History Encyclopedia* (Web Page, 2 March 2011) www.worldhistory.org/article/223/beer-in-the-ancient-world/.

26 Helena Korpelainen and Maria Pietiläinen, 'Hop (Humulus lupulus L.): Traditional and Present Use, and Future Potential' (2021) 75 (3) *Economic Botany* 302, 304. See also Bamforth (n 24) 35–42.

27 Lars Marius Garshol, 'The Early History of Hops', *Larsblog* (Blog Post, 6 December 2022) www.garshol.priv.no/blog/434.html citing Lars Larsson, 'Från tundra till skog. Miljöförändringar i norra Skåne under jägarstenåldern [From Tundra to Forest. Environmental Changes in Northern Scania during the Hunterian Stone Age]' (2009) 2 *Royal Vitterhets Academy of History and Antiquities* 146.

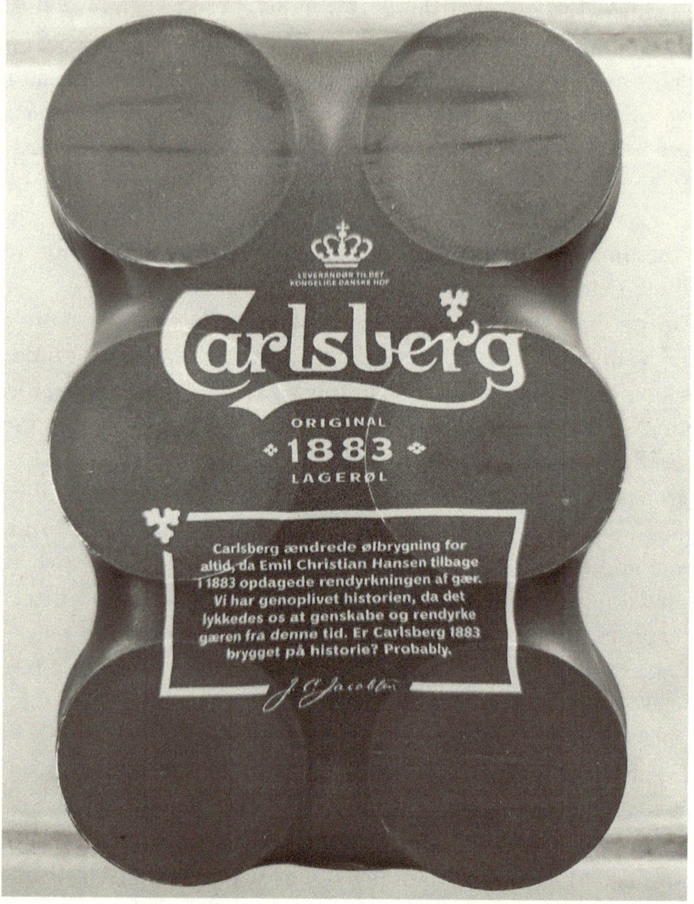

FIGURE 4.1 Carlsberg Original 1883.

BCE.[28] Speaking of hops, as already hinted at in Chapter 1, growing hops has been a duty established by law at least in Sweden, Finland, and Denmark since the early 1400s.[29] The reason is that, in the 1400s and 1500s, hops was a substantial and costly part of Sweden's imports. To break the dependence on imports, various laws were introduced requiring the cultivation of hops. Just how precious hops were seen to be is reflected in the fact that theft of hops was punishable by death.

[28] Garshol (n 27) citing Ult Hafsten, 'Jordbrukskulturens historie i Oslo of Mjøstrakten belyst ved pollenalytiske undersøkelser [The History of Agricultural Culture in Oslo of the Mjøstrakten Illuminated by Pollen Analysis]' (1958) 21 *Viking (Oslo)* 51.

[29] Rokka (n 4); Jens Eiken, 'The Oxford Companion to Beer Definition of Denmark', *Craft Beer & Brewing* (Web Page) https://beerandbrewing.com/dictionary/WBZ1ZDnezn/; Gabriela Bjarne Larsson, 'Stadgelagstiftning i senmedeltidens Sverige [Statutory Legislation in Late Medieval Sweden]' (Doctoral Thesis, Stockholm University, 1994).

FIGURE 4.2 Pripps beer sign.

The brewing industry in the Nordic countries has largely followed the trend seen in so many countries – from a huge number of small local breweries to a concentration of a small number of huge breweries, and then a counter-trend via the craft beer movement taking us back to a significant number of local producers. For example, from 2002 to 2008, Denmark grew from 19 to more than 100 breweries.[30] And in Sweden, there are now more than 400 breweries with their own production,[31] and non-alcoholic beer is the fastest growing market segment.[32]

The dominant player by far is Carlsberg, which was founded in 1847 outside Copenhagen. Via a series of mergers and takeovers, what is now the Carlsberg Group controls most major Nordic brands, such as Sweden's Pripps and Falcon, Norwegian Ringnes and Munkholm, Finnish Karhu and Koff, and Danish Tuborg (Figure 4.2). This gives the Carlsberg Group near total control of the

30 Eiken (n 29).

31 Swedish Breweries, 'Bryggerirapport [Brewery Report]', *Swedish Breweries* (Web Page, 2023) https://sverigesbryggerier.se/statistik/#bryggeristatistik.

32 Ibid.

mainstream Nordic beer market, except when it comes to Iceland. But Carlsberg's market share extends far beyond the Nordic countries. As of 2022, it was the sixth biggest brewery in the world and had an annual revenue of US$9.95 billion.[33]

4.4 TYPES OF BEER IN THE NORDIC COUNTRIES

There was a time, not so long ago, when Swedes generally ordered their beers by the simple phrase '*en stor stark*' (one big strong). No brands were mentioned, merely the quantity of standard-sized strong beers had to be articulated to place an order. The customer would then be served a glass (which started as a pint but has gradually decreased to 400–500 ml, and even down to 330 ml in some cases) of whatever pale lager was on tap (typically at least 4.5 per cent ABV, although all beer with an ABV over 3.5 per cent is now classed as *starköl* (strong beer)). This habit has, however, changed as the beer scene has become more 'sophisticated', although it is still possible to order a beer in this way. In 1999, work started on a law to standardize what a consumer could expect by way of volume and strength when ordering *en stor stark*.[34] However, in 2003 the government concluded that there was no need for standardization in this regard.[35] This conclusion is somewhat surprising. Could you, for example, imagine the law allowing petrol stations to sell petrol without the consumer knowing exactly how much and what type they would get for their money? Or what about a carton of eggs that may contain three to six eggs of some size not known to the consumer in advance?

Danish pale lager is doubtless the most prominent Nordic beer on the international stage. Looking at the Beer Judge Certification Program (BJCP) style guide and the style guide for the commercial brewing sector (for example, the Brewers Association 2023 Beer Style Guidelines), only two uniquely Nordic beers are included: the historical beer style 'Sahti', described as 'A sweet, heavy, strong traditional Finnish farmhouse beer usually with rye and juniper, and a banana-clove yeast character', and the similar Swedish 'Gotlanddricke'.[36] Interestingly, 'The

[33] Chris Kolmar, 'The Ten Largest Beer Companies in the World', *Zippia* (Web Page, 19 April 2023) www.zippia.com/advice/largest-beer-companies/#:~:text=The%20largest%20beer%20company%20in,market%20size%20of%20%24690%20billion.

[34] Tanja Linderborg et al, 'Standardregler för stor stark [Standard Rules for Large Strong]', *Sveriges Riksdag* (Web Page, 30 September 1999) www.riksdagen.se/sv/dokument-och-lagar/dokument/motion/standardregler-for-stor-stark_gn02l710/.

[35] Tasso Stafilidis et al, 'med anledning av prop. 2003/04:38 En ny prisinformationslag m.m [In Connection with Bill 2003/04:38 A New Price Information Act, etc]', *Sveriges Riksdag* (Web Page, 2 December 2003) www.riksdagen.se/sv/dokument-och-lagar/dokument/motion/med-anledning-av-prop.-20030438-en-ny_gr02l1.

[36] For a detailed discussion of Gotlandsdricke, see Lars Marius Garshol, 'Gotlandsdricke – An Overview', *Larsblog* (Blog Post, 8 January 2017) www.garshol.priv.no/blog/363.html.

first Finnish commercial microbreweries were Sahti brewers who received their licenses from the government in 1987'.[37] Sahti may be produced without hops, and juniper provides much of the flavour.[38] In fact, historically, juniper was used in nearly all farmhouse ales in Norway, and it was widely used in at least parts of Sweden.[39]

It is obvious that a style like Sahti is taking us to the outer limits of what most people would regard as beer. Indeed, versions brewed without hops would fail to qualify under several of the legal definitions of beer discussed at the end of Chapter 1.

So, it is only fitting to also note some of the 'near beers' of the Nordic countries. In Sweden, something called svagdricka used to be a common alternative to beer. Svagdricka is a dark, sweet, malt-based low-alcohol drink. In fact, as it typically is less than 2.25 per cent alcohol by volume, it is not subject to the sales restrictions that apply to beer. Interestingly, it was commonly mixed with milk, as was beer up until the mid-1900s. A similar drink, just called 'Malt', is enjoyed in Iceland. And around Christmastime, the Icelandic Malt is mixed with orange juice to make the Icelandic Christmas favourite of *Malt og Appelsin*.

[37] Rokka (n 4).

[38] Mika Laitinen, 'Sahti and Related Ancient Farmhouse Ales', *Brewing Nordic* (Web Page) www.brewingnordic.com/farmhouse-ales/ancient-homebrew-sahti/.

[39] Lars Marius Garshol, 'Danish Farmhouse Ale', *Larsblog* (Blog Post, 16 August 2015) www.garshol.priv.no/blog/334.html.

5

Beer Seen through Intellectual Property Glasses, and Intellectual Property through Beer Glasses

5.1 INTRODUCTION

Beer has a long history marked by both tradition and innovation, relies in its marketing on ever-changing imagery, reflects rapidly evolving tastes and market structures, and has both local and global appeal. Intellectual property (IP) in its multiple forms can serve as illuminating lenses or glasses[1] through which some features of the evolving beer markets become apparent.

Many market and product developments, whether in advertising for beer or brewing beer, are indeed highlighted through IP, often associated with illustrative stories and battles, as shown below. At the same time, beer turns out to be a laboratory for the study of the deployment of IP protections over the ages, and testing their limits and policy goals. In this chapter, we discuss beer-related developments through IP, and how some market and product trends around beer, such as the attraction of craft beers, highlight typical issues within the IP field. We focus mainly on trademarks and patents, which have played a prominent role in the marketing and production of beer.

Before we embark on our analysis of beer markets (between local and global), of tensions between Big Beer and craft brewers, of conflicts around geographical names, and of innovations in beer, a reminder that trademarks have a long tradition of association with beer.

[1] Speaking of glasses, we will see their shape and variety constitute an important ingredient in the experience of Belgian beers (see Chapter 6 on Belgium). In Chapter 6, we visit, among others, some cultural features linked to beer enjoyment, such as the art of pouring and the shapes of glasses and bottles, some of which could mobilize various IP rights, including copyright.

Beer Trademarks from Great Britain to the Czech Republic and Back in Time in Belgium

In Great Britain, after the passing of the Trade Marks Registration Act in 1875, the first trademark to be registered *for any product*[2] was the Bass red triangle (Figure 5.1), which still today remains the distinctive sign for this pale ale:

FIGURE 5.1 Beer marks in history. (a) The old sign that had been protected previously as an unregistered trademark (under common law) has travelled in time and space; (b) Bass bottles in a Japanese store (taken from Wikipedia, author Brian Adler, 2007); (c) Back in the nineteenth century, this pale elixir was already used on the other side of the Channel to animate hot Paris nights at Folies-Bergère, as shown in this Edouard Manet painting of 1882 (*Un Bar aux Folies-Bergère*). Two Bass bottles (one on the left, one the right) stand out among the other bottles through the distinctive logo; other beverages such as Champagne and absinth are discernible, not because of the presence of a logo but the shape or colour of the bottle. The Bass logo has inspired other painters (such as Picasso in his cubist *Bouteille de Bass, verre et journal*) and attracted the attention of Bloom, James Joyce's character in Ulysses (1922), which indicates that the red triangle had become a true synonym of beer.

2 The legend goes that as the applications for trademark registration opened on 1 January 1876, a Bass employee was sent to queue overnight so as to be able to get the first registration the next morning. There is no good beer without a ® TM!

Throughout the twentieth century, the Bass Brewery took over many other large breweries, and merged with Charrington at the end of the 1960s. The then largest UK brewery was acquired in 2000 by the Belgian Interbrew company. This corporation became AB InBev (today, the world's largest brewer: see box below: 'Interbrew Taking over Anheuser-Busch'); it was obliged to divest the Bass brewery (and other brands) because of competition concerns, but it kept the Bass trademark (relocated probably for tax reasons to a Luxembourg subsidiary, Brandbrew SA[3]), then renamed it (to Bass Trademark No. 1) before putting it up for sale for between £10 and £15 million, a bargain price according to *The Standard* newspaper (in April 2012). As in other industries, the trademark can follow another journey than the manufacturing facilities and acquire a value independently of any physical asset. This illustrates the trend towards an economy based on intangible assets, even when we are dealing with real drinks.

FIGURE 5.2 An early Czech beer mark. The register of the Czech IP Office indicates the filling date (23.4.1859) as well as the many renewals.
Source: https://znakitowarowe-blog.pl/old-uploads/2017/12/Najstarsze-zarejestrowane-znaki-na-%C5%9Bwiecie-czeski-PILZNER.pdf.

But, back in time, it appears that the Bass trademark is not the first registered trademark (for beer), it is rather the Czech trademark Pilsner from 1859[4] (*Messieurs les anglais, vous n'étiez pas les premiers!*) (Figure 5.2).

Some, however, claim that the first beer trademark (not registered at that time), Stella Artois, comes from Belgium (Figure 5.3).

Of course, in 1366 Belgium did not exist, but a tradition of brewing beer was established in Leuven. Figure 5.3 also shows a very real issue with the communication around beer: there are quite stringent rules on alcohol advertising, in particular for young people, that constrain how the promotion and even information on beers, including their trademarks, can be made (online or offline).

[3] A filing such as the Securities and Exchange Commission information for Ambev shows the complexities of the trademark and IP arrangements within a large conglomerate of brewing companies. See 'American Beverage Co Ambev – "20-F" for 12/31/04 – EX-4.17', *SEC Info* (Web Page) www.secinfo.com/dsVs2.zgh.7.htm#1stPage. This is typical of the important place of trademarks in the globalization of certain economic sectors.

[4] See Mikołaj Lech, 'The Oldest Registered Trademarks in the World', *Kancelaria Patentowa 'LECH'* (Web Page) https://znakitowarowe-blog.pl/the-oldest-registered-trademarks-in-the-world/.

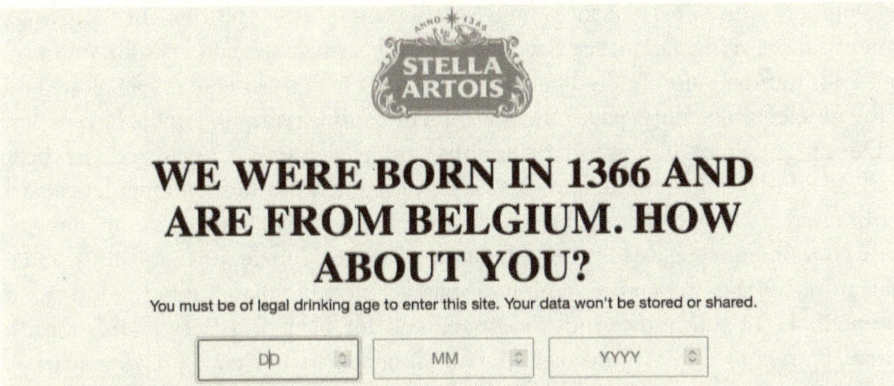

FIGURE 5.3 A webpage referring to the birth of the Stella Artois (and the need to check age for accessing webpages on beer).
Source: www.stellaartois.com/en_gb/heritage/.

5.2 BEER MARKETS BETWEEN GLOBAL AND LOCAL

We address here the quite recent meta-evolution in the beer market: from specialist to generalist brewers and back again to craft brewing.

5.2.1 *A Quick Reminder of the History of Beer*

In medieval times beer brewing was a very local pursuit. Brewed beer was kept in open containers, often having been brewed in homes or in very small village establishments. The beer either served the purposes of the brewers themselves (including serving visitors and travellers), or of a very local community. Beer was not adapted to preservation, packaging, and transportation for long periods and distances.[5] The ability to brew beer was connected to the more generalized ability of women to make fermented drinks of various kinds, for preservation and consumption in the home. Brewing was almost exclusively a female pursuit.

In the early Middle Ages, the monasteries took over the task of brewing beer (and men started to take over from women in that context). Most beer brewing nonetheless remained within the home and was undertaken by women, who had the skill of dealing with fermentation in preparing food and drink. This combination of domestic brewing and a nascent beer economy around monasteries was then replaced in more recent times by commercial brewers – and 'brewing centres' appeared around cities in England (London), Germany (Hamburg, Lübeck, and Munich), and the Low Countries (around Leuven, Bruges, Ghent or Haarlem, and Gouda).[6] Several

[5] Johan Swinnen (ed), *The Economics of Beer* (Oxford University Press, 2011).
[6] Ibid 3–28.

developments in beer making and conservation (the process of 'lagering', pasteurization, refrigeration; see Section 5.5.1 for beer patents) and later the improvements for transportation (including the invention of the crown cork or cap at the end of the nineteenth century) paved the way for a true industrialization in the beer sector.

During much of the twentieth century, external forces reorganized the beer markets into large general oligopolies, which triggered the sudden emergence of a 'partitioned off' crowded market segment of small specialists known as craft brewers. This phenomenon leads to a consideration of the role of brands (and thus trademarks) in this shaping and reshaping of markets, and the dynamics of brand-based competition. In the homogenous mass markets for beer, Big Beer brands form a potent barrier to entry, protecting the incumbents; in the craft brewing market, supported by a more sophisticated public, the huge multitude of breweries, combined with the growing scarcity of desirable brands, can also erect barriers to participation for new entrants. This alerts us to the tension between appropriation (IP) and cooperation (agreement) in brewing. It also calls for an exploration of the tension between tradition and innovation in brewing and beer consumption, and how IP rights impact it. Finally, it is a story of the local and the global, where again some areas of IP, in particular trademarks, contribute to further globalization, while geographical indications in principle favour businesses anchored in a local 'terroir'.

5.2.2 *Market Concentration and the Battles for Trademarks*

Multiple sources describe the mutation of the beer market in the twentieth century. Initially rapid concentration in beer brewing and distribution was triggered by economies of scale in production, technological change, expanded availability and reduced cost of transport, and expansion of advertising reach. These factors resulted in very significant concentration in brewing both in Europe and the US, with a rapid drop in the number of breweries, and in first national and then international oligopolies. For instance, by 2003 the big brewers Anheuser-Bush, Miller, Coors, and Pabst 'accounted for over 98% of sales in the macro sector of the US market'.[7] In 1934, that sector contained close to 800 breweries according to the same source. Following a merger frenzy all over the world, the world's largest brewers (AB InBev, SAB Miller, Heineken, and the Carlsberg Group) in 2011 accounted for over half of global beer production.[8]

Big brewers are generalists, their main product characteristically being a bland, international pilsner-style light beer (on the pilsner style, see

[7] See Victor J Tremblay et al, 'The Dynamics of Industry Concentration for US Micro and Macro Brewers' (2005) 26(3) *Review of Industrial Organization* 304, 310. See also Ignazio Cabras and David M Higgins, 'Beer, Brewing and Business History' (2016) 58(5) *Business History* 609.

[8] Johan Swinnen and Thijs Vandemoortele, 'Beeronomics: The Economics of Beer and Brewing' in Johan Swinnen (ed), *The Economics of Beer* (Oxford University Press, 2011) 335, 347.

Chapter 2), brewed in large volume and supplied at relatively low cost due to economies of scale. The multiple smaller regional breweries that existed in national markets almost vanished in the process of concentration. Product characteristics were no longer a real point of differentiation as all focused on the 'international pilsner' market. That type of bland and unchallenging beer appealed to the largest common consumer denominator and thus fit perfectly with a competitive dynamic focused on economies of scale. Its main attractions were ease of drinking and low price.

The remaining oligopolists were those who adopted this volume production approach earliest and most efficiently. Some of them, in particular in large countries, had focused their growth strategy by acquisition on their national market, others, in particular in smaller countries such as Denmark (with Carlsberg), the Netherlands (with Heineken), and Belgium (with Interbrew), as well as in South Africa (with SAB), were early adopters of an international growth strategy. As seen above, for example, the largest UK brewery, Bass-Charrington, was taken over by Interbrew in 2000; in 2002 a new entity, SABMiller, emerged from the merger between SAB and the second largest US brewery, Miller; in 2004, Interbrew merged with the Brazilian AmBev before swallowing up Anheuser-Busch in 2008, another Big Beer exponent in the then largest market, the US (and the acquisition spree continued with the Grupo Modelo, owner of Corona, in 2012 and with SABMiller in 2016).

Interbrew Taking Over Anheuser-Busch: A Sleepy Local Goliath Surprised by Globalization

Anheuser-Busch (or A-B) is an iconic American brewing company dating back to the 1850s when an ambitious German immigrant, Adolphus Busch, met Eberhard Anheuser, a successful soap manufacturer in St Louis. Relying on his connections in the brewing sector and on new technologies (mechanical bottling and pasteurization), Busch managed to create a national brand based on a very effective sales network all over the country (benefiting among others from the new refrigerated railcars, but also from dubious practices of price fixing). He even managed to ship its flagship beer, Budweiser, to Europe (an early move towards global markets that later resulted in trademark disputes at the highest level, see below). After Adolphus's death in 1913, August Busch Sr took the reins of the company through the difficult period of Prohibition (see Chapter 11). Then Adolphus Busch III took over until 1946, when another Busch, August II, took charge, before being ousted by his son, August III, through a palace coup in 1974. The later volatile relationship between August III and IV was not a model of harmony either. Clearly a family business, but a difficult family with colourful characters, secrets, and scandals. And also a history of unfair trade practices (see Chapter 7) that, among others, led to accusations, indictments, and a massive settlement in 1977; and still in the 1990s a dubious (but not uncommon) practice mandating its wholesale distributors to eject non-A-B brands from their portfolio. The competition with the arch-rival Miller Brewing Company intensified in the US, including in courts, in the media, and at the Federal Trade Commission over deceptive advertising (around the German brand Löwenbrau brewed by Miller for the US). It even 'got very personal', with Miller's president allegedly keeping a voodoo doll with the name 'August' in his office.[9] But the threat unexpectedly came from the Belgian Beers Barons[10] when, in late 2008, Interbrew, renamed in the meantime InBev, made a hostile takeover offer. A-B was bought a few months later for around $52 billion.

Interbrew had also started as a family business with years of collusion and price fixing.[11] However, after the merger between Belgium's largest breweries, Jupiler and Stella Artois, to form Interbrew in 1987, the families kept controlling shares, but stepped back from any role in the management and left CEOs to make the strategic moves and M&As. The takeover of A-B, in the state of which something was probably rotten, is not only interesting for comparing corporate governance models, but is also a 'story of globalization',[12] with 'beer kings' neglecting to realize that the competition game had become global.

The World's Local Brewer: Copyright and Trademark Battles around (Beer) Slogans

AB InBev now holds three of the most global brands: Beck's, Budweiser, and Stella Artois, but it also owns many local stars such as Brahma and Skol (Brazil), Bud Light and Michelob (US), Quilmes (Argentina), Bass and Boddington (UK), Klinskoye and Siberian Crown (Russia), Labatt (Canada), Franziskaner and Spaten (Germany), Jupiler, Leffe, Belle-Vue, and Hoegaarden (in the company's seat, Belgium). At some point, the big brewer looked for a messaging campaign that could best express its corporate identity, combining global brands sold over the planet and local ones reserved to certain markets. With the help of a branding expert, Interbrew developed the motto identifying the company as 'The world's local brewer'. When one of the most globalized banks, HSBC, started to rebrand itself as 'The world's local bank' in 2002 with a memorable global campaign,[13] it did not please AB InBev, which

9 We closely follow here the colourful presentation of 'Anheuser-Busch' by Randy Mosher in Garrett Oliver (ed), *The Oxford Companion to Beer* (Oxford University Press, 1st ed, 2012), who relies on various books. See, e.g., Peter Hernon and Terry Ganey, *Under the Influence: The Unauthorized Story of the Anheuser-Busch Dynasty* (Simon & Schuster, 1991); Julie MacIntosh, *Dethroning the King: The Hostile Takeover of Anheuser-Busch, an American Idol* (John Wiley & Sons, 1st ed, 2011).

10 This is the title of a book (subtitled *The Story behind Anheuser-Busch InBev*) by Wolfgang Riepl, devoted to the families leading Interbrew. The original version is in Dutch (*De Belgische Bierbaronnen* (Roularta, 2019)).

11 See Johan Swinnen and Devin Briski, *Beeronomics: How Beer Explains the World* (Oxford University Press, 2017) 55.

12 Ibid 56.

13 See Melissa Renteria, 'Executing a Global Strategy, Locally: Lessons from The World's Local Bank', *Columbia Business School* (Web Page, 15 March 2023) https://business.columbia.edu/cgi-marketing/chazen-global-insights/executing-global-strategy-locally-lessons-worlds-local-bank. But the story of globalization is less attractive now, in particular after the financial crisis of 2008, and HSBC has since abandoned the motto. See Alexandra Gibbs, 'Why HSBC Chose to

decided to initiate parallel proceedings in three countries. The court actions were based on copyright infringement of the slogan: the trademark argument was not available as the product/services of the two giant companies could not be more distant. But the recognition of the copyrightability of short sequences of words (four in the case of 'The world's local brewer') is also problematic. While it cannot fly in the US, where free speech would probably bar such copyright claims, there are some possibilities to keep copyright control on a title or slogan, in particular when it contains an original twist, as here an internal opposition (the world's local).[14] In the end, the world's largest brewer lost the copyright battle around its motto.

However, some other slogans in the beer sector have been recognized as protected under trademark or copyright law. For instance, the slogan 'Matten. Makkers. Maes', used to promote the pils beer under the Maes brand (and considered at one point the most well-known ad tagline in Flanders), was considered by the Antwerp Court of Appeal to be protected by copyright.[15] That such sequences and word play can suddenly come to mind without any effort is for that court not a reason to disqualify copyright protection.

5.2.3 *The Impact of TV and Other Media on Beer Marketing*

Interesting from an IP perspective in accounts of this evolution is the importance of the cost of advertising on the national and then global scale. The trigger was the rollout of national commercial television in most markets. Advertising on this national medium was expensive and dynamic, and the investment only made sense for brewers that marketed nationally. Local brewers did not have the capacity to pay for such advertising or the ability to take advantage of its extra-regional reach. Because of its high cost and national audience, television advertising favoured a small number of national brands, or nationally registered trademarks.[16] In other cases, large multinational brewers accumulated a portfolio of brands whose production costs were kept down by multi-use brewing operations, and whose advertising budgets far outweighed those available to new entrants. The cost of national television advertising would squeeze local brewers out of the market, and consumer loyalty to the national beer brands, bought by advertising, became an additional

Move on from Being 'The World's Local Bank', *CNBC* (Web Page, 17 August 2016) www.cnbc.com/2016/08/17/why-hsbc-chose-to-move-on-from-being-the-worlds-local-bank.html.

14 See the sinuous case law on titles and slogans in France: André Lucas, Agnès Lucas-Scloetter, and Carine Bernault, *Traité de la propriété littéraire et artistique* (LexisNexis, 5th ed, 2017). On the contrary, short sentences cannot be protected by copyright in the US or Australia.

15 Court of Appeal of Antwerp, 29 June 2009, A&M, 2010, 187 ('Maten, Makkers, Maes').

16 See Erik Strøjer Madsen and Yanqing Wu, 'Advertising and Concentration in the Brewing Industry' (Economics Working Papers, Aarhus University, October 2014); Christian Garavaglia, 'Industry Evolution: Evidence from the Italian Brewing Industry' (2022) 26(1) *Competition and Change* 75.

and powerful barrier to entry and also pushed regional brands out of the market. This resulted in a ringfenced market dominated by a handful of large national brewers. The only possible new players in such national markets were large foreign brewers that commonly entered by way of acquisition of some of the remaining breweries, resulting in further market concentration on a global scale.

Of course, today we have entered a new era where national television advertising no longer monopolizes the promotional spend of big brewers or any other corporations. The internet-based, more personalized advertising that now claims a substantial part of promotional budgets has probably another impact on the market's evolution. As advertising by social networks relies more on peers' consumption and communication, it might lend itself to the emergence of craft brewers that do not directly compete with Big Beer.

The New Imagery around Beers, and the Instagram Effect's Needs and Risks

For economists, 'the commercial TV factor can explain why extreme consolidation occurred much earlier in the US than in Europe':[17] the availability of TV sets and multiple channels expanded rapidly in the US after World War II, while commercial television came much later (at the end of the 1980s) in Europe as national public broadcasters long enjoyed a monopoly and were often prohibited from engaging in advertising. It is interesting to realize that evolving media laws have thus impacted the beer market.

Promotion always had to adjust to the medium. Today, the internet and social media form the new medium. While TV was an excellent vehicle for mass-marketed brands with a national appeal/audience, social networks now allow for more edgy and targeted promotion of beers towards individual consumers (often knowledgeable amateurs) who, in turn, will influence the dissemination of some promotional messages through digital and real-world 'word of mouth'. The creators of brand identities, as always, have to identify the primary demographic or focus for the brand's strategy, then develop a basic message taking into account the product's peculiarities (beer is not wine or liquor, for example). Today businesses have to find a brand design that consumers can identify with and will be tempted to share with their friends on Instagram, Facebook, or TikTok.[18] Will those new channels allow new entrants to reach consumers or will they enable further consolidation of the beer markets? The answer is not yet clear.

Being in the spotlight of social media also means promotion has to factor in new risks: contrary to television's one-way communication, all receivers of social media messages are also potential senders. This opens the way for misinformation or other

[17] Lisa M George, 'The Growth of Television and the Decline of Local Beer' in Johan Swinnen (ed), *The Economics of Beer* (Oxford University Press, 2011) 213.

[18] See, eg, Shutterstock, 'Bottling a Brand: How Alcohol Branding Differs from Beer to Wine to Liquor', *Shutterstock* (Web Page, 5 July 2016) www.shutterstock.com/blog/bottling-brand-alcohol-branding-differs-beer-wine-liquor.

information excesses to circulate more widely. This is what AB InBev experienced in the US after using a transgender actress and TikTok influencer for a 2023 ad campaign around the Bud Light beer. The media outrage and strong online reactions resulted in a culture war (typical for the US) involving right-wing politicians and celebrities flagging AB InBev as a 'woke company', then calling for a boycott.[19] To please a wide range of potential customers online is more complex than on TV. Inclusiveness, which is on everyone's lips, does not allow the launch of global campaigns that ignore some national, local, or idiosyncratic sensitivities.

5.2.4 *The Role of Trademarks in the Concentration of (Beer) Markets*

Interesting here from an IP perspective, in particular trademarks, is the importance of incumbent brands as a barrier to entry. If a new entrant intends to compete with established brands, it is likely that the advertising and promotional expenditure required to displace the incumbent brands makes the whole exercise uneconomic. Contrary to some theories, trademarks prove to be incapable of fulfilling a dynamic competitive role; they serve to reinforce concentration in the market by drawing up further defences to new entrants. They fail to achieve their oft-mooted function as a signalling shortcut benefiting consumers, informing them about new products and new entrants.[20] Trademarks were once thought of as key contributors to market concentration and therefore in the sights of anti-trust authorities,[21] but have more recently been seen as largely benign: the account of market concentration in beer brewing undermines that benign view.

The emergence of an oligopolistic 'Big Beer' market also draws attention to the role of trademarks in a homogenous market around the same pale and light 'international pilsner' beers. Trademarks are intended to serve as shorthand messengers about the origin and the qualities of a particular provider's products, but in this market they seem to do nothing of the kind. That is because the products are almost indistinguishably homogenous. So why is it rational for the oligopolists to spend so much on advertising and promotion? The question might be asked differently: when the big brewers develop and use trademarks as vessels for advertising, what purpose does this actually serve? Rather than showcasing different products, are they in fact just erecting a barrier to new entrants that benefits *all* incumbents? If their

[19] See Eri Sugiura, 'AB InBev Chief Blames Social Media as Transgender Spat Drains Bud Light Sales', *Financial Times* (Web Page, 8 May 2023) www.ft.com/content/dc63c64c-d32e-460a-afdc-458c94860c93; John Gapper, 'AB InBev Should Defy the Bud Light Culture War', *Financial Times* (Web Page, 28 April 2023) www.ft.com/content/3a84b28c-912a-4805-b942-13e597766a93.

[20] See Richard A Posner and William M Landes, 'The Economics of Trademark Law' (1988) 78 *Trademark Reporter* 267.

[21] See Sigmund Timberg, 'Trademarks, Monopoly and the Restraint of Competition' (1949) 14(2) *Law and Contemporary Problems* 323.

individual messaging is not directed against each other, then what *is* their rather uniform brand messaging aimed at? One argument is that the marks in this type of market serve also as an instrument of coordination between oligopolists whose interests are aligned. That interest does not lie in competing with each other but in competing with other products that *are* inherently heterogenous or different: beer brewers compete with wine makers for the hearts and minds of consumers. It was Galbraith himself who made the point that 'If advertising affects the distribution of demand between sellers of a particular product, it must also be supposed that it affects distribution between products'.[22]

In other words, the relevant market should be reconceived and reconstituted more carefully. It might include products that are genuinely heterogenous (an international pilsner vs a Trappist beer for instance) on one level but sufficiently similar on another (both are beers). From this perspective, the main effect and perhaps interest of the 'beer cartel' is to increase beer drinking by their concerted and factually coordinated advertising efforts aimed at non-drinkers (e.g. the young), drinkers from other alcoholic beverages to drinking their general kind of beer,[23] thus growing their market, which is in their common interest.

5.3 'PARTITIONING' THE BEER MARKET BETWEEN BIG BEER AND CRAFT BEERS

What in fact happened in the beer world is a process of what is sometimes referred to as '(market) partitioning'. When the craft beer revolution started, this was not in competition with Big Beer, although obviously it concerned 'beer', but about a new and separate market, 'partitioned' from Big Beer. The reason craft beers sprang up was because consumers were bored with the homogeneity of the Big Beer brews; because domestic brewing was deregulated in many markets; because localism became popular; and because of the emergence of an 'authenticity' movement which rejected commercialism, mass production, and profit-making in favour of society, localism, and craft values. Knowledge about beer history and beer styles, and the endless possibilities of brewing different beers was shared amongst craft brewers. We discuss the origins of the craft brew revolution in more detail in Chapter 10 addressing North America.

[22] John Kenneth Galbraith, *The New Industrial State* (Houghton Mifflin, 1967) 205.

[23] The growth of the craft beer product category contradicts Duffy's theory (Martyn H Duffy, 'Advertising and the Inter-product Distribution of Demand' (1987) 31(5) *European Economic Review* 1051) that advertising has no impact on product category demand, which itself was posited to contradict the view in Galbraith (n 22). A glaring difficulty with Duffy's approach is that he does not justify how he chooses a product category (they are all established alcoholic beverages, as opposed to, for instance, alcoholic beverages vs soft drinks or established vs new alcoholic beverages).

Trademarks formed no barrier to entry into this partitioned craft beer market: there were no brand-based incumbents. The existing Big Beer brands were simply sidestepped. What developed was a 'greenfield' market, although in some countries such as Belgium traditional and local/regional beers had survived to a greater extent than, for instance, in the United States. Although the emergence of this market had positive causes, it was because of consumer reaction *against* existing 'Big Beer' with its dull, choiceless products and stereotypical marketing images. That market appeared monolithic to many consumers. Intellectual property in the form of trademarks did nothing to disturb the equilibrium in that market, as the incumbent brands deterred new entrants of any kind. Instead, the new craft brands established a distinct and separate market with its own different dynamics, interactions, products, messaging, and loyalties.

5.3.1 *The Growing Market for Craft Beers and Desirable Brands as a Limited Resource*

Whereas the existing Big Beer market made a virtue of homogeneity, blandness, price, universal availability, and traditional values (around maleness, vacationing, camaraderie, romance), the emerging craft brew market made a virtue of variety, taste, smallness, localism, individuality, and edginess. Craft brewing structurally favours brewers remaining small and local, so that its dynamics are the opposite of those found in the international pale pilsner market; growth comes not only from individual brewers increasing capacity but more often from additional breweries creating new capacity. The consumer's expectations, understanding of craft beers, quest for variation, and individuality drive this fragmentation of supply. Crucial in this tale is the cost/price relationship. Brewing smaller volumes with quality ingredients using more traditional methods is relatively expensive, and that expense would tend to militate against a craft beer market emerging. However, it appears in part that the take-off and growth of this sector of the beer market coincided with a general rise in disposable income in relevant markets, and with changing drinking patterns. Whereas Big Beer profitability is centred on cost reduction and standard, low-end pricing, craft brews can viably command higher prices and turn a profit from smaller volumes – at least up to a point.

In a market that emphasizes the local, the traditions, the variability, and small runs there is considerable consumer resistance to amalgamations, takeovers, upscaling, and so on. Competition is not through generating economies of scale and erecting barriers to entry in the manner of Big Beer described above. There is no incentive to spend on national or even global advertising, so information and persuasion costs are kept low. What is phenomenal about this market is not its rapid growth in volume of consumption, but its astonishing growth in the number of separate suppliers.

In the initial stages of the craft beer revolution that, depending how one calculates, started in the 1980s with renewed interest in beer styles such as porter, pale ales, stout, and bitters, there was plenty of clear space for emerging new brewers – in terms of geographical spaces, product spaces, image spaces, and suchlike.

But as more and more entrants piled in (and the figures are striking),[24] the various resources for identifying correctly all those beers became more finite. What interests us here is brands and thus, in legal terms, trademarks as one of those resources; at the simplest level, this is about names for new breweries and beers. Initially, when there were fewer entrants and the collaborative and community-based, non-commercial attitude to craft brewing was strong, there were fewer conflicts about brands and those that did arise tended to be settled in constructive and collaborative ways.

However, with an increasingly congested craft-brewing space, conflict over trademarks/brands began to emerge: more overlaps and coincidences and less consensual, more adversarial and law-driven resolution. In terms of IP rights, the traditional dividing line between distinctive marks and descriptive terms is the tool used to moderate such conflicting interests. In the background lies the recurring question whether trademarks are a finite or infinite resource. The traditional view is that since marks must be distinctive to be registered, they are invented signs, and the scope for invention of signs (whether literary marks, device marks, or composite marks) is infinite, and therefore the supply of registrable trademarks is infinite. However, the craft beer saga seems to confirm that *desirable* signs available for registration as trademarks are *a finite resource*.

The battle amongst the growing multitude of new craft brewers in large part concerns control of common, technical, heritage, or geographical terms in beer brewing. But it also concerns edgy, alternative, excentric, sometimes allusive terms that suit the image of craft beer brewing as individualistic, original, surprising, and memorable. There is a certain 'vibe' about craft beer, and breweries in this segment like to develop their brands around terms that aim to reflect it. The relaxation of trademark rules in the mid-1990s, allowing colours, shapes, and packaging to be trademarked, added to the mix, since much of what is suggestive and desirable is figurative rather than literary in nature.

The trademark requirement of distinctiveness in principle preserves the freedom to use linguistic resources for communication: descriptive terms cannot be registered as trademarks since their use by other traders acting faithfully should not be impeded. Nonetheless, since 1995 even wholly descriptive terms can be registered if they *acquire* distinctiveness – if consumers have come to see them as performing a trademark function, as brand names rather than descriptive terms. Many signs with descriptive elements can thus be trademarked. For example, 'Stella Artois' is a well-known trademark all around the globe: 'Stella' (star) is the kind of laudatory epithet that is normally excluded from trademarking and 'Artois' is a region in northern France. Nonetheless, no consumer sees its ordinary meaning any

[24] See, eg, Christian Garavaglia and Johan Swinnen, 'The Craft Beer Revolution: An International Perspective' (2017) 32(3) *Choices* 1.

longer.[25] Even more: because of diverging promotion campaigns around this pilsner beer, the same trademark can be associated with a premium beer for a particular public, such as in the US, while it is marketed and perceived as a standard and common 'pils' elsewhere, for example in Belgium. It just depends on how a business uses its mark, and to what extent.

Non-Used Trademarks: Does the 'You Use or You Lose' Rule Really Work to Free the 'Beer Drop'?

Trademark law contains another filter aimed at preserving a 'commons of signs': according to the 'you use or you lose' rule embedded in trademark law, the non-use of some trademarked signs automatically frees the symbolic resource after the passing of time. But the application of the rule might be tricky. For instance, a start-up craft beer retailer, The Beer Drop, was faced in 2020 with opposition from Coles, the large food and liquor chain, on the ground it applied in Australia for a trademark substantially similar to the 'Wine Drop' trademark registered by Coles (in 2012 and thus valid until 2022).[26] To make a robust claim, Coles would have had to prove the average consumer would be confused, but it is not easy (or possible) to prove confusion as to the products when they are quite dissimilar (wine is not beer!). Thus, Coles claimed to have a trademark with reputation that was so extensive that it could extend its blocking effect when used for non-similar products. But Coles (which had quite a large portfolio of more than 1,000 marks) had apparently not really used its 'Wine Drop' brand over the years. To prove it might be complicated, however. Claims and oppositions by trademark owners are multiplying as the trademark watch services, now automatized and facilitated by artificial intelligence tools, are available to anybody. It also depends on what the law considers to be similar products – in the US, beer and wine are considered so similar that the US Patent and Trademark Office (USPTO) tends to disallow a trademark application for beer if the same or similar trademark is registered for wine (or vice versa), because it surmises that consumers would think they came from the same source;[27] in the 'Barefoot Radler' case in Australia, beer and wine were also considered to be 'goods of the same description'.[28]

Insufficient Prior Use to Oppose the 'Gigabier' Registration

Prior use is also difficult to establish, and a few tweets, even from Elon Musk, did not suffice to validly oppose the registration of 'Gigabier' as a trademark. The story starts with the inauguration on 9 October 2021 of Tesla's Gigafactory close to Berlin and the

[25] *Cantarella Bros Pty Ltd v Modena Trading Pty Ltd* (2014) 254 CLR 337.

[26] Clare Burnet, 'Craft Beer Retailer in Trademark Battle with Coles', *Brews News* (Web Page, 12 May 2020) https://brewsnews.com.au/craft-beer-retailer-in-trademark-battle-with-coles/.

[27] See 'Craft Beer Trademarks: Beer vs Wine', *David Lizerbram & Associates* (Blog Post, 2 December 2014) www.lizerbramlaw.com/2014/12/02/craft-beer-trademarks-beer-vs-wine/.

[28] See *E & J Gallo Winery v Lion Nathan Australia Pty Limited* (2009) 175 FCR 386, overturning the trial Judge's decision on this point.

announcement made by the magnate Elon Musk that 'we're even gonna have a beer' to be distributed in very fancy cybertruck-inspired bottles (Tesla's cybertruck is an electric light-duty truck).[29] The next day, a German company (Juicyphant), applied to the EU IP Office for registration as a trademark of the term 'Gigabier' in relation to products such as 'beer, alcoholic beverages and brewing services'. Tesla then tried to oppose the trademark registration by claiming a prior use in the course of trade, but it had not much evidence, mostly some social media posts and video screenshots of Elon Musk's speech at the Gigafest. A brief announcement at an event (even though attended by around 9,000 people) does not qualify as a real use for the relevant public; it is only a preview of mere local significance. Another takeaway from this: Even a tech-focused company and billionaire is attracted by a beer that can reinforce the 'lifestyle' messaging of completely different products and services. This flexible beer attraction is facilitated by the fact that a liquid can be marketed in any 'adjusted suit'.

In more recent times, as the number of new entrants has grown, it seems that the supply of desirable trademarks has tended to become exhausted. Sources document the rise in conflicts about signs that end up being litigated or at least settled with lawyers' involvement. This demonstrates that trademarks are in fact a finite resource, because most theoretically available totally distinctive marks are not realistic targets of appropriation, and in particular are ineffectual competitive tools in a market where image is increasingly significant.

This beer market experiment, both in the Big Beer segment (brands as barriers to entry) and in the Craft Beer part (finite supply of desirable marks), tends to confirm that trademarks have a competition effect: as barriers to entry through scarcity and cost.

5.3.2 *Big Beer's Reaction to the Threat from Craft Beers*

The emergence of the craft beer segment presented Big Beer with a conundrum, initially perhaps dismissed as minor because of the small volumes involved. The craft brewers presented a dual threat: as it was a growth segment, Big Beer wanted a slice; and as it ate into their own volumes, they needed to respond. It might also be that the financial returns on craft beers are potentially much higher. However, the challenge was a conundrum: craft brewing does not accord with cost reduction by scaling; and the craft-brewing image was totally at odds with the universalized homogeneity of international pilsner beers produced by giga-breweries.

[29] See Julie Canet, 'Tesla Has Beer but No Trademark', *Lexology* (Web Page, 16 October 2023) www.lexology.com/library/detail.aspx?g=54fbd78c-7d40-45b5-bb23-8015769a0b93. See also 'Elon Musk-Backed Tesla GigaBier Beer Is Here, Pack of 3 Priced over Rs 8K', *The Economic Times* (Web Page, 31 March 2023) https://economictimes.indiatimes.com/magazines/panache/elon-musk-backed-tesla-gigabier-beer-is-here-pack-of-3-priced-over-rs-8k/articleshow/99144270.cms?from=mdr.

So Big Beer faced the challenge of acquiring authenticity without being authentic, smallness while being large. Two options presented themselves, each challenging from a consumer persuasion perspective. First, to acquire existing craft breweries; second, to start craft breweries or to brew craft beers with their own established methodologies. Each of these strategies have clear branding and messaging problems; and in terms of intellectual property law, they interface with the law of passing off and consumer deception (unfair competition). Where Big Beer acquires craft breweries, the consumer requires some persuasion that these somehow remain true to the craft beer ideology. Starting to brew craft beers is probably more attractive to Big Beer, as their technological prowess and know-how allow them to brew craft-style beers of excellent quality and consistency. But in the result, consumers face the increasing difficulty of distinguishing between authenticity and spuriousness in beer brewing and distribution.

More negative strategic options presented themselves to Big Beer, enabled by their oligopolistic market power, resources, and multiple competencies: leveraging control over distribution, advertising infrastructure, and beer drinking establishments to squeeze out craft beer competitors. This they can do because their powerful position allows them to strike contractual bargains that make life difficult for craft breweries, in particular for those seeking to grow and move beyond their regional origins. By denying 'Little Beer' access to consumers, for example by monopolizing pubs and distribution (see also Chapters 7 and 9), the Big Beer breweries stymie the emergence and availability of real alternatives, drive their costs up further, and create space to invade the craft brew markets with the devices described in the previous paragraph. A particular practice is to reserve 'taps' in bars and cafes for the big breweries by offering discounts if the bar does not also provide products from other breweries, including craft breweries, and at the same time offering craft-style brews of the big breweries' own devising, or which they have acquired by taking over some of the larger craft breweries interested in selling out for a sometimes handsome profit.[30]

5.4 BEER STYLES EMBEDDED IN GEOGRAPHICAL TRADEMARKS AND INDICATIONS OF ORIGIN

During the Industrial Revolution, beer-brewing technology developed, as did the ability to preserve, package, refrigerate, and transport beer. Beer became a branded product that was in various ways made available over wider areas, although by modern Big Beer standards still quite localized. Still, consumers came to know beers by their brand names and styles, signs that taught drinkers what to expect. Most brewers developed the ability to brew a number of different beer styles. Certain regions had particular beer styles and regulations, had easy access to characteristic ingredients, and

[30] Rachel Clun, 'The Fight Brewing Over the Beer Giants That Have Captured the Australian Market', *Sydney Morning Herald* (Web Page, 29 April 2024) www.smh.com.au/politics/federal/the-fight-brewing-over-the-beer-giants-who-have-captured-the-australian-market-20240425-p5fmju.html.

became somewhat known for these styles. Beer bottling allowed beer to travel, and beer brewing became in part disconnected from supply to tied houses.

As a result of the extra-regional spread of beer brands, they began to be referred to by employing regional references or signs. At the same time, more people travelled or migrated over long distances, in particular to the Americas and also to Australia, South Africa, Canada, and New Zealand. As is the case with other food and beverage products, a trichotomy developed: on the one hand, geographical references were used to describe those styles of beer that had become associated with or originated in that particular place. On the other hand, geographical terms became or were integrated in beer corporate brands; and finally, some geographical terms became signs that purported to guarantee geographical origin and the special character that results from it (like geographical indications or GIs).

An interesting question is whether beer can ever have a totally inimitable and unique character because of the singular geographical (geological, climatological, and associated human) characteristics of a place of brewing. There appears to be little doubt about that, as some beers are naturally fermented (such as the Gueuze Lambic in the region around Brussels) and the particular microbiological profile of the relevant area is nowhere exactly replicated. The same could perhaps be said about water, barley, hops, and so on from particular areas. However, although this method of open fermentation of beer and sourcing its components may have been the standard in the early days, almost every component of brewing became commodified, traded, and widely available in more recent times. Natural fermentation was replaced by reliance on commercially supplied yeasts. Most beer styles could therefore successfully be brewed anywhere. Many in the brewing industry maintain that yeast is the key differentiating ingredient in beers, but this is controversial.

In time, these facts have resulted in recurrent disputes: about place names as brands; about place names as GIs; and about place names as styles (or terms that allude to place names). At the same time, some non-geographical signs (analogous to 'traditional expressions' in wine law, or particular bottle shapes, glass shapes and suchlike) have also become closely associated with certain regions; for instance, some abbey-brewed beer styles are closely associated with Belgium (see Chapter 6 on Belgium).

5.4.1 *Trademarking Placenames: The Battles around Bavaria and Budweis*

5.4.1.1 Is Bavaria in Holland?

Two illustrative cases that have reverberated around the world involve the 'Bavaria' and Budweiser brands, which both are geographical place names. As for the Bavaria brand, surprisingly perhaps, this is a beer brewed for a long time in Holland. The Bavaria sign has thus lost its initial geographic meaning (referring to the region and state in southern Germany). As a beer brand, the term 'Bavaria' had some initial difficulties: normally geographical terms referring to places where such goods do or reasonably might originate are difficult to register as trademarks. This is because consumers would see them not as a badge indicating corporate origin, but as indicators of geographical origin. Nonetheless trademark laws tend to recognize that such terms might become registrable if they have been used as trademarks over a considerable period. In other words, the law imagines that at some point the mark morphs in the mind of the consumer from a descriptive geographical term to a distinctive trademark. How quickly that happens will depend on the evidence of trademark use the mark owner can muster. It also depends on the nature of the relevant consumers: what they are imputed to know, how discerning on average they might be, and so on. It should also be noted that a geographical term might be recognized as distinctive (i.e. not descriptive of geographical origin) not just through use but because it has been embellished or rendered in a distinctive manner. Not the term simpliciter but a more complex or composite mark.

This was the case with the Bavaria trademark, at least in Australia. In that jurisdiction, the mark's eligibility for registration was contested, not only in relation to distinctiveness, but because the mark was also said to be misleading as to the place of brewing. The actual mark at issue was a label mark which included the term 'Bavaria' centrally displayed but was in the shape of a label with some writing running around an external scroll. That writing included the terms 'Beer Brewed in Holland'. Ultimately, the court held that the mark was not deceptive since the average Australian consumer of a speciality beer would not know where Bavaria might be, or that it was even a place name. They might just as well think it was in Holland, or they would at worst not make anything of the term. This may no doubt be seen as a poor reflection on Australia's geography teachers. In any case, in terms of distinctiveness, the court ruled that the mark (being the label) was sufficiently distinctive because of its embellishments, and another indication of that fact was that other brewers used the term Bavaria in relation to their beer.[31]

In Italy, the Dutch brewer also won the right to continue to use and own the Bavaria trademark in question.[32] The Italian decision meant (perhaps perversely) that the Dutch brewer was able to prevent Italian brewers from using the term Bavaria in relation to their beers. The issue also played out in Ireland, where the Dutch company sought to register a composite mark containing the dominant terms Bavaria (and Holland), which was opposed by the Bavarian beer brewers. The opposition was rejected on the basis that the Dutch brewer already had rights to 'Bavaria' as its brand previously, and that was sufficient basis for its present right to register and own the composite Bavaria Holland brand.[33] The key to all the successes of the Dutch brewer was that it had used this term incorporated in or as

[31] See Natalia Blecher, 'Bavaria NV v Bayerischer Brauerbund eV', *Lexology* (Web Page, 10 August 2009) www.lexology.com/library/detail.aspx?g=3604c878-d1df-4122-b47c-9ca409618390e.

[32] Bavaria NV, 'Final Victory in Italy for Dutch Brewery Bavaria in Trademark Battle', *PR Newswire* (Web Page, 24 September 2012) www.prnewswire.com/news-releases/final-victory-in-italy-for-dutch-brewery-bavaria-in-trademark-battle-171044421.html.

[33] See *Bavaria NV v Bayerischer Brauerbund eV* [2009] FCA 428.

its trademark for a very long time.[34] This just goes to show that with some persistence and in the absence of others using the same sign in the relevant market, almost anything can be registered as a trademark. The Bavarians were simply too slow to react and therefore lost their monopoly over the descriptive term 'Bavarian' for beer, something the real state of Bavaria is extremely well-known for (think of the Oktoberfest in Munich, the capital of Bavaria).[35]

5.4.1.2 Is Budweis in America?

The well-known 'Budweiser' brand has been used for a beer brewed in the US but also in the historical city of Budweis or České Budějovice in the Czech Republic. The US and Czech brewer fought for control of the mark after the collapse of the Soviet sphere of influence. Interestingly, and contrastingly, when it comes to the Budweiser mark, a court decision in Italy went against AB InBev, the owner of the famous American 'Budweiser' brand. It was not allowed to use the Budweiser brand because it was considered deceptive by the court. Instead, InBev declared that it would use the mark 'Bud' until any further decision in its favour. The town of České Budějovice was known as Budweis in 1898 when the Czech brewery, victorious in Italy, was started.[36] In addition, the American brewer lost its battle to stop the Czech brewer from using the terms Bud and Budweiser in the UK.[37] In Australia, as in many other jurisdictions, there was also a fight between these two companies over the Budweiser mark:[38] the Federal court ultimately held as follows:

> I would make these orders because of the use of other words, less prominently displayed on the labels. These words are 'Budweiser Budvar' which are used on the labels as part of the first respondent's name 'Budweiser Budvar, National Corporation'. The first respondent has various versions of its name. 'Budweiser Budvar, National Corporation' is one. 'Budějovick[yacute] Budvar, Národní Podnik' is another. Thus, whilst I have found that the primary trade mark usage of 'Budějovick[yacute] Budvar' on the bottles in question was not, and is not, unlawful, the desire of the first respondent to use its so called 'English' corporate name, should, I think, be restrained, for the reasons I have given in my reasons for judgment.[39]

[34] On disputed but not in Australia, see 'Budweiser Trademark Dispute', *Wikipedia* (Web Page, 28 July 2024) https://en.wikipedia.org/wiki/Budweiser_trademark_dispute.

[35] 'Welcome to Oktoberfest', *Oktoberfest Munich* (Web Page) www.oktoberfest.de/en.

[36] In relation to the Italian victories of Budvar, see 'Budweiser Budvar Has Won Two Lawsuits in Italy', *Budweiser Budvar* (Web Page, 23 August 2023) www.budejovickybudvar.cz/tiskove-zpravy/budweiser-budvar-has-won-two-lawsuits-in-italy.

[37] 'US Beer Giant Loses Bud Trade Mark Battle', *Pinsent Masons* (Web Page, 18 February 2003) www.pinsentmasons.com/out-law/news/us-beer-giant-loses-bud-trade-mark-battle.

[38] Christopher Heath, 'The Budweiser Cases: Geographical Indications v Trade Marks' in Dev S Gangjee (ed), *Research Handbook on Intellectual Property and Geographical Indications* (Edward Elgar , 2016) 396.

[39] See *Anheuser-Busch, Inc v Budějovick[yacute] Budvar, Národní Podnik & Ors* [2002] FCA 390.

What is the correct approach? By analogy with the Bavaria case, it could be said that 'Budweiser' had become so shorn of its geographical signification over time that it had become a pure trademark: consumers seeing it as a badge of corporate origin and either not realizing it had anything to do with a place in the Czech Republic or that, if it ever had, it no longer did. In that sense, the Budweiser mark was both distinctive and not deceptive. But who owned the mark? A principle of trademark law maintains that the company that uses a sign as a trademark is its owner; that would make InBev and its predecessors the owners, since they did not use it in a descriptive but in a purely trademark manner. That is also why the Dutch brewery is the legitimate owner of the term 'Bavaria' as a trademark. But that seems to allow companies to 'steal' geographical terms that by rights 'belong' to the inhabitants of the actual region. Trademark law allows this odd appropriation based on its acceptance of a shift in meaning from general and descriptive to distinctive and brand-based.

5.4.2 *Protecting the Geographical Indication 'Bayerisches Bier'*

The Bavaria brand and other terms referring to a geographical place raise another interesting IP issue: the interplay between the protections of trademarks and GIs. 'Bayerisches Bier' is a registered geographical indication (a protected GI or PGI) in Europe. That means the registered terms can only be used in relation to beers that comply with the underlying specifications (not only brewed in Bavaria, but also to certain prescribed standards[40] embedded in '500 years of purity and tradition'). Any other use in relation to beer is ipso facto an infringement, whether or not consumers are actually misled; thus, 'Bavarian-style beer brewed in Belgium' would still infringe the GI, even though it would be very clear to a consumer that it did not come from Germany. Here a worldwide conflict between GIs and trademark rights has come to the fore: Europe argues that GIs should trump trademark rights, whereas the US and its allies on this topic argue that trademark rights (as private property rights) should prevail. In the Bavaria case in Europe, the Bavaria PGI was at issue, as it was in the Australian case. Despite this protection, the trademark was allowed to stand. Particularly noteworthy is that the addition of '-style' is outlawed by GI rules: Bavarian-style beer is not allowed other than for beer that meets the PGI requirements. Some terms are registered as GIs, while others are not: for instance, 'Belgian (or Belgium) beer' is not. Some terms are registered as 'Traditional Speciality Guaranteed', such as 'Gueuze' (for a Belgian type of beer). Registration in one language usually brings with it a monopoly extending to translations. Thus, some terms that are closely associated with certain places are not afforded special protection, whereas others are. This has come about haphazardly and for historical reasons: many regional or associated terms have 'flown the coop'; a very good example is the term 'pils'

[40] See 'Bayerisches Bier', *European Commission* (Web Page) https://ec.europa.eu/agriculture/eambrosia/geographical-indications-register/details/EUGI00000013270, which provides prescribed characteristics of the beer (as well as requiring Bavarian origin).

or 'pilsner', whose origin lies in the Bohemian city of Plzeň (German: Pilsen): it is a very commonly used term, descriptive of a certain style, that no consumer would expect to describe only a beer that actually comes from Plzeň. Such terms have become common descriptors: for instance, in beer-brewing competitions, many of the categories have styles that are in origin geographical terms.[41] In the list of the Brewers Association, many beers are 'Belgian Style', 'American Style, 'British Style'. Thus, the globalism of the craft beer market relies on the freedom to use many geographical references in a style-linked manner. If these terms were protected as GIs, then the use of them in conjunction with '-style' would be prohibited but for those beers brewed in those regions and meeting the gazetted specifications.

It should be noted that the absolute, no-proof-of-deception-required nature of GI protections also differ from trademarks in that there are few defences: in trademark law, a defendant can argue that the mark is not used as a mark; that the similar sign is used in good faith; that the user has a prior right; that the mark has become generic. In GI law no such excuses exist; therefore, if a geographical term has been incorporated into a registered trademark, a rival might still legitimately include on its label a reference to the actual location of the brewery in the same place – as long as that is done in good faith. This is illustrated for instance by the Australian Budweiser case; there is no such excuse for the user of a place name that is registered as a GI.

5.5 BEER MARKETS BETWEEN INNOVATION AND TRADITION, BY JEAN-MARC DELTORN

IP not only relates to the protection of goodwill, but also aims to promote and protect innovation.[42] Here too beer is an interesting laboratory for testing IP theory. Although brewing is a traditional craft going back thousands of years, it is still in many aspects the subject of continuous innovation, whether concerning the making (technological improvements regarding containers; chilling and heating; brewing know-how related to the production of different beer styles, focused on flavour, colour, mouth feel, alcohol content, or the use of biotechnology for natural and artificial yeasts and spores) or transport and packaging (shapes of beer bottle and packaging, including functional aspects, such as screws and caps). The relevant areas of IP are mainly patents and trade secrets (confidential information). The (registered) designs and copyright aspects will further be addressed in Chapter 6 on Belgium.

5.5.1 *Beer-Related Inventions and Patents*

Innovations and technical developments have profoundly influenced the history of beer production by revolutionizing every aspect of brewing from fermentation to packaging.

[41] See, eg, '2023 Brewers Association Beer Style Guideline', *Brewers Association* (Web Page) www.brewersassociation.org/edu/brewers-association-beer-style-guidelines/.

[42] This section consists of the part on patents written by Jean-Marc Deltorn, Professor at CEIPI, Strasbourg. The intertitles and the structure have been revised by the main contributors to this chapter.

Today, innovation in the field of brewing technologies remains high. This activity is readily observable through patent filings. Patents have played a crucial role in the history of beer production, intertwining technological innovation with the brewing industry's evolution. Since 1838, more than 22,000 patents have been filed worldwide in the Cooperative Patent Classification (CPC) class C12C alone (characterizing the patents in the field of 'Beer; Preparation of beer by fermentation; preparation of malt for making beer; preparation of hops for making beer'), with China, Germany, the US, Japan, Denmark, Korea, and Belgium ranking as the top applicants.

An early patent related to brewing technologies was filed in the US by Thomas Behan and related to 'improvements in beer and ale' aimed at 'reducing the risk of failure of brewing beer and greatly improving its flavor' (US868A, 1 August 1838). During the brewing process, malted barley and hops are mixed in warm water to produce a liquid called 'wort'. The invention consisted of a double-walled boiler that allowed precise adjustment of the preparation of the wort, located in a closed central vessel, at an optimal temperature of 200°F (approximately 93°C) by controlling and adjusting the heating of water in the space between the central and an external vessel. According to the inventor, this technique enabled optimizing the extraction of essential oils and other aromatic elements from the hop. Since essential oils contribute to the aromatic profile of beer, extracting more of these oils results in a more intense and complex aroma. A beer thus produced would probably have a more pronounced hop character, a desirable trait in styles like IPAs, where a strong hop presence is a defining feature.

The Pasteurization of Beer

One of the earliest and most impactful advancements in beer production protected by patents was the result of the inquisitive mind of the French chemist and microbiologist Louis Pasteur.[43] In the mid nineteenth century, one of the main issues with beer production and distribution was its limited shelf life that prevented mass production and trade between countries. While studying the fermentation processes in beverages, Pasteur showed that the spoiling of beer was due to the growth of microorganisms. He then proceeded to develop a process whereby heating the beer at a minimum temperature of 55°C for a few minutes and immediately after cooling the liquid, most microorganisms were killed without affecting the gustative properties of the beer, a method now known as 'pasteurization'. Pasteur filed a series of patents first in France on 28 June 1871 and later in 1873 in Belgium with a patent entitled 'Procédés nouveaux de fabrication et de conservation de la bière' and in the US with a patent on the 'Improvement in brewing beer and ale' (see Figure 5.4). Pasteur improved his production method by 'performing the process of brewing without the presence in the wort of atmospheric air'. This process enabled brewers 'to produce a

[43] Some commentators hint that Pasteur was also motivated by the bitterness of the Franco-Prussian war and the loss of Alsace and Lorraine, and that he wanted to hit the Germans 'where it hurts most: in their beer glasses'. See John Verive, 'Gearhead: Pasteurization's Place in Craft Beer's Battle', *Craft Beer & Brewing* (Web Page, 9 May 2020) https://beerandbrewing.com/gearhead-pasteurizations-place-in-craft-beers-battle/.

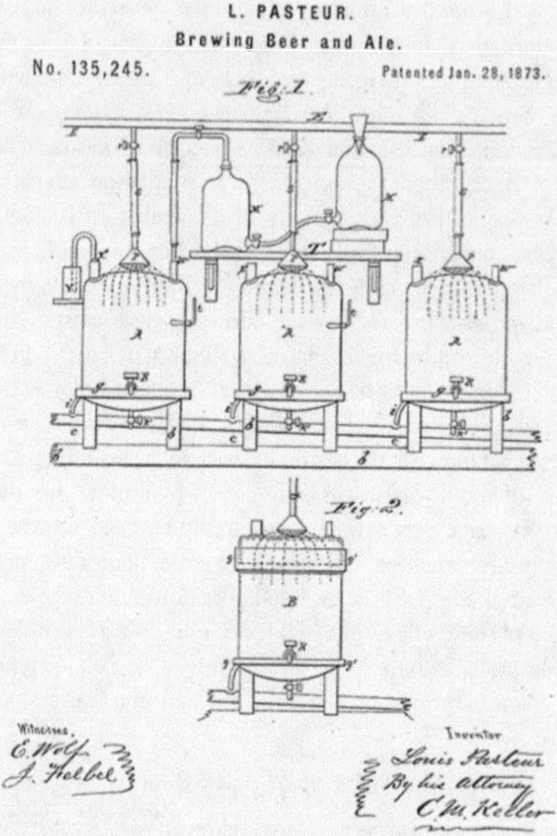

FIGURE 5.4 Drawing for the L. Pasteur (Brewing Beer and Ale) patent No. 135,145 (1873).

better quality and greater quantity of beer from the same quantity and quality of wort and to afford a beer which shall also embody the quality of greater degree of unalterableness during time and changes of climate in transportation and use'. Pasteur indeed claimed that, 'by my new process the beer produced possesses in an eminent degree the capacity of unchangeableness and can be transported without detriment or deterioration; and that in the use of my process by which I am enabled to brew in all seasons and in most any climate successfully the product is more aromatic and is perfectly limpid' (US135245A). This revolutionary technology enabled brewers not only to extend the shelf life of their beer products but also to drastically improve its consistency.

In the twentieth century, another key development in the beer industry was the development of canned beer. This alternative packaging option democratized beer consumption by making it more accessible and convenient, fostering the growth of a global beer market. The beer can was invented by the American Can Company, which patented 'Vinylite', a plastic lining for cans marketed under the brand name 'Keglined'. Patent US2028798A, filed on 30 August 1934 and granted on 28 January 1936 to Charles K. Beck, describes a method of lining the inside of cans. The description recognized that 'In the packaging of beer in metallic containers, it has been found that the exposure of the tin forming the outer surface of the metal when exposed even in small quantities chemically reacts upon the beer to change its appearance, making it cloudy and unmarketable'. Faced with this problem, the patent claimed 'a method of fully lining the can surfaces of a can to be used for beer and the like' to prevent contact between the beer and the metal. This innovation effectively addressed the issue of metal-induced spoilage, ensuring that the beer retained its clarity and taste. The lining material described is a type of plastic resin, specifically Vinylite, which is applied as a thin, continuous film covering the entire interior surface of the can. Vinylite is a copolymer of vinyl chloride and vinyl acetate known for its inertness and resistance to chemical reactions. As a result, canned beer became a practical and popular choice for both breweries and consumers. The introduction of canned beer led to an explosion in beer consumption due to its portability, durability, and extended shelf life compared to bottled beer. By the mid twentieth century, canned beer had become a staple in the beverage industry, contributing to the expansion of major breweries and the globalization of beer brands. This packaging revolution not only made beer more widely available but also played a crucial role in shaping modern beer marketing and distribution strategies.

5.5.2 *How Regulations Other than Patent Law Encouraged Beer-Related Inventions*

Patents have not only captured key transformations of the brewing process, but they have also followed the transformations of the legal landscape controlling the production of beer. For instance, in June 1816, the British government enacted a law that prohibited the use of all types of ingredients for colouring beer.[44] This legislation was part of a broader effort to address public health concerns and ensure the purity of food and drink. Indeed, during the early nineteenth century, there was increasing awareness and concern about the adulteration of food and beverages. Brewers often used various additives to colour and flavour beer, some of which were harmful. These additives included substances like toxic metals and chemicals that could pose serious health risks to consumers. The prohibition was aimed at protecting consumers by ensuring that beer was made from traditional safe ingredients such as malt, hops, water, and yeast. Breweries producing darker beers like porters and stouts, which sometimes used additives to achieve their dark colour, were directly impacted. Faced with this new regulation, Daniel Wheeler came up with a solution based on one of

[44] See Martyn Cornell, 'The Porter Brewer and the Peterloo Massacre', *Zythophile* (Web Page, 22 November 2018) https://zythophile.co.uk/2018/11/22/the-porter-brewer-and-the-peterloo-massacre/.

the main ingredients of beer: malt. The idea was to roast malt in a manner similar to roasted coffee using heated cylindrical drums. His 1817 patent described 'a method of drying and preparing malt so that the greater part of the saccharine and amylaceous principles of the grain become changed into a substance resembling gum and extractive matter of a deep brown colour readily soluble in hot or cold water.' (British Patent No. 4112, 29 June 1817). The end product is a 'black malt' that can be used as a natural colouring agent. In response to the law and the need for a natural way to achieve the stout's characteristic dark colour and rich flavour, companies such as Guinness began using roasted barley and malt. Roasting provided a natural and compliant solution, allowing Guinness to maintain the quality and distinctiveness of its stout without relying on prohibited substances. This shift not only adhered to the legal requirements of the 1816 law but also likely affected the taste of the beer. Roasted barley contributes to a distinctive flavour profile that includes elements of bitterness, coffee, and chocolate, which are characteristic of modern Guinness stout. More recently, innovations in malt production, including the development of new kilning techniques and the introduction of speciality malts, have expanded the range of flavours available to brewers. Patents on these processes and products have allowed for more complex and varied beer profiles, influencing modern brewing trends.

The introduction of prohibition laws in the US, enacted by the 18th Amendment in 1920, which banned the production, sale, and transportation of alcoholic beverages, spurred the development of non-alcoholic beer as breweries sought to stay in business. In this context, Patent No. 1551979, filed by Henry Deckebach in 1919, shortly after the ratification of the National Prohibition Act in 1919 and before Prohibition went into effect, described a method for producing non-alcoholic beer by removing alcohol through a process of vacuum distillation. In its description, the patent discloses a 'means of removing alcohol from beer [without affecting its taste] and recovering the alcohol that is removed'. The invention thereby allowed breweries to produce 'near beer' containing less than 0.5 per cent of alcohol and complying with Prohibition laws while maintaining some of the flavour characteristics of traditional beer (what was done with the recovered alcohol is not discussed in the patent). Still, near beer lacked the full flavour and complexity of traditional beer. The vacuum distillation process and other methods used to remove alcohol often resulted in a taste that many consumers found unsatisfactory compared to regular beer. Despite its shortcomings in taste, near beer saw substantial production and consumption due to the absence of legal alcoholic alternatives. Statistics from the Prohibition era indicate that near beer production was significant. For instance, by 1921, production of near beer reached around 300 million gallons annually, and major breweries such as Anheuser-Busch and Pabst shifted a significant portion of their production to near beer to stay afloat. Anheuser-Busch's near beer brand 'Bevo' became particularly well-known. However, overall consumption and satisfaction were lower compared to pre-Prohibition levels. Many consumers turned to illegal alcohol (bootlegging) and speakeasies for traditional alcoholic beverages, leading to a significant black market for alcohol.

5.5.3 *Patents on Beer Fermentation and Selection of Yeast Reactivate the Debate on Biotech Patenting*

One significant innovation in beer production in the second half of the twentieth century was the development of continuous fermentation systems, patented by Morton Coutts in 1953, which revolutionized the brewing industry by enhancing both efficiency and consistency of the brewing process. This process revolutionized the brewing industry by allowing for a constant flow of beer production, which significantly shortened the brewing time by as much as several weeks and improved overall efficiency. Coutts's invention separated the yeast growth stage from the alcohol production stage, maintaining a continuous flow between the two. This method allowed for raw materials to be added continuously, producing a steady supply of beer. The world's first brewery to use this method was established in Palmerston North, New Zealand, in 1957. This innovation not only improved production efficiency but also enhanced the consistency and quality of beer. Continuous fermentation is especially suitable for producing large quantities of a single beer type, and it has been adopted by several major breweries worldwide, including Guinness.

More recent innovations have enabled brewers to achieve unprecedented consistency and quality through the selection of genetically modified yeast. These techniques – some leading to patented inventions – have opened new horizons for flavour and brewing efficiency. The case, involving an application jointly filed by Carlsberg and Heineken at the European Patent Office (EPO), centred on the contentious issue of patenting naturally occurring mutations in barley plants used for brewing beer. Carlsberg and Heineken, two of the world's leading beer producers, sought patents on specific barley varieties that they claimed produced superior beer due to their naturally occurring mutations. These patents (EP2384110 and EP2373514) covered barley plants with particular genetic mutations that resulted in improved brewing properties, such as enhanced taste, longer shelf life, and reduced malt usage.

The nature of these patents sparked considerable controversy. Unlike genetically modified organisms (GMOs), these patents focused on mutations in barley found through traditional breeding techniques. The scope of the patents, which included claims on the barley plants, the brewing processes using these barley varieties, and the beer produced from these processes, raised concerns among various stakeholders. Critics argued that such broad patents could encompass a wide range of natural barley mutations, potentially stifling innovation and restricting the use of these natural genetic resources. Furthermore, by covering specific genetic traits that could occur through mutation and selection processes, these patents were, for their detractors, essentially protecting the result of an evolutionary process that, in time, would have occurred without any human influence.

Indeed, these patents raised significant opposition, notably from environmental organizations, farmers, and breeders, contending that granting these patents would limit access to natural plant varieties and hinder agricultural research. They argued that the patents were overly broad and that naturally occurring mutations should not be subject to patent protection. Erling Frederiksen, a representative for the NGO Friends of the Earth in Denmark (NOAH), stated in opposition to the patents that 'There should be no patents on beer and barley. Breeding plants and brewing beer are not inventions, but based on centuries-old tradition'.[45]

Despite the opposition, the EPO eventually ruled in favour of the validity of the patents in a restricted form: while the original patent covered barley plants bred without genetic engineering, the limited patent only concerned the plants characterized by specific mutations. The case highlighted the tension between encouraging innovation through patents and protecting access to natural genetic resources. This ruling underscored the complex balance between the need to incentivize technological advancements and the imperative to safeguard public access to naturally occurring genetic materials. The decision has set a precedent that could influence future patent applications and disputes in the agricultural and brewing industries, emphasizing the ongoing debate over the limits of intellectual property rights in relation to natural organisms.

5.6 KNOW-HOW AND TRADE SECRETS IN BEER BREWING

The brewing craft is a subtle one, with infinite possible variations in style and composition of beers and in brewing techniques. Nonetheless, it is capable of standardization and homogeneity of production, as we can see in the Big Beer sector; in modern times this is in part due to monitoring technology. Bamforth puts it succinctly when he refers to the 'brewery control center': 'The facility is fitted from start to finish with in-line sensors that can monitor all the key pulses of the process and relay the information back to the computer screen in "space HQ". Thus, the most fabulous control is achieved and tremendous consistency is possible in the products.'[46]

Nonetheless, although the brewing craft is ancient, it still lends itself to human ingenuity and imagination which produces beers of different styles – from the subtly distinct to the radically different. A recent example is the sudden appearance and development of fruit beers: addition of fruit and fruit flavours to beers to create a different category of drinks. There is much experimentation involved, but also reliance on brewing experience, knowledge of the subtleties of technique and personal know-how, and understanding of how to translate an idea or concept into a reality. In this environment, where particularly in craft brewing there is demand for constant new brews and also for high-quality (and consequently relatively highly priced) drinks, what knowledge is shared and what is not? What gives an edge or advantage? Can knowledge be documented or is it 'tacit': How is knowledge shared or transmitted? And in our context, what does the law say about this sharing of skill, knowledge, experience,

[45] 'No Patents on Beer! Carlsberg Claims Barley and Beer as Its Invention', *No Patents on Seeds* (Web Page, 17 November 2016) www.no-patents-on-seeds.org/en/node/372.

[46] Charles W Bamforth, *Grape vs Grain: A Historical, Technological, and Social Comparison of Wine and Beer* (Cambridge University Press, 2008) 104.

and information? Basically, the critical legal distinction is between free 'know-how' and proprietary trade secrets – but about the law more below.

In the early days of craft brewing, know-how was recognized as critical but was often shared between master brewers from different brands. Brewing was commonly a collaborative pursuit.[47] But more recently the craft sector has become more mature, crowded, and competitive; it is now more rivalrous and exclusionary. There is more incentive to appropriate and attempt to control new ideas, techniques, and even the most subtle and personal know-how. We described above how, in the early days of craft brewing, branding was non-exclusionary and not contested, while it is now more directly linked to competition and proprietary rights in trademarks. In a similar way, the brewing craft itself has changed as the sector has matured. A key to competitiveness is now individual control over know-how, trade secrets, the tacit knowledge of individual brewmasters, and their creative skills. But at the same time beer brewing remains an ancient skill with fundamental elements and it remains desirable in the market to signal qualities of not only of creativity and novelty, but also of tradition and continuity. Innovation is not a selling point per se for beer as it is in other areas. Continuity is important too and it is thus advisable to promote a product that combines elements of craft, tradition, and novelty in a subtle manner. The personality of brewers is thus an important component of relevant advertising and promotion, and in any case their personal skills can make the difference between an appealing and an appalling beer.

In other words, in the contemporary craft scene, brewers and their personal know-how have become a vital asset in an increasingly competitive market. Who the brewers are in Big Beer is largely unknown, because there are few attempts and little incentive to stamp Big Beer with a particular brewmaster's individuality and radical novelty. When it comes to craft beer, by contrast, individual brewmasters are often a well-known and crucial part of the character and marketing of a brewery: there are celebrated brewers in many countries, leaders of the craft and speciality beer movement, such as Theo Musso in Italy and Phil Sexton in America, or Rudi Ghequire of the famous Rodenbach brewery in Belgium. But there are also the small family breweries with brewmasters such as Daniel Thiriez of Brasserie Thiriez in Esquelbecq, France, and a long tradition, as is the case for the Maes family of the 'De Halve Maan' brewery in Bruges, Belgium.

But how does the law allow all this brewing skill and knowledge to be appropriated and controlled? We saw above that one way is through patents – but the more common (and inevitable) way is through the law of trade secrets. Traditionally that law draws a distinction between 'trade secrets' and 'know-how'. Trade secrets are bits of information that can be clearly identified that a brewery (in the present context) has treated as secret

47 Dan M Forman, 'Courts Help Brewers Protect Their Recipes and Techniques from Employee Theft', *CDF Labor Law* (Blog Post) www.callaborlaw.com/entry/courts-help-brewers-protect-their-recipes-and-techniques-from-employee-theft. See also 'Causing a Brouhaha: Trade Secrets Disputes in the Craft Beer Industry', *Orrick* (Web Page, 4 February 2017) www.orrick.com/en/insights/2017/02/causing-a-brouhaha-trade-secrets-disputes-in-the-craft-beer-industry.

(e.g. by hiding it from most of its employees, or keeping it under lock and key, or getting employees to sign confidentiality clauses), and that gives it a competitive edge. Know-how, on the other hand, is the kind of information or 'tacit' undocumented knowledge that resides in the mind of a brewmaster (again in this particular context). Much of the subtlety of beer brewing lies in the field of know-how, rather than trade secrets. Basic ingredients. techniques, and processes are either well-known or traditional, and since brewing has increasingly become a skill acquired through formal education, much of it is the common stock of knowledge of all brewing graduates. However, equally important is the more subtle art of brewing that lies in the realm of personal know-how: the new ideas, the subtle touches, the background knowledge acquired by trial and error. The only manner in which such know-how can effectively be acquired or transition from one brewery to another is *by hiring the brewmaster concerned*. Know-how cannot really be clearly itemized, documented, and sold as information; it is mobile only because of the mobility of the employees who possess the necessary know-how. These days, breweries that value the know-how of employees therefore turn their minds to retaining or restraining their key brewmasters. Alternatively, they will sue for trade secrets breaches after employment – the line between free know-how and proprietary trade secrets is in many cases not easy to draw.

For that reason, they more commonly seek to enter into non-competition agreements with their brewers. These are clauses or restrictive covenants under which one party (the employee) agrees not to take on different brewing work during a certain period of time and a certain area after they quit. In more recent times such non-competition clauses have become an issue in the craft beer sector (but potentially also for Big Beer). They are particularly controversial because of the initially highly collaborative, sharing style of the craft beer community. As Paige Latham Didora says:

> For a long time, the craft beer industry seemed more defined by a spirit of collaboration than protectionism. That stance was evident not only in the normalization of collaboration beers, but on forums where brewers shared tips, through stories about breweries extending lab capabilities to and sharing materials with neighbors, and even via festivals based on co-brewed beers.[48]

But as that sector has become more crowded and competitive, brewers seek to appropriate and hang on to the competitive advantage derived from a particular brewmaster's skill. As Didora says, 'as craft beer has progressed from infancy, the lawsuits that have arisen from non-competes and nondisclosures can feel like a loss of innocence for the industry. Swanson [Averie Swanson, Master Cicerone and founder of Chicago's Keeping Together], sees this current era as a natural evolution'. '"Non-competes and NDAs are important. I think that this industry has definitely reached an adolescent or more mature phase over the last five-to-10 years", she says. She adds that an increasing

48 See Paige Latham Didora, 'What's Fair in Beer and Litigation? – The Role of Noncompetes, Nondisclosures, and Trade Secrets in Brewing', *Good Beer Hunting* (Web Page, 18 February 2021) www.goodbeerhunting.com/blog/whats-fair-in-beer-and-litigation-the-role-of-non-competes-non-disclosures-and-trade-secrets-in-brewing.

number of people started breweries, beginning in the mid-2010s, not because of a passion for homebrewing, but because of the perceived business opportunity.'[49]

Where the individual brewmaster represents that advantage, non-competition clauses which prohibit these individuals from working for a competitor for a set amount of time after the end of their employment are the most effective legal method to achieve this aim. But they are controversial in general and regarded with particular ambivalence in the craft beer sector; they are anathema to its traditional values. Of course. they do not exclusively or even principally apply to the brewmasters themselves, but often to sales personnel and in some cases to lower-level brewery workers.[50] An example much commented on in the United States relates to the litigious behaviour of the Boston Brewing Company (BBC), one of the largest American craft brewers, which has developed a reputation for suing its former employees,[51] whether for breach of non-competition clauses or misuse of trade secrets.[52] This is part of a broader trend that has attracted adverse attention from authorities – so much so that in the United States there is a move afoot to abrogate and prohibit all non-competition clauses. In other jurisdictions they are also being looked at anew by legislators. Abrogating non-competition clauses can only be a good thing for the craft brewing sector, ensuring it remains dynamic and innovative and does not go stale. In any case, brewers have alternative legal means to protect *genuine* trade secrets, be they commercial or technological, in particular non-disclosure clauses and confidentiality clauses in employment contracts.[53] On occasion, both craft and Big Beer brewers have been known to sue each other for trade secrets breaches, as for instance happened between Coors and AB InBev.[54]

49 Ibid.

50 See Dave Infante, 'When Brewers Enforce Non-Competes, Everybody Loses', *VinePair* (Web Page, 16 February 2024) https://vinepair.com/articles/hop-take-non-competes-in-brewing/.

51 Jessica Infante, 'Former Sales Reps Challenge Boston Beer's Non-Compete in Pair of Lawsuits, Allege Hostile Work Environment', *Brewbound* (Web Page, 7 February 2024) www.brewbound.com/news/former-sales-reps-challenge-boston-beers-non-compete-in-pair-of-lawsuits-allege-hostile-work-environment/; Katie Johnston, 'The Brewer behind Sam Adams Has Long Kept Former Employees on a Tight Leash. Now Some Are Suing to Break Free', *The Boston Globe* (Web Page, 8 March 2024) www.bostonglobe.com/2024/03/08/business/boston-beer-co-noncompete-agreements/.

52 Toppling Goliath also ran into some adverse publicity for litigiousness of this kind. See Keith Gribbins, 'Let's Talk Non-Compete Agreements in the Brewing Industry and Reflect on the Toppling Goliath Suit', *Craft Brewing Business* (Web Page, 6 August 2018) www.craftbrewingbusiness.com/featured/lets-talk-non-compete-agreements-in-the-brewing-industry-and-reflect-on-the-toppling-goliath-suit/. In relation to BBC, see Infante (n 51).

53 Robert G Young, 'The Secret Sauce: Protecting Brewing Recipes and Processes – The Role of Employee Agreements', *Bowditch & Dewey* (Blog Post, 8 December 2016) www.bowditch.com/craftbrewerylegalblog/2016/12/08/the-secret-sauce-protecting-brewing-recipes-and-processes-the-role-of-employee-agreements/.

54 See Celes Keene, 'Theft of Trade Secrets: The Newest Chapter in the War of the Beer Companies', *Klemchuk LLP* (Blog Post, 30 October 2019) www.klemchuk.com/ideate/beer-battle-over-trade-secret-theft-anheuser-busch-sues-coors. See also Justin Kendall, 'Anheuser-Busch Accuses MillerCoors of Stealing Confidential Beer Recipes', *Brewbound* (Web Page, 17 October 2019) www.brewbound.com/news/anheuser-busch-accuses-millercoors-of-stealing-confidential-beer-recipe-information/; Charles Riley, 'AB InBev Accuses Rival of Obtaining the Secret Recipe for Bud Light', *CNN Business* (Web Page, 18 October 2019) https://edition.cnn.com/2019/10/18/business/bud-light-secret-recipe-stolen/index.html; Forman (n 47).

On a final note, the development of brewing as a science and the subject of structured courses and education has also changed things: it has generated a corpus of shared knowledge, but that obviously also risks homogenization in the craft brew sector. From brewing guilds which were the main receptors of brewing knowledge (more of an applied kind) and main training bodies, we have evolved to a tertiary education model of learning the brewing craft. At the same time a, science of brewing has developed; as a science, it goes back to the employment by Guinness of the first company brewing scientist in history,[55] William Sealy Gosset. His story is a surprising one, as he became widely known as a statistician. His Wikipedia entry explains:

> In his job as Head Experimental Brewer at Guinness, the self-trained Gosset developed new statistical methods – both in the brewery and on the farm – now central to the design of experiments, to proper use of significance testing on repeated trials, and to analysis of economic significance (an early instance of decision theory interpretation of statistics) and more, such as his small-sample, stratified, and repeated balanced experiments on barley for proving the best yielding varieties. (Wikipedia)

The entry also points out that 'Gosset remained at Guinness throughout his life as Head Experimental Brewer, then Head of the Statistics Department he formed at Guinness, before his promotion to Head Brewer for the new Guinness brewery in London in 1935'.[56] However, it is only relatively recently that brewing has become the subject of tailored and specific university programmes, that of UC Davis often being advanced as one of the first.[57] Thus, beer brewing takes on the allure of a science rather than an art form, and the practice of brewing becomes a profession rather than a craft. Nonetheless, the personal skills and know-how of individual brewmasters, as well as their creativity, will always remain a vital component of the craft brewing sector. That sector competes by relying on a peculiar mix of tradition, skill, science, innovation, know-how, and trade secrets, as well as marketing image and promotion, which defies the traditional categories and policies of IP law.

[55] See 'William Sealy Gosset', *Wikipedia* (Web Page, 16 August 2024) https://en.wikipedia.org/wiki/William_Sealy_Gosset.

[56] See also Karen Lamb and David Farmer, 'The Genius at Guinness and His Statistical Legacy', *The Conversation* (Web Page, 16 March 2018) https://theconversation.com/the-genius-at-guinness-and-his-statistical-legacy-93134#:~:text=The%20first%20scientific%20brewer%2C%20Thomas,in%20particular%20crops%20of%20hops.

[57] See Tom Acitelli, 'The Origins of America's First University Degree in Brewing', *All About Beer* (Web Page, 11 June 2015) https://allaboutbeer.net/the-origins-of-americas-first-university-degree-in-brewing/. See also 'History of the UC Davis Master Brewers Certificate Program', *UC Davis* (Web Page) https://cpe.ucdavis.edu/areas-study/brewing/history-uc-davis-master-brewers-program; 'UC Davis Brewing Program History', *UC Davis* (Web Page) https://cpe.ucdavis.edu/areas-study/brewing/history-uc-davis-master-brewers-program.

6

Belgium as a Beer Country (or Beer as a Belgian Country?)

6.1 BEER CONSUMPTION IN BELGIUM

Belgium is to beer what France is to wine (or Cuba to cigars, to continue the list of addictive products!).[1] Belgium has a very long beer tradition – Stella Artois, sold all over the world, claims to be one of the first brands, dating back to 1366! Belgium has also acquired a worldwide reputation for craft beers – at least for the Anglo-American public – since Jackson's famous book *Great Beers of Belgium* was first published in 1991.[2] This beer expert[3] made the Lambics, White and Red Beers, as well as the Trappists, known outside Belgium. However, as in other countries, most beers sold in Belgium are a version of pilsner beer (such as the Jupiler, Stella, and Maes brands). Despite this, Belgian beers are associated in the minds of many consumers with top-fermented, 'spiced', strong, and Trappist beers. In Belgium, beer is also deeply and in many different ways associated with culture.

Beer Consumption in Belgum

Beer consumption in Belgium is 54 litres per capita per year, according to Statista's per capita volume sales in the beer market worldwide, by country, in 2023.

1 This presentation comes from the entry on Belgium in Garrett Oliver (ed), *The Oxford Companion to Beer* (Oxford University Press, 2011).

2 Michael Jackson, *Great Beers of Belgium* (Brewers Publications, 6th ed, 2008).

3 See 'Michael Jackson (writer)', *Wikipedia* (Web Page, 27 September 2024) https://en.wikipedia.org/wiki/Michael_Jackson_(writer).

6.2 FEATURES OF BELGIAN BEERS: CRAFTED, STRONG SOMETIMES BASED ON SPONTANEOUS FERMENTATION, AND WITH A ROBUST MONASTERY TRADITION

Belgium claims to have more craft beers and local brands than any other country: about 1,500 types of beer are brewed in Belgium (but Belgians do not drink as much beer in volume as Czechs or Germans[4]).

For Jackson, 'among the great brewing nations, Belgium was, for various historical reasons, the most parochial, and that helped it maintain its brewing traditions, its specialties, its Fine Beers'.[5] At the end of 2023, there were 417 breweries in Belgium, a relatively small country.[6] At the same time, Belgium hosts the world's biggest brewer (AB InBev: see Chapter 5 on IP) that distributes mass-market pilsners everywhere (including Budweiser, Stella Artois, and Labatt). This is the paradox of the Belgian beer country: associated with very distinctive and tasteful brews, while distributing and marketing the most standardized bottom-fermented beverages on a global scale.

Many Belgian craft beers are quite strong (for example, Duvel, a blond beer with 8.5 per cent ABV), but many triple craft beers (with between 7 and 10 per cent ABV) are today brewed outside Belgium (in the United States, for instance) and the strongest beers do not originate from Belgium.[7] The Huyghe brewery in East Flanders has chosen to brand one of its beers Delirium Tremens (8.5 per cent) – an obviously suggestive name (and therefore good trademark) as delirium tremens refers to the violent tremors experienced by alcoholics during withdrawal from alcohol – but the brewery also makes fruit beers with low alcohol by volume. In the United States, Delirium was at some point removed from stores nationwide as its reference to alcoholism was considered contrary to the law,[8] before being awarded the title of 'Best Beer in the World' at the World Beer Championships in Chicago in 1997. Obviously, the rules on promoting alcohol and the sensitivities around drinking differ a lot from country to country (see Chapter 3 on health and

4 See 'Beer Consumption by Country 2024', *World Population Review* (Web Page) https://worldpopulationreview.com/country-rankings/beer-consumption-by-country.

5 Jackson (n 2) 20.

6 The Brussels Times with Belga, 'Number of Belgian Breweries Drops for the First Time in 15 Years', *The Brussels Times* (Web Page, 13 January 2024) www.brusselstimes.com/874380/number-of-belgian-breweries-drops-for-first-time-in-15-years.

7 Many strong beers, such as the Brewmeister and BrewDog beers (Snake Venom, Armageddon, End of History) come from Scotland (perhaps the influence of whisky?), but this raises the question of what is to be considered beer, as BrewDog (and Schorschbräu in Germany) use an unconventional means, 'freeze distillation' (building on the tradition of Germany's Eisbock), to raise the alcohol levels. See Nick Hall, '13 Strongest Beers in the World for Serious Brew-Snobs', *Man of Many* (Web Page, 7 August 2023) https://manofmany.com/lifestyle/drinks/strongest-beers-in-the-world.

8 See William Albuquerque, 'Riding the Pink Elephant: A Kook at Delirium', *The Bowdoin Orient* (Web Page, 3 December 2010) https://bowdoinorient.com/bonus/article/5883/.

safety). Evoking a visit to the Brewers' House in Brussels, Jackson was amused by reading on a tall pennant the message for a moderate drinking campaign: 'A pint or two a day keeps the doctor away.' 'I especially liked the added, open-ended, qualifier: "or two"', writes Jackson. 'It is hard to imagine such as truthful slogan being permitted in my own country, the United Kingdom. Or the United States.'[9] (When the contributors of this chapter were young, it was usual for Belgian children to be served low-alcohol table beer – *bière de table* or *tafelbier* – also called small beer).

Craft beers are now widespread. Regarding beer making, however, something that was for a long time unique to Belgium, and in particular the region around Brussels, was spontaneously fermented beers. The lambic beers rely on the contamination of the wort in open containers by wild yeasts in the environment (see Chapter 1 on beer brewing). Typical for some spontaneously fermented beers is also the addition of fruits such as cherries for Kriek and the use of the 'Champagne method' (*méthode champenoise*) of combining beers from different periods for Geuze. This spontaneous fermentation style of brewing is also adopted elsewhere these days; because of the open vessel used to cool wort during fermentation, these are often referred to as 'coolship' beers.[10]

Since around CE 800, with the expansion of Charlemagne's empire to northern Europe, monasteries also spread in the Low Countries, and with the cooler climate switched from producing wine, as they did in southern Europe, to brewing beers.[11] The shift to monasteries as centres of brewing remains visible in Belgium (and Germany). However, many commercial brewers developed from the twelfth and thirteenth centuries, in part because of technological innovation, with the role of hops in beer conservation, and regulations, such as the exemption of monasteries from direct beer taxes, which in turn prompted the local rulers to favour commercial brewers (see Chapter 11 on tax and excises). Belgian beers today have often maintained some links with the monasteries, a strong tie in the case of the Trappist beers, or at least a symbolic tie, as many commercial beers still like to refer to abbeys, but often without any real connection to them.

6.2.1 *Abbey vs Trappist Beers*

Trappist beers are definitely linked with abbeys but are to be distinguished from abbey beers (Figure 6.1). To be allowed to use the Trappist® name and the label 'Authentic Trappist Product' (ATP), an abbey has to meet certain prescribed requirements: the beer (or other Trappist products, such as cheese or bread) must

[9] Jackson (n 2) 26.

[10] See, for instance, the list of coolship beers brewed by Allagash in Oregon at 'Results for "Coolship"', *Allagash Brewing Company* (Web Page) www.allagash.com/?s=coolship.

[11] Johan Swinnen and Thijs Vandemoortele, 'Beeronomics: The Economics of Beer and Brewing' in Johan Swinnen (ed), *The Economics of Beer* (Oxford University Press, 2011).

FIGURE 6.1 Logo of the 'Authentic Trappist Product'.

be made within the immediate surroundings of the abbey; under the supervision of the monks or nuns; and the 'profits should be intended for the needs of the monastic community, for purposes of solidarity within the Trappist Order, or for development projects and charitable works'.[12] Thus, without monks there is no Trappist label: when in January 2021 the last two monks left the Achel Abbey to join the larger community at the mother house of Westmalle, the brewery based at the Achel abbey lost its Trappist appellation. Also, if there is no charity (or solidarity with the Trappist community), there is no Trappist beer. Today, nine abbeys brew and sell Trappist beers, and Belgium remains their stronghold.[13]

Commercial brewers have attempted to capitalize on the attraction of the real abbey beers, and labels with cheeky monks with a goblet in hand and in the background some abbey walls or stained glass windows have invaded the market. This prompted the Trappist monasteries to take measures such as the creation of the International Trappist Association and the adoption of the ATP label referenced above. The Trappists even won a court decision on 6 September 1985 when the Brussels Commercial Court confirmed, 'it is now common knowledge that customers attribute special standards of quality to products made by monastic communities, and this is especially true of Trappist monasteries'.[14] From then on, the term

[12] 'Criteria for Obtaining the ATP Label', *International Trappist Association* (Web Page) www.trappist.be/en/about-ita/atp-label/#.

[13] The list includes the five Belgian abbeys of Chimay, Orval, Rochefort, Westmalle, and Westvleteren, as well as La Trappe, Mont des Cats, Cardena, Mount St. Bernard, Tre Fontane, and Zundert.

[14] Brussels Commercial Court, 6 September 1985, Revue de droit intellectuel, Ing.-Cons., 1985, p 408 (*Westmalle & alii v Labo-Pax*).

Trappist was to be reserved for Trappist monks, while 'abbey beers' could be used to refer to beers brewed at non-Trappist monasteries or even to monastery-inspired beers sold by commercial brewers. Belgian case law was much later confirmed by non-state rules when in 2021 the Beer Judge Certification Program, the previously mentioned international certifying organization for beer judges that defines style guidelines and parameters for beer competitions worldwide, renamed the 'Trappist Ale' category to the more generic term 'Monastic Ale'.[15] 'Trappist' is thus not a beer style, but a protected designation of origin (on beer and geographical indications, see Chapter 5 on IP).

Speaking of the BJCP style guide, we may here pause to note that Belgian styles are well represented. In fact, no fewer than fifteen distinctly Belgian beer styles are included in the style guide.

At any rate, as a result of all those developments noted above, the appearance of Trappist beer bottles remains aligned with the modesty of the religious order, while the abbey beers often exploit the monkish style! An excellent example is the Belgian Leffe beer, which is an AB InBev brand that taps into the monastic brewing tradition by suggestive messaging, but is in fact brewed in the Leuven facilities of AB InBev and distributed on a global scale without any involvement of monks – though royalties are still paid to the original abbey located in the city of Dinant.[16] Other craft abbey beers, such as the Pestoeër (Pastor in English) or Missjënaris (Missionary) from the brewer Klein Kloosterke (Small Monastery), have more genuine links with the local abbey of Maaseik.[17] Many brewers tap into the reservoir of monastic, or at least medieval, imagery, such as the US New Belgium beer called 'Abbey'.[18] This is not a recent trend, nor is it limited to Belgium, as shown in Figure 6.2.[19]

Sometimes the reference to a monastery is denied trademark protection, as with the judgment of the General Court of the EU confirming the refusal by the EU Intellectual Property Office to register 'Klosterstoff' as a trademark for a beer because of a lack of distinctiveness (the German term 'Kloster' refers to monastery and 'Stoff' to (narcotic) substance, and the combination was quite surprisingly found descriptive for alcoholic and beer products).[20] More generally, brewers have to worry about consumers' different levels of beer knowledge; it might be that Belgian consumers understand full well that 'Leffe' is not brewed in a monastery, but what about consumers in the US? A Florida man brought suit against AB InBev for consumer

[15] See Caroline Wallace, Sarah Wood, and Jessica Deahl, *Trappist Beer Travels, Second Edition: Inside the Breweries of the Monasteries* (Schiffer Publishing, 2nd ed, 2023) 19.

[16] See 'Leffe', *Wikipedia* (Web Page, 24 April 2024) https://en.wikipedia.org/wiki/Leffe.

[17] See 'Genieten van bier in een unieke brouwerij [Enjoying Beer in a Unique Brewery]', *Brouwerij Klein Kloosterke* (Web Page) www.brouwerijkleinkloosterke.be/#.

[18] 'Our Story', *New Belgium Brewing* (Web Page) www.newbelgium.com/company/story/.

[19] Oliver (n 1) 2.

[20] *Alpirsbacher Klosterbräu Glauner GmbH & Co KG v European Union Intellectual Property Office* (T 844/16) [2017] Judgment of the General Court (Ninth Chamber).

FIGURE 6.2 Beer labels and reproductions from various countries. All these labels come from the Pike Microbrewery Museum of Seattle, US; from top row, left to right: American beer label c. 1890; Brazilian beer label c. 1900; Scottish beer label c. 1940; American beer label c. 1933; Swiss illuminated manuscript, seventeenth century; German coloured lithograph c. 1900 (reproduced from Garrett Oliver, n. 1, p. 2).

deception arguing that he was misled into thinking exactly that; AB InBev has also been sued in the US in relation to two other of its brands – the Beck beer not being brewed in Germany and Kirin Ichiban not being brewed in Japan (cases that were later settled).[21]

6.2.2 *Pairing Beer with Food and Haute Cuisine: From Monasteries to New Chefs*

If the Trappists associate beers with cheese and other products (to be bought at the abbey, for instance as in Orval), many chefs now pair beers with food, or make food using beer. Although beer was once seen as food – some monks looked at it as 'liquid bread' (see also our introductory Chapter 1) – today Belgium has many traditional restaurants which specialize in *cuisine à la bière*, with recipes for rabbit, mussel, or beef stew. Lists of beers now also appear on the menu of haute cuisine restaurants along with the names of wines. To demonstrate the higher cooking status acquired by beers, Michael Jackson quotes several examples, including the wine-named beer 'Malheur Brut Reserve' that was served in 2001 at chef-patron Jan Buytaert's Michelin-starred restaurant De Bellefleur, at Kapellen, near Antwerp.[22] The metallic film wrapping with the wire cage, typical of Champagne bottles, is also used in beer bottling to propel the status of some craft beers into the realm of luxury. But the use in Belgium of champagne bottles might also be justified by the local taste for re-fermentation in the bottle, which requires heavy glass and wired corks to withstand the CO_2 pressure of the beer undergoing a second or third fermentation. These days drinkers can find a path through all the complexities, assisted by a 'beer sommelier'.

6.3 THE INDISPENSABLE INGREDIENTS OF BELGIAN BEER CULTURE

In Belgium maybe more than anywhere else, beer must be seen as a component of culture and described in its cultural, and sometimes very local, context. It is thus for good reason that the Belgian beer culture was in 2016 inscribed on the Representative List of the Intangible Cultural Heritage of Humanity by UNESCO.[23] This is justified, according to UNESCO, by the many cultural and social dimensions of beer production and consumption: several organizations of

[21] Stephanie N Grimoldby, 'Attorney Predicts Deceptive Labeling Class Actions Will Increase; Leffe Case Brewing in Florida', *Florida Record* (Web Page, 29 April 2016) https://flarecord.com/stories/510720031-attorney-predicts-deceptive-labeling-class-actions-will-increase-leffe-case-brewing-in-florida. See also Dan Svantesson, 'Australian Consumer Law Is Failing Beer Drinkers', *The Conversation* (Web Page, 11 October 2017) https://theconversation.com/australian-consumer-law-is-failing-beer-drinkers-85260.

[22] Jackson (n 2) 17.

[23] See 'Beer Culture in Belgium', UNESCO Intangible Heritage (Web Page) https://ich.unesco.org/en/RL/beer-culture-in-belgium-01062?RL=01062.

brewers exist, which work with communities (to ensure responsible beer consumption) and support sustainable practices (recyclable packaging). Transmission of expertise and skills is also ensured by master brewers who run classes and by university programmes (such as organized by the Centre for Malting & Brewing of the KU Leuven[24]). Beer is closely connected with the hospitality sector too, and this is for instance translated in the rituals around pouring, serving, and drinking beer (and its pairing with food in many restaurants and pubs).

6.3.1 *Pouring (Belgian) Draft Beer Is Enchanting (No Decanting Needed)*

While pouring wine in a glass is a rather straightforward operation, unless you need to filter and first decant the (old) wine, pouring beer usually involves more dexterity as you have to find the right balance between liquid and glass so as to ensure the right amount of foam.[25] At least for Belgian beers.

For a philosopher (and we share the view), 'the pouring of a beer; when it is competently done, can be a highly enjoyable experience itself, one that tells us a lot about a beer's quality even before we taste it'.[26] Pouring beer in a glass is also part of the ceremony required prior to the enjoyment of drinking. The action of pouring, if taken seriously, contributes to create an aura of authenticity, making the beer a true cultural artefact. Presented in a video for Stella Artois,[27] the pouring ritual has nine steps involving a dance between the Chalice glass and the Draught Master: first purify the Chalice in a cold water bath; sacrifice a few drops for the sake of freshness; hold the Chalice at 45 degrees to ensure proper bubbling; then straighten it up when it is 80 per cent full; when the glass is filled, tilt the skimmer at 45 degrees and skim the foam off, ensure 3 cm of foam, no more, no less; dip the Chalice in a cold bath removing the outer excess liquid – and it is ready to be served! The pouring experience together with the capturing of the liquid by the glass is also important because while most physical entities, like us humans, have relatively clear-cut visible physical boundaries, this 'is not true of beers', as Dale Jacquette reminds us. 'Beers exist communally in a keg all floating indistinguishably around one another in a volume of liquid, until one by one they are called forth into the world to enter a glass and are served to an appreciative drinker.' For Jacquette (and us – and you the reader?), 'That moment of being poured from the spigot is what I call the defining moment in the life of a beer. It is the exact instant of time when a beer is tapped

[24] KU Leuven has an AB InBev Chair in Malting and Brewing Sciences. See 'Postgraduate Programme Malting and Brewing Sciences', KU Leuven (Web Page) www.biw.kuleuven.be/en/study/programmes/postgrad/maltingbrewing.

[25] This part of the book consists of a slightly modified version of an intertitle in Dale Jacquette, 'Thirst for Authenticity. An Aesthetics of the Brewer's Art' in Steven D Hales (ed), *Beer and Philosophy: The Unexamined Beer Isn't Worth Drinking* (Blackwell Publishing, 1st ed, 2007) 18.

[26] Ibid 19.

[27] See Stella Artois (Web Page) www.stellaartois.com/en_gb/quality/.

from the cold darkened depths where it has lived in quiet anonymity like a baby in the womb, inseparably from all its brothers and sisters, until at that moment it finally becomes an entity unto itself, the glass of beer that has just been served.'[28] And that wasn't a few seconds before! What makes beer happen is thus also the adjustment of the liquid from tap (or from a bottle) to the beer glass. Their shapes thus play a not-so-minor role in the beer experience.

6.3.2 *The Multiple Shapes of Beer Glasses and Bottles*

Because of the pouring ritual, the shape of the receiving glass is of utmost importance. Many would agree that some beer drinking vessels are not suitable – for example, an ashtray, a milk carton, or a condom.[29] Beer must be drunk from a proper drinking glass. To drink it from a teacup leads invariably to a bad experience. Beer in Belgium – more so than anywhere else – is served in glasses of different shapes and sizes, from goblets and chalices to flutes and so-called tulips, some of those recipients have been intentionally designed to best accommodate beers of different colours, types, and with varying levels of foam.

Brussels has long had a House of Brewers[30] located at Number 10 of its iconic Grote Markt (Grand Place), where the Houses of other important medieval guilds and professions can also be found. Two other beer museums are worth mentioning. The Schaerbeek Beer Museum,[31] which opened in 1994 and is still operated by volunteers (and a not-for-profit association), contains a collection of around 2,500 bottles of Belgian beers and more than 5,000 glasses, showing the focus of brewers on the containers. Belgian Beer World,[32] which opened in 2023 with the support of more than 100 brewers (members of the Belgian Brewers Association), aims to offer an interactive experience around beer, this includes showing pairs of glasses and bottles.[33] Figure 6.3 shows photos from both museums.

The importance of the shape of glasses is also illustrated by Stella Artois' iconic chalice that the divine beverage deserves, according to the promotion (Figure 6.4).

[28] Jacquette (n 25), 17.

[29] For the examples provided by Dale Jacquette that we follow here, see Jacquette (n 25) 19.

[30] This House has a small collection of implements, brewing and fermentation tubs, a boiling kettle, so on, that can be viewed. See *House of Belgian Brewers 2024* (Web Page) https://beermuseum.be/en.

[31] See 'History', Musée De La Bière Schaerbeekois (Web Page) http://museedelabiereschaerbeekois.be/?lang=en.

[32] Belgian Beer World (Web Page) www.belgianbeerworld.be/en.

[33] While the first museum is hosted in a modest former school (see above footnote), the second one is located within the impressive building of the former Stock Exchange (La Bourse – De Beurs). See Belgian Beer World (n 32). Those two locations/operations probably are good symbols of the dual culture and economy of the Belgian brewing sector, with many small brewers run by amateur-connoisseurs and a (few) giant(s) that benefited from globalization through an early acquisition strategy.

FIGURE 6.3 Photos from (a) Schaerbeek Beer Museum and (b) Brussels Museum of Beer. Photos taken by A. Strowel (2023–2024).

FIGURE 6.4 Stella Artois advertising. Source: www.stellaartois.com/en_gb/heritage/.

To serve a beer in a special glass helps to emphasize and individualize the beer. The flute shape (with a 'stylish bulge just above the stem and a narrowing at the top that straps both the head and the aroma') is well-suited for beer with a *pétillant* carbonation, such a Belgian lambic or gueuze.[34] This shape is not so conducive for less carbonated beers, and such glasses are thus not used for most German beers.[35] For a Belgian (and a German), it is quite surprising that in many countries beers are commonly served in standard, straight-sided, wide-mouthed glasses – in the UK or US pubs, for example (but they serve mostly pilsner beers). A Belgian would agree with the view that 'drinking vessels can make the beer, just as clothes are sometimes said to make the person. They are both practical and emotional, and their shapes, size, and material are designed to match both the beer and the occasion'.[36] Brewers promote their glasses: to many Belgians 'Kwak' is a beer well-known for its inherent qualities but also for the peculiar pinched-waist style of glass; the original 'Kwak' glass had to sit in a wooden holder for it had no flat foot. The Bosteels brewery that produced Kwak was recently acquired by AB InBev and two new beers plus a new beer glass were launched in 2016 with the following slogan 'Iconic Kwak glass in a new jacket'. This glass has a foot but retains the pinched-waist style. Interestingly, trademark registration for this original (and truly quite striking) beer glass shape was refused in the United States, the Trademark Trial and Appeal Board holding that consumers would not see the glass as performing a trademark function.[37]

34 Ibid.

35 One can wonder why Bavarian beer is invariably drunk in the Munich Biergarten out of a special gigantic glass mug, the Maβ: this does not ensure that the beer remains at the right temperature for long (but we know that Germans drink higher volumes of beer, and the time to empty such Maβ is thus arguably shorter).

36 Entry by Tim Hampton on 'drinking vessels' in Oliver (n 1).

37 Ropes and Gray, 'Refusal to Register "Beer Glass and Stand" Mark Affirmed', *World Trademark Review* (Web Page, 24 September 2010) www.worldtrademarkreview.com/article/refusal-register-beer-glass-and-stand-mark-affirmed.

6.3.3 *Battles around Belgian Beer Glasses*

No wonder that beer glasses are also cherished by tourists (and local amateurs), who do tend to consider that the experience of drinking Belgian beers also includes the (not entirely legal) option of taking home some stylish and 'iconic' glasses. To fight this well-developed practice, pubs have devised different strategies.[38] Some involve tech (with security alarms in the stem of each glass), others rely on education of the public,[39] while others have added yet another trick to elevate the experience of drinking beer. For instance, in the Dulle Griet, a bar in Ghent, those drinking the house beer must hand over their shoes, which are then put in a basket that is pulled up to the ceiling. The basket is not only the guarantee that the glasses don't disappear at the end of the drinking session but it has become an attraction in itself. This is a smart way to ensure respect for civility and good manners. It is an interesting experience that should remind lawyers that to ensure compliance, there are other ways than legislating and enforcing! Often technical measures of protection are used to ensure compliance with the law (for example, anti-copying devices to ensure copyright/IP is respected), sometimes educating the public (such as with IP-awareness campaigns) might improve the situation, but there are clever ways to ensure people do not deviate from collectively beneficial behaviour. Designing the adequate contexts and 'choice architectures' must be part of the law's enterprise to nudge the behaviour of groups or individuals in the right direction.[40]

Unfortunately, at other times, and often connected to the alcohol in beer, glasses are not seen as a treasure to take home, but as a weapon to assault people at licensed premises. This practice is called 'glassing', and it requires other types of measures to reduce the risks.[41] However, for most Belgians, using plastic glasses, as sometimes happens for this purpose, would be complete anathema.

[38] See Daniel Boffey, 'Belgian Bars Put the Boot Into Tourists Who Steal Beer Glasses', *The Guardian* (Web Page, 15 March 2018) www.theguardian.com/world/2018/mar/15/belgian-bars-put-the-boot-into-tourists-who-steal-beer-glasses.

[39] See Maïthé Chini, 'Bar Goers in Belgium Asked to Stop Stealing Beer Glasses', *The Brussels Times* (Web Page, 18 October 2022) www.brusselstimes.com/307511/bar-goers-in-belgium-asked-to-stop-stealing-beer-glasses.

[40] On the nudge theory in law and the use of behavioural insights, see Alberto Alemanno and Anne-Lise Sibony (eds), *Nudge and the Law: A European Perspective* (Hart Publishing, 1st ed, 2015).

[41] For example, the rules in Queensland, Australia, where high-risk venues for glassing do exist apparently. See 'Ban on Regular Glass in High-Risk Venues', *Business Queensland* (Web Page, 29 November 2017) www.business.qld.gov.au/industries/hospitality-tourism-sport/liquor-gaming/liquor/compliance/banned-products/regular-glass.

6.3.4 *Litigation around the Shape of (Beer) Bottles and Glasses*

Due to the effort of brewers in designing proper glasses, it is thus not surprising that brewers pay attention to their IP rights over glasses and that Belgium has experienced quite a lot of litigation around the shape of glasses – and of bottles as well. Design registration is a possibility but so is obtaining a trademark registration for the shape or an aspect of the shape of a beer bottle. Sometimes a trademark consists of a verbal reference to a shape, such as the 'Tete de mort' mark registered by the Brasserie Du Bocq, which references its skull-shaped beer glass.[42] In the EU, the football trophy-shaped beer glass for which German brewery Erdinger sought protection as a registered mark was also rejected, the decision-maker requiring that the shape be very far removed from the usual to obtain registration (and thus a monopoly).[43] That a 3D mark must substantially depart from the shapes normally used in a particular sector before it can be registered as a trademark also stood in the way of a beer bottle with a centrally engraved pane being refused.[44]

Many decisions of the Court of Justice and General Court of the EU have refused a 3D trademark protection for the shape of bottles generally, not just for beers, because of a lack of distinctiveness, either as such or acquired through use (Figure 6.5).[45]

That not just the shape of the glass but also the shape of the beer bottle itself is an ingredient of the beer experience is well-known, and probably also stands in the way of trademark registration. Especially when beer is directly consumed from the bottle, which is common with certain beers – but not that common in Belgium (compared to other countries) – the bottle shape is an integral part of the drinking experience (rather than a distinct sign of commercial origin). This is, for instance, the case for the Mexican beer Corona, that is served without a glass but with a slice of lemon in the neck. This feature of Corona, owned by AB InBev, led the importer to file an application for a three-dimensional EU trademark on 'a transparent bottle, filled with a yellow liquid, having a long neck in which a slice of lemon with a green skin has been plugged' (Figure 6.6).

The CJEU dismissed the appeal from the judgment of the Court of First Instance of the EU that had already confirmed the European Union Intellectual Property

[42] 'Tête De Mort [Skull]', *European Union Intellectual Property Office* (Web Page) https://euipo.europa.eu/eSearch/#details/trademarks/017827296.

[43] 'Erdinger Beer Glass: No Trademark Protection as 3D Mark', *Meyer-Dulheuer MD Legal Patentanwälte PartG mbB* (Web Page, 29 September 2020) https://legal-patent.com/trademark-law/erdinger-beer-glass-no-trademark-protection-3d-mark/.

[44] *Unión de Cervecerías Peruanas Backus y Johnston SAA v Office for Harmonisation in the Internal Market (Trade Marks and Designs) (OHIM)* (T-323/11) [2012] Judgment of the General Court (Sixth Chamber).

[45] *Voss of Norway ASA v Office for Harmonisation in the Internal Market (Trade Marks and Designs)* (C-445/13 P) [2015] CJEU 303; *The Coca-Cola Company v Office for Harmonisation in the Internal Market (Trade Marks and Designs) (OHIM)* (T-411/14) [2016] Judgment of the General Court (Eighth Chamber).

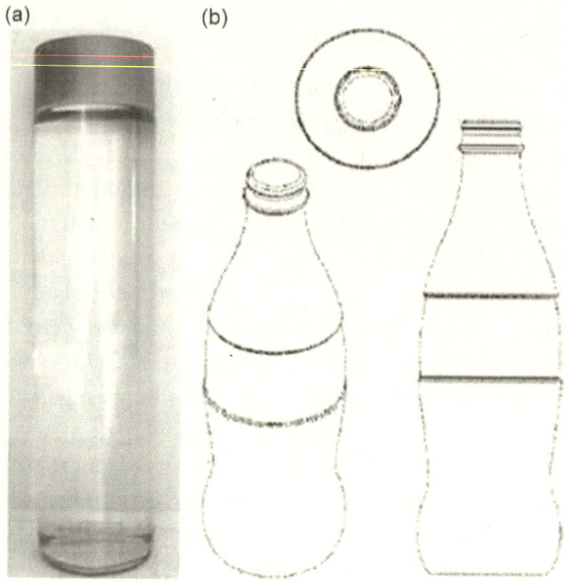

FIGURE 6.5 3D trademark reproductions from the CJEU and General Court of the EU decisions. (a) Cylindrical bottle with a non-transparent cap having the same diameter; and (b) the shape of the Coca-Cola bottle without flutes.

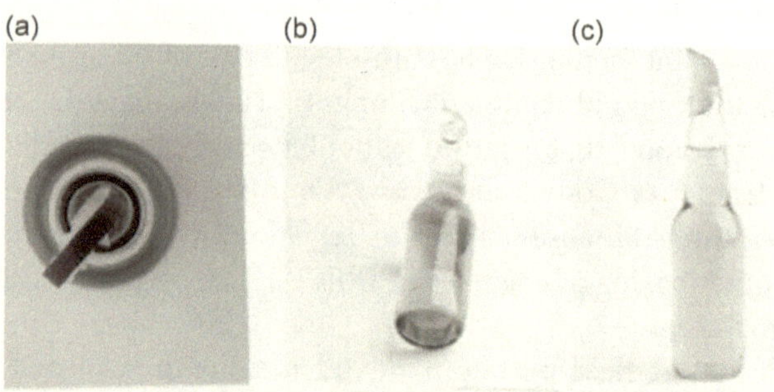

FIGURE 6.6 3D trademark reproductions for Corona beer from the CJEU decision.

Office (EUIPO) Board of Appeal's refusal of the registration of this 3D trademark.[46] The components of this composite trademark are indeed able to be commonly used for the presentation of the goods and will not be perceived by the public as an indication of origin; in addition, their combination 'represents the only way in which a drink can be decorated with a slice or a piece of lemon when the drink is consumed directly from the bottle'.

[46] *Eurocermex SA v Office for Harmonisation in the Internal Market (Trade Marks and Designs) (OHIM)* (C-286/04 P) [2005] CJEU 422.

6.3.5 *Beer Personalities in Belgium*

Especially for craft beers which have a local flavour, the personality of the brewmaster and, to a lesser extent, of the draught master can play a role in attracting the interest and building a long-term trust relation. Some brewmasters have acquired a worldwide reputation. For instance, Jean De Clerck, who became professor at the KU Leuven/UC Louvain brewing school and published in 1948 a canonical two-volume book (translated as *Textbook for Brewing*), developed the recipe for the Duvel beer (from the Flemish word for 'devil') brewed by the Moortgat brewery but also fine-tuned the Chimay Trappist beer brewed at the Notre-Dame de Scourmont Abbey – that he contributed to the 'devil' did not prevent him from being buried in the cemetery of the Scourmont Abbey, an honour usually reserved to the resident monks.[47]

Many other personal stories around beer are embedded in the Belgian beer culture. As put by Garrett Olivier,

> perhaps what defines Belgian beer more than anything else is a sense of stubborn individuality. Belgian brewing is a realm of non-conformists and *garagistes*, many of whom seem content to tirelessly tilt at the windmills of change, sometimes for decades. If this means keeping a day job and brewing at the weekends, so be it ... Many brewers seem to be radical and conservative at once, unwilling to try anything new, yet still creating beers that taste like no one else's.[48]

6.3.6 *Get the Belgian Beer Experience in Dubai, Singapore, Adelaide (Australia)*

Yes of course you can get a Belgian beer experience in Belgium, for instance by undertaking a Belgian beer tour (Figure 6.7); or by visiting one of those pubs that have an enormous list of different beers to choose from – at the Delirium Café Brussels you can find 2,004 beers.[49]

But in fact the Belgian beer experience is (apparently) not confined to Belgium. Belgian beer cafés, which commonly feature Belgian beers but also French fries and mussels (although many Belgians actually pop over the border to Holland for their mussels), are to be found all around the world. For instance, there is a Belgian Beer Café in Melbourne, Australia,[50] a Brussels Belgian Beer Café in Ulaanbaatar,

[47] See Nick Kaye's entry on Jean De Clerck in Oliver (n 1). See also 'Jean De Clerck', *Wikipedia* (Web Page, 7 March 2024) https://fr.wikipedia.org/wiki/Jean_De_Clerck.

[48] See the entry on Belgium in Oliver (n 1).

[49] 'Delirium Café Brussels', Delirium Village Brussels (Web Page) www.deliriumvillage.com/bar/delirium-cafe/.

[50] Belgian Beer Café Melbourne (Web Page) www.belgianbeercafemelbourne.com.au/.

FIGURE 6.7 Belgian beer tour. Photo taken by A. Strowel.

Mongolia,[51] a Belgian Beer Café at the Al Hamra Golf Club in Dubai, which promises 'an authentic taste of Belgium, defined by the country's finest beers and heartiest dishes',[52] and a 'Kingdom of Belgians' restaurant in Singapore where 'Belgian food and drink rule' and 'Chef Stroobant reveals his fun side with an amazing 40 beers available'.[53]

What does this mean for consumers in those jurisdictions? What are their expectations of a Belgian beer café in Adelaide or Dubai? On the one hand, the consumers might be misled since there are no *Belgian* beer cafés in Belgium (no need to add the claimed *Belgian* origin for a café located in Belgium). And if such a (Belgian) café did exist in Belgium, what would it be associated with? Deception might depend on the detail of the consumer messaging, but if all the café does is

[51] 'Brussels Belgian Beer Café' (Instagram) www.instagram.com/brussels.belgianbeercafe/?hl = fr.

[52] 'بلجيان بير كافيه [Belgian Beer Café]', *Visit Ras Al Khaimah* (Web Page) https://visitrasalkhaimah .com/ar/discover/food-drinks/belgian-beer-cafe/.

[53] *Kingdom of Belgians* (Web Page) www.kob.com.sg/. See also Regula Ysewijn, 'My Books: Belgian Café Culture', *Miss Foodwise* (Web Page, 20 October 2016) www.missfoodwise.com/ 2016/10/belgian-cafe-culture-book.html/; Daniel Fallon, 'Why Belgian Beer Tastes Different (and Better) in Belgium', *Sydney Morning Herald* (Web Page, 11 August 2023) www.smh.com .au/traveller/inspiration/why-belgian-beer-tastes-different-and-better-in-belgium-20230721-p5dq89.html.

replicate the visual style of a Belgian café and serve chips and some Belgian beers, and if at least some of the beers actually come from Belgium, then probably there is no deception. Belgian beer culture may be inscribed on the UNESCO list of Intangible Heritage (see above), but that does not provide it with any particular legal protection, or establish some exclusivity in relation to its 'use' or imitation or following outside Belgium.[54] However, the protection of the Belgian beer café concept is pursued worldwide through a franchise system put in place by the giant AB InBev company and its subsidiary Creneau Int, a hospitality management and consultancy firm (based in Belgium and Dubai).[55]

On the contrary, it does not seem that Belgian authorities are particularly concerned about Belgian beer culture popping up around the world in various guises, including Belgian beer cafés. Perhaps it's all effective advertising for the real thing and therefore good for tourism. The Italian authorities have taken a more aggressive stance, by comparison, in relation to 'Italian restaurants', with the availability of certification by reference to standards[56] such as requiring the use of oil, flour, dairy products, and cured meats of Italian origin; and an Italian minister calling for 'a ratings system for Italian restaurants around the world to show they use "genuine Italian" products and to help diners tell them apart from establishments serving food "that has nothing to do with Italy"'.[57] Nothing comparable is (yet) proposed for Belgian beer cafés and restaurants, but there are rather fewer of those than Italian pizzerias around the globe.[58]

54 'Beer Culture in Belgium', *UNESCO* (Video) www.unesco.org/archives/multimedia/document-4390.

55 See 'Belgian Beer Café Franchise' (Web Page) https://belgianbeercafefranchise.com/; 'Belgian Beer Café', *Creneau International* (Web Page) www.creneau.com/work/belgian-beer-cafe.

56 'Made in Italy Enhancement', *Asacert* (Web Page) https://asacert.com/en/made-in-italy-2/.

57 Clare Speak, 'How Italy's Government Wants to Rank Italian Restaurants Abroad', *The Local Italy* (Web Page, 9 May 2023) www.thelocal.it/20230509/how-italys-government-wants-to-rank-italian-restaurants-abroad.

58 There were said to be 76,000 pizzerias in the United States alone in 2017. See 'Pizza', *Wikipedia* (Web Page, 7 October 2024) https://en.wikipedia.org/wiki/Pizza.

7

Consumer Protection and Unfair Competition Law

7.1 INTRODUCTION

In the end, beer is produced to be consumed, so beer consumers are the ones who drive beer production. This alone may be seen as enough to justify consumer protection for beer drinkers, a concept with a long history. In 1156, for example, a decree passed in Augsburg, Germany, declared that 'a brewer who makes bad beer or pours an unjust measure shall be punished'.[1] Lawmakers in the 1100s were concerned about beer being poured in the proper quantities – when, as we noted in Chapter 4, the modern Swedish lawmaker thinks it is fine that consumers do not know in advance how much beer they will receive when ordering 'en stor stark'. Perhaps laws do not always get better over time.

In Chapter 3, we covered consumer protections that address health aspects of beer law. Here, we discuss consumer protection more broadly, together with the related field of unfair competition law.

Unfair competition law is conceptually and materially diverse around the globe.[2] It complements antitrust law; both aim to protect competition as an institution. Initially, its protection was directed at the honest entrepreneur and, as early as 1900, was anchored in Art. 10bis of the Paris Convention as early as 1900, so far the only provision in international law on this subject. After World War II, a strong notion of consumer protection was added, culminating in the European Directive on Unfair Commercial Practices in 2005 (UCP Directive), which only applies to business-to-consumer (B2C) trade practices.

In the US, Art. 43(a) Lanham Act and section 5 FTC Act as well as state common law provide the source of unfair competition law. In Australia, the Australian

[1] Mark Dredge, *A Brief History of Lager: 500 Years of the World's Favourite Beer* (Kyle Books, 1st ed, 2019).

[2] See generally Frauke Henning-Bodewig, 'Unfair Competition Law – An Introduction to a Complex Topic' in Frauke Henning-Bodewig (ed), *International Handbook on Unfair Competition Law* (CH Beck, 1st ed, 2013) 1.

Consumer Law regulates similar issues. We can think of preserving the institution of competition as the clamp bundling together different interests.

Unfair competition is not always recognized as a separate field of the law, either. That has led to highly diverse regulation. While some countries still work with a core tort law approach, others are vested with a patchwork of specific regulations, and yet others have comprehensive unfair competition laws.

As such, we can identify core unfair competition rules, with specific provisions varying between countries. Starting from Art. 10bis of the Paris Convention, these 'core rules' include confusion, disparagement, and misleading practices. Unfair competition law is also strongly affiliated with trademark law, but, today, goes far beyond it.

Relating to consumer protection, Arts. 6–8 of the UCP Directive lay down two pillars: misleading practices and aggressive practices.[3] Other rules also relate to the protection of competitors, such as disparagement, slavish imitation, impediment, and breach of laws. However, there is no clear dividing line between B2B and B2C protection as advertising is a communication process on the market and unfair practices will mostly affect both groups, if to different degrees. The goal of regulation is to level the playing field by giving consumers undistorted choices and letting companies compete fairly.

Accordingly, this chapter will cover the most relevant provisions relating to marketing and advertising as concern beer, as well as rules protecting competitors and specific consumer protection provisions adjacent to unfair competition law. In general, there is no specific unfair competition law for beer marketing, but there are common practices that can be evaluated across legal systems. Unfair competition law borders antitrust law on one side and IP law on the other. Its impact on the beer market can be analysed through this lens as well.

7.2 MARKETING AND ADVERTISING

7.2.1 *Misleading Practices*

At the heart of unfair competition law is the ban on misleading and deceptive practices, as spelled out in Arts. 6 and 7 of the Unfair Commercial Practices Directive (UCPD) and Art. 3 of Directive 2006/114 in Europe.

[3] *Directive 2005/29/EC of the European Parliament and of the Council of 11 May 2005 Concerning Unfair Business-to-Consumer Commercial Practices in the Internal Market and Amending Council Directive 84/450/EEC, Directives 97/7/EC, 98/27/EC and 2002/65/EC of the European Parliament and of the Council and Regulation (EC) No 2006/2004 of the European Parliament and of the Council* [2005] OJ L 149/22. See also *Decision No 854/2005/EC of the European Parliament and of the Council of 11 May 2005 Establishing a Multiannual Community Programme on Promoting Safer Use of the Internet and New Online Technologies* [2005] OJ L 149/1.

Article 6 UCPD defines misleading actions as false information or practices that are likely to deceive the average consumer, whereas Art. 7 covers misleading omissions as a practice that omits material information necessary for the average consumer to take an informed transactional decision and that is likely to cause the average consumer to take a decision they would not have taken otherwise. Article 7 (2) of the UCPD also bans providing information in an unclear, unintelligible, ambiguous, or untimely manner.

Similar provisions against misleading practices are included in Art. 18 of the Australian Consumer Law, common law doctrines of passing off, and specific federal and state laws against misleading and deceptive practices in the United States.[4]

7.2.1.1 Geographical Deceptions

Very often misleading advertising cases centre around designations of location and origin and thus complement trademark law and the law of geographical indications. In a German case, the Supreme Court (BGH) stated that the EU Directive on geographical indications did apply in this case and would prevent the application of the unfair competition law on misleading advertising even if the location is not associated with a special quality. The Warsteiner Brewery (from the town of Warstein) bought a brewery in Paderborn, which is 40 kilometres away from Warstein. The Court found that the designation 'Warsteiner' was not misleading as long as the actual production site was sufficiently clear and the brewery had a legitimate interest in using the designation.[5] The 'legitimate interest' was that Warsteiner Brewery, which had built a reputation around its designation, should be allowed to expand production to other regions while keeping its central establishment in Warstein.

In a somewhat divergent decision, the Court of Appeals of Munich found the designation 'Chiemseer', which refers to the Chiemsee lake around Munich, was misleading.[6] In fact, the brewing, which was unrelated to the lake, was done in a different town in Bavaria (Rosenheim), 16 kilometres away. Adding the name 'Rosenheim' to the designation was not considered enough to avoid the likelihood of deception – the beer was distributed outside of Bavaria, and the average consumer

4 See Dennis Corgill, '§ 26 United States' in Frauke Henning-Bodewig (ed), *International Handbook on Unfair Competition Law* (CH Beck, 1st ed, 2013) 621, 640.

5 Bundesgerichtshof [German Supreme Court], I ZR 54/96, 19 September 2001 reported in NJW 2002, 600; *Schutzverband gegen Unwesen in der Wirtschaft eV v Warsteiner Brauerei Haus Cramer GmbH & Co KG* (C-312/98) [2000] EuZW 2001, 125. The 'de-localizing' information was found on the back of the label for beer brewed in the new brewery in Paderborn and was held sufficient in light of the European consumer standard.

6 Oberlandesgericht München [Munich Court of Appeal], 29 U 3187/15, 17 March 2016 reported in GRUR-RR, 2016, 272.

does not have reason to obtain additional information and will not always know local areas. The Court did not find any legitimate interests for use.

In another decision, the Munich Court found that the designation of a beer as 'Neuschwansteiner' was not misleading. The average consumer knows that Neuschwanstein Castle is a museum – since the death of its builder King Ludwig II at the end of the nineteenth century and, due to its hilly location, not really suitable for hosting a brewery.[7] Moreover, it is a supreme tourist attraction and due to its location on a hill not really apt to host a brewery.

The decisions taken together demonstrate that the application of the ban on misleading advertising is vested with uncertainties and the information duties of the consumer stemming from the average consumer standard may differ depending on the case and court. The European Court of Justice for some time put a high burden of information on the consumer by attributing knowledge in the abstract from labelling information even if printed in small type on the back of the package. However, more recently a more realistic and empirical consumer model was applied taking account of the real behaviour concerning information in a specific transactional situation and referring to the overall impression of the packaging or advertising.[8]

Bavaria is a rich source of potential beer-related misleading advertising and designation. The Supreme Court found the designation 'Königl. – Bayerische Weisse' (Royal Bavarian White/Whit Beer) misleading with respect to four different possible interpretations by the average consumer:

- The brewery is owned by the royal family.
- It is allowed to use the designation by way of permission from the royal court.
- is the official purveyor for the royal court.
- It uses brewing traditions from royal times.[9]

As the brewery was only bought by a member of the royal Bavarian family after World War II (when Bavaria had been a democracy for some time), none of those interpretations were true. The case should have been dismissed, because none of the interpretations would be relevant to consumer decisions, but the Court found that the use of old brewing traditions or an official position might connote a certain level of quality.

7 Oberlandesgericht München [Munich Court of Appeal], 29 U 885/17, 1 February 2018 reported in GRUR-RR 2018, 381.

8 See *Purely Creative Ltd and Others v Office of Fair Trading* [2012] (C-428/11) CJEU 651, where the Court of Justice of the European Union stated that actions and decisions of the consumer are 'not always rational'. See also *Bundesverband der Verbraucherzentralen und Verbraucherverbände – Verbraucherzentrale Bundesverband eV v Teekanne GmbH & Co KG* (C-195/14) [2012] CJEU 361.

9 Bundesgerichtshof [German Federal Court of Justice], I ZR 106/89, 21 February 1992 reported in GRUR 1992, 66.

In another decision, the German Supreme Court found the designation 'Klosterbräu' (monasterial brew) to be irrelevant. The term implied the beer was brewed in a monastery or used the brewing traditions of monks, which was found to be of little relevance to consumer decisions.[10]

Marketing can mislead through more than just geographical terms. Sometimes, the inclusion of additional references can also suggest a genuine connection with a place. In the 'Byron Bay Bitter' case, the name 'Byron Bay' was used on a beer brewed elsewhere, and the label included a map identifying Byron Bay. Together, these designations were considered enough to imply that the beer was brewed in Byron Bay. After all, consumers know beer trademarks might contain geographical references that do not serve as geographical indications of origin.

The use of geographical references – textual and visual – is extremely common in craft brewing; obviously, brewers see value in evoking such connections for consumers. For instance, one study found that, of 118 craft beer brands in Wales, 51 (43.2 per cent) included 'provenance indicators', and 56 of 124 craft beer breweries did the same in Brittany.[11] In this sense, beers are similar to local foods, where provenance indicators are also very common in labelling and promotion. Representations can be on a local, regional, or national level.

In a similar vein, suit was filed against an advertising campaign for Benediktiner Helles, a lager brewed by a company in Hessia (which is displayed on the label as well).[12] However, the ad showed a Bavarian Alps landscape and Ettal Abbey, which suggested that the brewing took place in Bavaria. The company replied that its main establishment was in Ettal, and the cooperating Ettal monks ensured that the beer was brewed according to the traditions of Benedictine monks. The case is still pending, and the Court in Munich will have to evaluate whether the information on the label is sufficient and how this plays in combination with the ads. Again, the question can be posed whether the location of the brewing process has any relevance for the transactional decision if the monks supervise the adherence to traditional brewing traditions. At least the purpose of preserving quality is not affected by this.

7.2.1.2 Other Types of Misleading Practices, Especially about Method of Production

Various other practices may also count as misleading advertising. If innkeepers regularly fail to fill beer glasses to the calibration mark, for example, they may be

[10] Bundesgerichtshof [German Federal Court of Justice], I ZR 276/99, 7 November 2002 reported in GRUR 2003, 628.

[11] See Robert Bowen and Maggie Miller, 'Provenance Representations in Craft Beer' (2022) 57 (10) *Regional Studies* 1995.

[12] Von Tillmann Neuscheler, 'Streit um Benediktiner-Bier [Dispute over Benedictine Beer]', *FRAZ.NET* (Web Page, 18 May 2023) www.faz.net/aktuell/wirtschaft/unternehmen/vorwurf-der-herkunftstaeuschung-streit-um-benediktiner-bier-18902325.html.

liable for unfair competition penalties in addition to contractual remedies.[13] This only applies if the practice is systematic – that is, intended to achieve an unfair advantage in competition. Calibration marks are often regulated by law. In the EU, Directive 2004/22/EC requires the volume to be provided if drinks are served for immediate consumption.[14]

An example of specific provisions on misleading advertising in food law is Art. 7 (1a) of Regulation 1169/2011 on food information. It provides that information on the method of food production, among other things, should not be misleading.[15] A brewing company marketed a beer in a champagne-style bottle with the words 'Brewed after the time-honoured Méthode Royale' on the packaging. The German Court found this misleading and assumed that the average consumer would expect, on the basis of this designation and the high price, a special method of brewing, making the beer a luxury product.[16] The designation created associations with 'méthode champenoise'; special methods of in-bottle beer fermentation exist as well. In fact, the beer was brewed according to a traditional method for Märzenbier, a style commonly sold for less than one euro per half-litre.

Under the same provision, 'Original Rotbier' (Original Red Beer) was found to be misleading.[17] The designation 'original' implied traditional brewing adapted with modern knowledge. In fact, the defendant had blended normal beer with red beer and not used traditional wooden barrels for the ripening process.

A designation as 'eco-beer' is only allowed in the EU if production conforms to Art. 30 of Regulation 2018/848, which requires that 95 per cent of farmed ingredients be produced under a specific control system and without chemical pesticides or fertilizers.[18]

13 Bundesgerichtshof [German Federal Court of Justice], I ZR 30/81, 21 April 1983 reported in GRUR 1983, 451; Bundesgerichtshof [German Federal Court of Justice], I ZR 136/84, 10 December 1987 reported in GRUR 1987, 180.

14 Directive 2004/22/EC of the European Parliament and of the Council of 31 March 2004 on Measuring Instruments [2004] OJ L 135/1. See also Council Decision (EU) 2021/651 of 19 April 2021 on the Signing, on Behalf of the Union, of the Agreement in the Form of an Exchange of Letters Between the European Union and the Argentine Republic Pursuant to Article XXVIII of the General Agreement on Tariffs and Trade (GATT) 1994 Relating to the Modification of Concessions on All the Tariff-Rate Quotas Included in the EU Schedule CLXXV as a Consequence of the United Kingdom's Withdrawal from the European Union [2021] OJ L 135/01.

15 *Regulation (EU) No 1169/2011 of the European Parliament and of the Council of 25 October 2011 on the Provision of Food Information to Consumers, Amending Regulations (EC) No 1924/2006 and (EC) No 1925/2006 of the European Parliament and of the Council, and Repealing Commission Directive 87/250/EEC, Council Directive 90/496/EEC, Commission Directive 1999/10/EC, Directive 2000/13/EC of the European Parliament and of the Council, Commission Directives 2002/67/EC and 2008/5/EC and Commission Regulation (EC) No 608/2004 Text with EEA Relevance* [2011] OJ L 304/18.

16 Oberlandesgericht München [Munich Court of Appeal], 29 U 885/17, 1 February 2018 reported in GRUR-RR 2018, 381.

17 Landgericht Nürnberg-Fürth [Regional Court Nürnberg-Fürth], 4 HK O 5207/19, 23 July 2021.

18 *Regulation (EU) 2018/848 of the European Parliament and of the Council of 30 May 2018 on Organic Production and Labelling of Organic Products and Repealing Council Regulation (EC) No 834/2007* [2018] OJ L 150/1.

Eco-beer is trendy and is used in many mixed drinks. In a recent case, the Court of Justice of the European Union (CJEU) ruled on the distribution of a mixed drink consisting of 55 per cent wine and 10 per cent beer. The Court applied the Regulation on aromatized wine products, which protects consumers from quality- and production-related deceptive practices.[19] Article 3(4) of the Regulation requires that an aromatized wine-product cocktail includes at least 50 per cent grapevine products with no added alcohol. 'Alcohol', in the sense of the Regulation, also includes beer, regardless of whether the actual alcohol level is raised by the addition.[20]

7.2.1.3 Sales Promotion and Social Sponsoring/Sustainability

In modern advertising, beer may be subject to certain practices that fall under unfair competition law. One practice is greenwashing as well as sustainability claims; these appeal to the environmental consciousness of consumers and try to cash in on that. In the EU, legislative initiatives are underway to limit greenwashing and promote transparency and substantiation of sustainability claims.[21] Positively this legislation may also support the function of advertising to contribute to environmental protection and sustainability.

Again, the basic conflict underlying unfair competition becomes apparent. At what point does marketing exceed its function in market communication, requiring the law to step in to preserve competition? Beyond that, the question also arises whether unfair competition law may serve other public purposes beyond preserving competition, such as sustainability.

A prominent German case touches upon that fine line. A well-known German TV moderator was hired to promote Krombacher Bier in an advertising campaign. The ad showed rainforest as a background and read: 'With every box of Krombacher you purchase, you will protect 1 square metre of tropical rainforest in Dzanga Sangha sustainably. This will be secured by WWF Germany.'[22]

With respect to the constitutional limits of advertising, freedom of speech also protects commercial speech. Consequently, there does not need to be a direct relationship between the subject of the advertising (such as the rainforest) and the

[19] *Regulation (EU) No 251/2014 of the European Parliament and of the Council of 26 February 2014 on the Definition, Description, Presentation, Labelling and the Protection of Geographical Indications of Aromatised Wine Products and Repealing Council Regulation (EEC) No 1601/91* [2014] OJ L 84/14.

[20] *Hauser Weinimport GmbH v Freistaat Bayern* (C-216/23) [2024] CJEU 393.

[21] *Proposal for a Directive of the European Parliament and of the Council on Substantiation and Communication of Explicit Environmental Claims (Green Claims Directive).*

[22] Bundesgerichtshof [German Federal Court of Justice], I ZR 33/04, 26 October 2006 reported in NJW 2007, 919; Bundesgerichtshof [German Federal Court of Justice], I ZR 97/04, 26 October 2006 reported in GRUR 2007, 251.

product (such as Krombacher). One of the main issues in this case was whether the direct reference to protecting the rainforest was misleading.

The first step in a case of misleading advertising is to identify the relevant meaning of the ad, then evaluate whether this meaning conforms to the facts. The Supreme Court identified that the average consumer might interpret the ad in two possible ways:

1. A real piece of land is acquired to protect it.
2. Extensive funding is provided and mediated by an organization active in the country.

As a general rule, if the ad is not clear, the Court will take the interpretation most unfavourable to the advertiser. If the second interpretation applies, the advertising would only be misleading if much less funding was provided than the consumer would expect when viewing the ad. Similar rules apply when tying beer sales to a very attractive product. That advertising will only be misleading if the consumer is likely to get a wrong impression of the value of the goods involved.

We can also look at the case as one of misleading by omission. When is an advertiser obliged to provide additional information to avoid misleading consumers? There is no general duty to inform consumers about any characteristics of a product or service, but this is limited to such features essential for the transactional decision. In the case at hand, the advertiser would only need to provide extra information if the ad created certain expectations for the average consumer that are not backed by the facts.

7.2.2 *Aggressive Commercial Practices*

The 'Krombacher' case also has a second facet. Social or environmental sponsoring means that the advertising company supports social or environmental initiatives or institutions financially and this is permitted, and advertising can contribute to achieving societal goals. However, unfair competition law is mainly about preserving the free choice of consumers. That freedom could be impaired by the emotional impact of sponsoring, inducing consumers to buy products they would not have otherwise.

However, is this not the goal of advertising in general? The problem, again, is where to draw the line. In the last thirty years, under the influence of European law, German courts have become very reluctant to intervene. Advertising is only inappropriate when it more or less excludes the rational consumer decision. Beyond that, the consumer is free to base their transactional decisions on notions not directly connected to the product itself, such as sponsorship.

In the Krombacher case, the emotional appeal was found not to be strong enough to exclude rational decision-making. However, the EU is now switching to a stronger regulatory approach. That approach will require that certain sustainability-related claims and ads be approved before use, adding administrative enforcement to purely civil law systems.[23]

Social or environmental sponsoring is a modern way to persuade consumers to buy the product. In the past, this was done by offering free beer. In 1910, 'treating people with free beer' to draw business was considered to be inappropriate.[24] Today, the average consumer is rational enough not to be overly influenced by that tactic – or are they?

The same is true for other forms of sales promotion, like rebates, free prizes, and membership programmes, which would be unlawful only in extreme cases or if they are misleading.

7.2.3 *Comparative Advertising*

Around the world, comparative advertising laws are quite liberal and apply to beer marketing as well. Basic requirements are that like is compared with like, the characteristics are substantially comparable, and the result is accurate and does not give a wrong overall impression.[25] This framework is in line with Art. 4 of Directive 2016/114/EC and misleading and comparative advertising, the second European directive in the field of unfair competition.[26] Truthful and undistorted price comparisons are at the heart of comparative advertising.

7.3 PROTECTION OF COMPETITORS

The protection of competitors – beyond misleading and comparative advertising – varies widely. One core protection prohibits product denigration and disparagement. Another, the protection against imitation and parasitic behaviour beyond trademark law, is partly provided by extended theories of passing off and misappropriation that remain scattered and rudimentary in most jurisdictions. Even in strict unfair competition law systems like the German one, that protection is partly considered to be pre-empted by trademark and copyright law. As to theories of protection and against free-riding without further elements of confusion or reputation, their status remains shaky at best. As for beer production and marketing, they do not play a major role. The principle applies that no protection for investments as such should be granted.

The same is true for impeding competitors. 'Impeding' can include boycotts, inducing employees or customers to breach contracts, and other actions that stop a

[23] Ibid.

[24] See Ansgar Ohly, 'Das neue UWG – Mehr Freiheit für den Wettbewerb? [The New UWG – More Freedom for Competition?]' (2004) *GRUR* 889, 895.

[25] See Holger Buck, '§ 6 France' in Frauke Henning-Bodewig (ed), *International Handbook on Unfair Competition Law* (CH Beck, 1st ed, 2013) 98.

[26] *Directive 2006/114/EC of the European Parliament and of the Council of 12 December 2006 Concerning Misleading and Comparative Advertising* [2006] OJ L 376/21.

competitor from freely offering products or services to consumers. In some countries, this field is covered by antitrust law.

7.4 SPECIFIC CONSUMER PROTECTION LAWS RELATED TO BEER

7.4.1 *Preventing Alcohol Abuse*

In addition to misleading advertising laws, beer is also subject to health-related regulation, as we have already discussed. Often, administrative laws try to prevent excessive alcohol consumption. Section 5 of the German *Gaststättengesetz* (Restaurant Statute) allows for imposing conditions on pub owners when guests' health is threatened – such as when the owner supports alcohol abuse.

Alcohol abuse exists when alcohol is consumed excessively, resulting in considerable risks to health. According to the Administrative Court of Hesse:

> It may be taken into account that it is hard to draw general lines of abuse due to the different physical conditions of people and the different grades of habituation to alcohol. Excessive consumption may be assumed if guests are so strongly alcoholised that they display striking behaviour or resort to assaults. This does not exclude abuse also in cases of 'silent drinkers'.[27]

Pub owners can be liable when they actively support excessive drinking *and* when they provide further alcohol to guests while knowing those guests have had enough.

Owners' pricing schemes can also support alcohol abuse. This could be the case if alcohol is sold at a very low price. However, the freedom to set prices is also guaranteed and cannot be supplanted by an administrative order. The line may be drawn where a price leads consumers to drop rational behaviour and consume alcohol in excessive quantities.[28] This could be assumed in extreme cases like *flat-rate* (all-you-can-drink) parties.

7.4.2 *Health and Transparency Regulations*

Many countries have administrative law provisions relating to consumer health protection and transparency, either found in general food law or applying directly to alcohol or beer. Infringement can lead to administrative or criminal law sanctions. These specific statutes may also include specific clauses on misleading advertising. Beer is subject to the general labelling and information requirements in food law, which means packaging must state the type of beer, the name of the producer, a list of ingredients, the 'best before' date, the share of alcohol in per cent per volume up to one decimal, and volume.[29]

[27] Hessischer VGH [Hesse Higher Administrative Court], 6 B 31/09, 25 February 2009.

[28] Ibid.

[29] See, eg, *Regulation (EC) No 178/2002 of the European Parliament and of the Council of 28 January 2002 Laying Down the General Principles and Requirements of Food Law,*

The EU introduced a very strict health claims Regulation, which covers information in advertising and on labels.[30] Article 4(3) provides that beverages containing more than 1.2 per cent by volume of alcohol cannot be the subject of health claims, defined in Art. 2(5) as 'any claim that states, suggests or implies that a relationship exists between a food category, a food or one of its constituents and health'.

Nutrition claims (which refer to particular beneficial nutritional properties) are also not allowed unless they refer to a reduction in the alcohol or energy content. Advertising a beer as 'digestible', for example, is prohibited under this Regulation.[31] The same prohibition applies to positive claims relating to wine – that is, claims suggesting that drinking wine will lead to no negative health consequences.[32]

Beyond that Regulation, national unfair competition law can allow claims when laws that mainly exist to maintain fair competition are breached. For example, under section 3a of the German Statute against Unfair Competition (UWG), a company can make an unfair competition claim if a competitor breaches any legal provisions that aim to regulate competitive behaviour. The effect is that broader civil law enforcement is provided in relation to the breached law with suits not only to be brought by the directly injured party but also by consumer organizations and organizations protecting competition, thus considerably affecting the enforcement of the various statutes outside of unfair competition law.

The EU health claims Regulation was acknowledged as a relevant law by the courts and, as such, companies that infringe it may be subject to unfair competition claims. This is especially relevant as the health claims Regulation provides strict requirements for labelling, presenting, and advertising beer. Article 6 requires nutrition and health claims to be based on scientific evidence that a business operator or marketer can produce. Articles 7 and 10 provide further information duties. Nutrition claims must be listed in the annex of the Regulation in order to be permitted. In certain cases, health claims must be authorized as per Art. 13 of the Regulation.

Laws around health claims restrict beer advertising in general. A German court prohibited the advertising of alcohol-free beer with the claim that the beer would be 'vitalizing'.[33] 'Vitalizing' was found to be health-related – it means 'vital' and, as such, refers to healthy people. 'Vitalizing' would, therefore, imply an improvement in the health of a person. As per Art. 10(3) of the Regulation, a non-specific claim

Establishing the European Food Safety Authority and Laying Down Procedures in Matters of Food Safety [2002] OJ L 31/1 .

30 *Regulation (EC) No 1924/2006 of the European Parliament and of the Council of 20 December 2006 on Nutrition and Health Claims Made on Foods* [2006] OJ L 404/9.

31 Bundesgerichtshof [German Federal Court of Justice], I ZR 252/16, 17 May 2018 reported in GRUR 2018, 1266.

32 *Deutsches Weintor eG v Land Rheinland-Pfalz* (C–544/10) [2012] Judgment of the Court (Third Chamber).

33 Oberlandesgericht [German High Court], 4 U 19/14, 20 May 2014 reported in GRUR-RR 2014, 465.

must be accompanied by a specific claim listed in Arts. 13 and 14 of the Regulation. As this was not the case, the claim was held to be prohibited.

7.4.3 *What Is a 'Biergarten'?*

Austria has its *Heuriger*, Germany its *Biergarten* (beer garden). But what exactly is a beer garden? Don't think it is not regulated. A restaurant in Munich was granted the right to run a restaurant and included a beer garden. When the noise emissions of the garden at night exceeded the limits, there were a lot of complaints. According to section 2 of the Bayerische Biergartenverordnung (Bavarian Beer Garden Regulation), beer gardens may be run until 11 p.m., after which stricter noise emission rules apply. As such, it mattered whether the defendants were running a beer garden in the sense of the Regulation.

The Administrative Court of Munich found that beer gardens differ from other outdoor places in two ways: their special character as a garden and their special way of operation. A special way of operation may include, for example, bringing your own food (*Brotzeit*) and a certain independence from the rest of the restaurant, indicated by a different menu and/or a separate beer dispenser.[34] A 'garden' in the sense of the Regulation may not be present where a yard is surrounded by different buildings for living and commercial activities or streets and lacks greenery, even if there are a few trees.[35]

7.5 CONCLUSION

Given the long history of beer production and distribution, general unfair competition or fair trade practices cases centre around traditions connected to locations and brewing methods in advertising and marketing and mirror the cultural importance as well as conflicts with health and morals around beer. Beer may be strongly connected to morality, but good morals no longer play such a big role in unfair competition law, the orientation of which is functional. The goal of protecting consumers as well as competitors ultimately serves the purpose of preserving the competitive process with respect to the notion of its fairness. Rules are directed at the behaviour of market participants. The cases we have discussed show that unfair competition law effectively protects the quality of beer production.

Even in civil law countries with strong unfair competition statutes, courts have a lot of discretion in applying general clauses, in contrast with strict administrative food law regulations. In Europe, though, this is changing. Statutory law is becoming more concrete, and the European Commission is more actively regulating marketing, especially in relation to health and environmental claims.

[34] Bayerischer Verwaltungsgerichtshof [Bavarian Administrative Court], 22 CS 23.1265, 22 August 2023 reported in GewArch 2023, 469.

[35] Ibid.

This also begs the question: do other public goals impact laws around advertising, and can those laws be used as a regulatory instrument to achieve those goals? For health and sustainability issues, the answer is 'yes'. To the same end, codes of conduct and self-regulation will play an increasing role even in countries where this hasn't been widespread before. Unfair competition law can support adherence to and effectiveness of these instruments of indirect regulation.

8

Czech Beer Culture

The Urquell and 'Going for One'

8.1 HISTORY AND MARKET DEVELOPMENT

The Czech Republic (or Czechia) mostly consists of three historical lands: the original kingdom of Bohemia, the Margraviate of Moravia, and, partly, the Duchies of Silesia. Human presence on these lands dates back 600,000 years, and the first documented settlement by a defined 'nation' was Celtic oppida in the sixth century BCE. Remains of Celtic settlements have been found mostly in today's south-western Bohemia, which later became the region of Plzeň (Pilsen) or České Budějovice (Budweis).[1]

The Celts brewed beer but did not use hops for flavouring. Hops were introduced as a key brewing ingredient by the Slavs, who settled in the area around CE 550. The region quickly became known for beer brewing, mostly because it provided – besides an abundance of water sources – ideal terroir and weather conditions for all key ingredients. Local varieties of hops were considered so unique and essential to the flourishing beer economy that various hops sapling export restrictions, including those enforced by capital punishment, applied from the early Middle Ages until the nineteenth century.

Beer Consumption in the Czech Republic

Per capita beer consumption in the Czech Republic is the highest in the world. According to Statista's per capita volume sales by country in 2023, the Czechs consume 138 litres per person per year. That figure reached its peak in 2005 at nearly 165 litres per capita and has since declined. Steeply rising prices in pubs and restaurants caused on-trade sales to drop below 30 per cent, which means most beer is drunk outside of public houses.

[1] For a complex overview of the history of beer production in the Czech countries, see Jaroslav Novák Večerníček, *Historie piva – od zrození až po konec středověku* [*History of Beer – From the Origins to the End of Medieval Age*] (Computer Press, 2009).

The first known formal records of beer brewing in Czech countries were also connected to hops. Dukes and kings mandated tithes of hop production for monasteries, for which beer brewing represented an important source of income. Some sources report that monks in the oldest Czech monastery of Břevnov (still existing and still brewing beer) were so captivated by beer that Bishop Vojtěch temporarily banned them from brewing and drinking it, to restore their focus on more spiritual affairs.

Besides tithes, other beer law instruments also had great economic and political importance – and are familiar even today to the general Czech public. Examples include brew titles (*právo várečné*), one-mile monopoly (*právo mílové*), and tap title (*propinační právo*).[2] These titles and monopolies were so economically and politically important that a dispute about brewing and serving beer, which arose between burghers, nobles, and knights in 1484, failed to be settled at thirty-three consecutive national assemblies and ended only in 1517 with the Treaty of St Wenceslas.[3]

The dispute implies that, in the Middle Ages, the main societal concern regarding beer was availability. A significant focus on technology and quality (or clarity) emerged only from the eighteenth century and was linked to František Ondřej Poupě, a brewer, innovator, author, and scholar whose publications became the cornerstone of modern Czech beer production. František, whose innovative and scientific approach to beer brewing was first neglected and ridiculed, later became hugely successful as the head brewer in the city of Brno, where he also founded the world's first beer brewing school.

Another brewer who greatly influenced the Czech beer culture was Josef Groll, a Bavarian. In 1842, he was invited to help establish the production of Bavarian-type lager in the new Pilsner municipal brewery. When he realized Pilsner ingredients were different to those in Bavaria – softer water, lighter English-type malt kilning, and specific red hops from Žatec (called 'Saaz' in German, which is why these hops are often known as Saaz hops) – he decided to adapt the brewing procedure.[4]

The resulting light-golden lager became an immediate hit, and the pilsener, or pils, has become the most popular beer type in Czech countries (although, as discussed below, the Czech countries have also given the world some other significant beer styles). The 'original source' pilsner – Pilsner Urquell – is still in production at Pilsner Urquell Brewery (Plzeňský Prazdroj) and is considered the 'gold standard' in the Czech Republic (Figure 8.1).

[2] See Filip Vrana, 'Právovárečná měšťanstva – část 1: Historie a právní vývoj [Brewing-Law Burghers – Part 1: History and Legal Development]' (2018) 64(1) *Kvasný Průmysl* 29.

[3] See 'Historie piva v Čechách [History of Beer in Bohemia]', *BeerWeb* (Web Page) https://beerweb.cz/o-pivu/historie-piva-v-cechach#:~:text=Ran%C3%A9%20exporty%20piva%20byly%20zah%C3%A1jeny,pln%C3%AD%20tak%20sv%C3%A9%20vlastn%C3%AD%20kapsy.

[4] See Roger Mittag, 'Geographic Appellations of Beer' in Mark Patterson and Nancy Hoalst-Pullen (eds), *The Geography of Beer* (Springer Dordrecht, 1st ed, 2014) 68.

FIGURE 8.1 The first Pilsner Urquell beer was drawn in 1843.

Eighteenth-century innovations led to consolidated beer production and fewer breweries (from nearly 1,500 active breweries in 1850 to under 900 by the end of the nineteenth century), but higher quality and greater consistency and volume. Industrialized beer production soon moved from monasteries and municipalities to dedicated beer brotherhoods, societies, and corporations.

Of course, not all beer ventures were successful. In 1889, the London-based Bohemian Breweries Limited acquired three Czech breweries. British shareholders, motivated by the phenomenal success of Guinness shares, 'expected the shares of the Czech breweries [to] becom[e] valuable somewhat like of some African gold mine',[5] but the actual result was a total failure.

The developing beer industry suffered its first major hit during World War II, when more than 100 breweries, more than 60 per cent of hop production capacity, and nearly 30 per cent of barley production capacity were destroyed.[6] After the war, Czechoslovakia fell into the Soviet Bloc, which meant the totalitarian rule of the Communist Party of the Soviet Union (CPSU), nationalized production facilities, and a state-controlled economy.

During Communist rule, beer was meant to be a generic cheap alcoholic drink. The price of beer was uniformly set by the CPSU, and serial beer drinking became a standard leisure activity for men. Investments and innovations were very modest, so brewing facilities became badly outdated over the four decades of Communist rule.

The situation can be illustrated by bottled beer. While export bottles still bore labels indicating their manufacturers, bottled beer in Czechoslovak shops regularly had none – it was just plain, generic beer, and consumers were not meant to ask where it came from. In this sense, the Czech beer scene during Communist rule was a pioneer of the 'plain packaging movement', albeit for reasons other than those driving the movement today.

After the end of Communist rule in 1989, all parts of the beer production chain went private. The only large brewery that was not privatized and is still state-owned is Budějovický Budvar (Budweiser).

The development of the beer market between 1990 and 2010 was quite turbulent. Most large breweries were acquired by international groups and remodelled their production chains for greater efficiency. Often, that led to a decline in quality. Overall beer consumption steadily decreased, while demand for craft beers rose.

From 2010 to 2020, the number of craft breweries producing less than 10,000 hectolitres a year rose from under 100 to more than 500. Large breweries reacted by acquiring small breweries, focusing on exports, and, thankfully, improving the quality of their products.

8.2 IT'S ALL ABOUT PILSENER

Pilsener has been so popular in the Czech countries that consumers are still used to ordering beer not by type but by available degrees (see Chapter 1). Traditionally, the

5 The story was originally published in the national newspaper *Národní listy* and is explained in detail in the contemporary paper Libor Hruška, 'Bohemian Breweries limited – Zlatý důl nebo past? [Bohemian Breweries Limited – Goldmine or Trap? Part 1: The Founding of Bohemian Breweries in 1889]' (2013) 59(5) *Kvasný Průmysl* 134.

6 See 'Historie piva v Čechách [History of Beer in Bohemia]' (n 3).

most common varieties are 10- or 12-degree beers. The degree indicates the percentage of fermentable extract in the wort, not the actual alcohol content. While there are several variables (including the type of yeast used and the fermentation temperature), the higher the degree, the longer the fermentation normally takes (resulting in a higher percentage of alcohol). Higher degrees also have proportionally more residual unfermented extract, which gives pilsener its typically rich flavour.

Ten-degree beer has 3.5–4.5 per cent alcohol, while most 12-degree beers have 4.9–5.3 per cent alcohol. The original pilsener, the Pilsner Urquell, is exceptional, with 11.7 degrees (popularly rounded to 12 degrees) but only 4.4 per cent alcohol – which results from a shorter fermentation than other 12-degree beers.[7]

Lower-degree beers (typically 8 degrees or less) used to be popular for specific uses, like curing the thirst of glassblowers who worked in temperatures of around 60°C. Today, these low-degree beers are produced mostly by craft breweries and are especially in demand during the summer.

The percentage of fermentable extract is also the basis for the Czech legal classification of beer,[8] where *ležák* (lager) indicates 11–12-degree beer and *výčepní pivo* (tap beer) indicates 7–10-degree beer. These two types dominate the Czech market, with lager taking more than 50 per cent of beer sales and tap beer around 43 per cent. Over the past two decades, ales, porters, and weaker beers have become more popular, but their percentage of overall sales is still in single digits.

If we look at the beer styles the Czech Republic has contributed to the international scene, we can see that style guides – such as the Beer Judge Certification Program's *2021 Beer Style Guidelines* – include entire sections on Czech lager.[9] These sections include both the famous pilsner style (normally labelled as 'Czech Premium Pale Lager') and weaker, less flavoursome styles such as Czech Pale Lager, Czech Amber Lager, and Czech Dark Lager.

Tap beer is served everywhere from gastronomic restaurants to pubs and bars, whereas, from the early 2000s, pubs started to differentiate between those serving big beer brands and those serving craft beers. Large breweries attempted to hold market share by offering pubs partnership programmes – which featured incentives like loans and advantageous equipment leasing – in exchange for long-term exclusivity and even delivery obligations.[10] Some of those practices effectively prevented small,

7 The formula of Pilsner Urquell remains a well-kept secret. Brewmasters work in sections and only very few of them are aware of the complete composition of ingredients and details of the brewing procedure. The historical consistency of the quality of the product is maintained also thanks to regular visits of pensioned brewmasters to the brewery.

8 See Decree of the Ministry of Agriculture No. 335/1997 Sb.

9 See Gordon Strong and Kristen England, '2021 Beer Style Guidelines', *Beer Judge Certification Program* (Web Page) www.bjcp.org/download/2021_Guidelines_Beer.pdf.

10 This practice is not far from the problematic model of tied houses. See Koen Deconinck and Johan Swinnen, 'Tied Houses: Why They Are So Common and Why Breweries Charge Them High Prices for Their Beer' in Ignazio Cabras, David Higgins and David Preece (eds) *Brewing, Beer and Pubs* (Palgrave Macmillan, 1st ed, 2016) 231.

FIGURE 8.2 Pours with different levels of foam are said to affect the taste of the beer.

independent breweries from competing for the most attractive pub market and were sanctioned by the Czech Office for the Protection of Competition (ÚOHS).[11]

In any case, those practices did not stop the appearance of independent pubs, which serve either craft beers from independent breweries or beers brewed on-site. Interestingly, they sometimes offer both craft and large-brand beers. Why? Because the Czech beer community is traditionally inclined towards some well-established brands – and because even large brands can still make products that impress highly demanding beer connoisseurs.

All proper Czech pubs offer draught beer. Bottled or canned beer is for the home or places where ordering a beer is uncommon, such as cafés or cocktail bars. As draught beer requires specific technology and care, most pubs only offer a few brands or a few variants of one brand on tap.

Generally, there are two ways of serving the traditional pilsener. The first, *na hladinku* (levelled), involves pouring all the beer into the glass at once, starting with a tiny amount of foam and then carefully adding the desired volume (Figure 8.2). That technique was originally more popular in Bohemia and typically delivers a rich, dense, moist foam and sharper taste.

The second serving method, *nadvakrát* (twice), is traditional in Moravia and Silesia. At first, a larger amount of foam is poured into the glass and, after sitting for a little while, the rest of the beer is added underneath. The resulting beverage has

[11] See, for example, Case No VO II/S063/01, where the Czech Office for the Protection of Competition sanctioned two large breweries for tying 'advertisement' agreements with mandatory subscriptions.

a dryer, softer foam and milder taste, making it smoother to drink. This level of attention to the 'details' (that is, the pouring method) is a clear illustration of just how committed the Czechs are to their beer culture. Where else can you order a beer by reference to how it should be poured?

Today, most pubs offer beer served *na hladinku* partly for efficiency and partly by popular demand. Consumers always expect that properly served beer has foam on top – a head indicates freshness and protects the beer from quick oxidation.

Czech beer tradition refers, a bit pejoratively, to serving beer without foam as '*čochtan*'. The English equivalent is something like 'a splasher'. However, foamless beer is hugely uncommon and, unless explicitly ordered, would be turned down by a reasonable Czech patron.

8.3 CZECH BEER CULTURE: 'GOING FOR ONE'

Some cultural assets, to use a UNESCO term, have defining features that enable them to be recognized, documented, and eventually registered on a cross-border basis. Beer culture, however, is different, and so we should rather speak about national 'beer cultures'.

Belgian beer culture (discussed in Chapter 6), which was registered in 2016 by UNESCO as the first beer-related intangible asset,[12] is typically defined by traditionally broad varieties of beers, specific social institutions (such as Trappist monasteries), and the various ways beer is popularly used, including in cooking and cheese-making. German beer culture (discussed in Chapter 2), which is currently aspiring to similar recognition, is defined by its technology and traditional focus on production purity.

By contrast, beer historians in the Czech Republic found the defining features of Czech beer culture are mostly historical and societal.[13] These include hop production traditions, the overwhelming popularity of pilsener, and the broader social effects of beer.

Beer was originally produced in relatively small communities that included monasteries and burgher beer mansions. These mansions were not only places where beer was brewed but also where it was served. Limited transportation options and small production volumes led to beer being drunk, as original sources put it, 'around the chimney', and so pubs and tap houses became natural centrepieces of local communities. Even later, when beer production was industrialized, it often remained a communitarian business dominated by beer brotherhoods and similar societies.

[12] See Intergovernmental Committee for the Safeguarding of the Intangible Cultural Heritage, 'Decision of the Intergovernmental Committee: 11.COM 10.B.5', *UNESCO* (Web Page) https://ich.unesco.org/en/decisions/11.COM/10.B.5.

[13] See Libor Zajíc, 'Pivo jako předmět bádání v rámci humanitních věd [Beer as an Object of Research in the Humanities]' (2023) 70(2) *Studia Historica Brunensia* 7.

Pubs also served as community institutions for various professions. In cities, it was quite common for members of professional communities to meet in dedicated pubs after work. Pubs and guesthouses also popped up around trade routes and were used as community spots for travelling professions. Timber-rafting culture, for example, grew around beer-serving venues.[14]

All those social aspects can be summarized in the Czech phrase '*jdeme na jedno*' (let us go for one), which serves as a call to meet over a beer. It is used as a general phrase, even by people who do not drink beer, to suggest meeting in an informal environment. It is also used to suggest a collective reward – for example, following a work accomplishment or personal achievement – and to deal with a difficult, unresolved task, in the sense of 'we are stuck but let us go for a beer and try to solve it there'.

'Going for one' also became a statement of modern Czech politics. The first post-Communist Czech president, Václav Havel, was known for his extraordinary talent of 'going for one' to mark historical events and to unblock difficult political tasks. For Havel, unlike his predecessors and successors, these occasions felt very easy and natural, because he was, throughout his life, a regular to several Prague pubs. Havel originally preferred wine but changed to beer when he worked in Trutnov Brewery (now Krakonoš Brewery), unable to find employment anywhere else under Communist rule.[15]

The most specific meaning of '*jdeme na jedno*', and the most difficult to explain, is a call to just go for a beer. It may not mean that the speaker wants to meet and talk about something particular, or even to talk at all. It may just be a call to go to a pub and drink beer – because drinking beer is worthy enough. The value of 'going for one' normally lies in meeting others and the inevitable pub interactions, but it is an integral part of Czech beer culture that going for a beer makes sense per se.

[14] Timber rafters – whose specific professional culture was also recognized as an intangible asset by UNESCO upon the petition of Austria, Czech Republic, Germany, Latvia, Poland, and Spain – were keen beer drinkers in all of those countries, except Spain. Dedicated beer pubs served as places where members of this travelling profession met and developed their stories and traditions. See Intergovernmental Committee for the Safeguarding of the Intangible Cultural Heritage, 'Decision of the Intergovernmental Committee: 17.COM 7.B.4', *UNESCO* (Web Page) https://ich.unesco.org/en/decisions/17.COM/7.B.4.

[15] Havel was employed there as an 'unskilled manual labourer' for fourteen years, and the experience served as an inspiration for one of his most famous plays, *The Audience*.

9

Contracts, Competition, International Trade, and the Environment

9.1 INTRODUCTION

The world has seen many major trading empires. Vikings from the Nordic countries with trade routes stretching from Constantinople to Greenland, and from the warm Mediterranean to the icy waters of the far north. The Hanseatic league – centred around the Baltic Sea – dominated trade in northern Europe in the thirteenth to fifteenth centuries, with Hamburg being known as 'the Hanseatic League's Brewhouse', already exporting some 133,000 hectolitres of beer in 1369.[1] The Dutch commanded the largest fleet in the world, with a trading empire stretching from New York to Jakarta in the sixteenth and seventeenth centuries, and it has been noted that '[t]he rise of The Netherlands to this height was accompanied by the formation of a brewing industry unmatched in its time'.[2] The English took over and dominated international trade from the eighteenth century. Ale was a standard article of the sea ration and Henry VII established a naval brewery at Portsmouth in 1492.[3]

So, what did all these trading empires have in common? Well, trading skills, courage, and a willingness to embark on great – and often risky – long-distance voyages. But for our purposes, there is another important thing they have in common, as is hinted at above – beer, and more specifically hopped beer![4] Hopped beer lasts longer (at least in the sense of staying drinkable longer) and therefore extends the possible range for seafarers – an obvious competitive advantage:

1 Franz G. Meussdoerffer, 'A Comprehensive History of Beer Brewing' in Hans Michael Eßlinger (ed), *Handbook of Brewing: Processes, Technology, Markets* (Wiley-VCH, 1st ed, 2009) 16.

2 Ibid 20.

3 Ibid 22.

4 Ibid. As far as England is concerned, there was initially considerable resistance to hops. However, 'hop growing was legalized by an Act of Parliament in 1554 and hopped beer slowly established itself alongside ale in England during the first half of the sixteenth century'.

> At the latest after a series of stunning military misfortunes due to lack of beer and near catastrophes like the one caused by tainted beer during the battle with the Armada, the significance of beer in building an empire became evident to everybody. Beer was not only a rather stable beverage during sea voyages, but was also indispensable for the sailors' health.[5]

This chapter highlights a selection of different international trade issues and agreements regulating beer. As societies evolved and trade routes and trading partners were identified, the trading of goods and services became an age-old tradition. Because of trade, there needed to be a common ground for buyers and sellers for the exchange of goods and services. In a way, there was a need for a communal set of rules to govern the purpose of basic trade – rules to enable buyers and sellers to reach agreements on transactions with assurances that the buyer will receive the goods in the quality, quantity, and time frame specified in the order and the seller will receive payment, or penalties for breach of contract will be imposed.[6]

This chapter also seeks to draw attention to the environmental law side of beer law. Like the matter of cross-border trade, this is clearly an international issue.

However, first, we will examine two key contract law topics in the beer industry; namely licencing and collaboration agreements. We also delve into the related area of competition law.

9.2 CONTRACT LAW

The contract plays a central role in all commercial activities and the beer industry is no different. Contracts regulate the breweries' purchases of ingredients, equipment, and consumables such as electricity. Contracts play a central role in the employment of staff, the establishment of a brewery, the rent or purchase of the building housing the brewery, and the distribution of the beer. Consumers ordering a beer in a pub or a retail outlet enter into contracts with the seller. These are just some examples. Contracts are everywhere.

Lawyers would commonly advise a brewery start-up to at least consider the following types of contracts:

- ownership and formation documents;
- intellectual property and brand protection agreements;
- commercial leases;
- equipment purchase and lease agreements;
- supply agreements; and
- distribution agreements.[7]

[5] Ibid 22.

[6] Ann Krueger, *International Trade: What Everyone Needs to Know* (Oxford University Press USA, 2020) 22.

[7] Hillary St Jean, 'Key Legal Considerations for Breweries, Part I: Transactional and Contract Matters', *Rogoway Law Group* (Web Page, 15 March 2024) www.rogowaylaw.com/transactional-contract-matters-breweries/.

Two areas of contract law of particular significance in the beer law context are licensing and collaboration agreements. We will focus on them here.

9.2.1 *Licensing*

Consumers are used to seeing beer brewed under licence. If you, for example, visit a 'bottle shop' in Australia, beers such as Stella Artois, Budweiser, Carlsberg, Coors, and Heineken are all brewed locally under licence. Others are brewed overseas, but not in the country one might expect – what would you say about Mexico's Corona being brewed in China? In contrast, some breweries have made a point of maintaining all manufacturing in the one location. That is the case when it comes to Pilsner Urquell of the Czech Republic, for example, a fact reflected in their marketing

Licensed brewing is governed by complex contractual arrangements. Drafting such contracts requires specialist knowledge and some law firms specialize in the brewing industry. Furthermore, the larger companies obviously also rely on skilled in-house lawyers. We will not discuss such contracts in detail here.

Licensed brewing comes with several advantages. In many cases, it creates local jobs where the beer is consumed. It typically cuts down transportation costs – a benefit for both the company and the environment. And consumers get a fresher beer. At the same time, licensed brewing also comes with a few issues; some of them potentially of a legal character.

Even where a 'foreign' beer is brewed locally 'under supervision of' or 'under licence from' the original creator, the branding typically still emphasizes the link to the country where it was originally brewed. One example of this is found in the famous 'Anno 1366' on a bottle of Stella Artois. Such references have the potential to cause a careless consumer to assume that the beer was imported. Then again, when you buy beer in a shop, you can, in most cases, check where it has been brewed. But this is not always clear, and it may be overwhelmed by branding.

For instance, some years ago, a person buying a carton of Asahi beer in Australia would see the text 'Japan's No. 1 Beer' appearing prominently on the box and, at two different locations on the box, the text 'Imported by Asahi Premium Beverages a division of Independent Distillers (Aust) Pty Ltd' would appear.[8] Taken together, these two statements may certainly have caused an ordinary and reasonable consumer to believe the beer in question was brewed in Japan. But once the box was opened, the fine print on the bottles revealed that the beer was brewed in Thailand under licence from Asahi (at the time, a quick check of the Asahi website showed that the company then had breweries in numerous countries, including Thailand,

8 See Dan Svantesson, 'Australian Consumer Law Is Failing Beer Drinkers', *The Conversation* (Web Page, 11 October 2017) https://theconversation.com/australian-consumer-law-is-failing-beer-drinkers-85260.

Malaysia, and China). So, yes, the beer was, indeed, imported as the box promised. But not from the place one might have expected.

The problem of knowing what you get is arguably even worse when it comes to ordering beers at a restaurant or pub. On menus, the likes of Peroni, Heineken and Carlsberg are often listed as 'imported beers', even when they are in fact brewed under licence in Australia. And when the beer is on tap, where is the 'fine print' to read?

It is of course possible to argue that the foreign beer brands that have their products brewed in Australia take sufficient steps to make their beer taste similar enough to the original product. And if the beer tastes the same to the average beer drinker, what is the big deal?

However, even if the taste is the same, the place of origin still matters. If you buy an expensive Swiss watch, surely it matters that it was made in Switzerland and not in China. Can't we feel the same about beer?

9.2.2 *Collaboration Brewing Agreements*

Apart from adding unusual ingredients like avocado, oysters, and bulls' testicles[9] to their beers, there are other ways for breweries to stand out in the crowded marketplace. One option that has increased in popularity is various forms of collaborations (or 'collabs'), either with other breweries or with partners outside the brewing industry, such as sports teams, influencers, or producers of things that can be added to the beer, such as spirits.

Surprising Collabs

Oregon-based brewery '10 Barrel' paired with the last remaining Blockbuster video store to create a beer.

A Stone Brewery collab with rock band Metallica resulted in a pilsner named 'Stone Enter Night Pilsner'.

The Danish brewery 'Mikkeller' created a trio of beers in collaboration with film director David Lynch.

Interestingly, law – and more precisely a desire to avoid litigation – seems to have played a major role in driving the uptake in brewing collaborations in the early years. This is particularly well illustrated by the background to what became Collaboration Not Litigation Ale:[10] '[T]he use of the word [collaboration] in a brewing context really caught on in 2004, when Russian River and Avery blended two Belgian-style

[9] Andy Young, 'Top 10 Weirdest Beer Ingredients', *The Drinks Business* (Web Page, 22 February 2013) www.thedrinksbusiness.com/2013/02/top-10-weirdest-beer-ingredients/.

[10] See 'Collaboration Not Litigation Ale', *BeerAdvocate* (Web Page) www.beeradvocate.com/beer/profile/30/34877/.

beers they'd independently named Salvation and called it Collaboration Not Litigation Ale."[11]

Brewing collaborations are now very much an established part of the brewing scene, not least amongst craft brewers. Sometimes these collaborations come about through well-planned marketing initiatives. However, there is also a trend of collaboration built on mutual admiration for each other's products or work, or simply as a result of friendships.

At least in these latter cases, it may be tempting to avoid formal agreements. They may be seen as too costly, too complex, and simply unnecessary. However, as history has taught us, as soon as money is involved, a good contract may be better than a good friendship at ensuring an ongoing harmonious relationship. In other words, also in simple 'collab' arrangements between friends, it is useful to clearly map out the parties' expectations in the form of a contract. Doing so may in fact make the relationship both more manageable and more efficient, and of course more lasting (Figure 9.1).

So, what should such a contract contain? Well, some things are obvious. The contract must address the following questions:

- What beer will be brewed (including agreement on every necessary detail of the brewing process)?
- When and where will the beer be brewed?
- Who will source the ingredients and from where?
- Who will brew the beer?
- How much beer will be brewed?
- In what form will the beer be sold (kegs, cans, bottles)?
- Who covers what costs?
- Who sets the price?
- How is the profit divided?
- What are the tax implications?
- How will the beer be branded, and who is responsible for the branding?
- How will the beer be marketed, and who is responsible for the marketing?
- How and where will the beer be sold, and who is responsible for this?

Apart from these obviously necessary aspects of the agreement, there are clauses that may be included to deal with risks. For example, the agreement may address liability issues in case the production, or the beer itself, leads to litigation by a third party:

- Who is liable if someone is injured during the production of the beer?

[11] Martin Cizmar, 'The Etiquette of Cooperation: 7 Simple Ground Rules for Successful Collaboration Beers', *BeerAdvocate* (Web Page, February 2016) www.beeradvocate.com/articles/13375/the-etiquette-of-cooperation-7-simple-ground-rules-for-successful-collaboration-beers/.

FIGURE 9.1 Collab between Pivovar Thrills Brewing and Svantesson Brewing.

- Who is liable if the beer makes people ill (e.g., due to the inclusion of undisclosed allergens)?
- Who is liable if the branding leads to litigation, for example due to it being offensive or violating a third party's trademark?

In addition, there are other important matters to consider, in particular as part of future-planning. Interestingly, the importance of these questions stem not so much from the risk of the beer failing, but rather from the possibility of the beer becoming a success:

- Who owns the branding of the beer?[12]
- Should the agreement include any confidentiality clauses?
- Should the agreement include any restraint of trade clauses?
- Should the agreement include any clauses regulating trade secrets?
- Is the contract aimed at a one-off production of one batch, or an ongoing brewing arrangement?

[12] See further Chapter 5.

These lists of matters to consider when entering into a collab arrangement may, no doubt, seem rather intimidating. However, at least for some types of collaborations, the pragmatic approach may be for the collaborating partners to simply agree that the brewery where the beer is made carries all costs and reaps all the financial rewards. Where the collaborators adopt this approach – combined with co-labelling and taking turns brewing at their respective breweries – an ongoing fruitful collaboration can be put in place with minimal legal complexity.

In many ways, a brewing collab agreement is similar to other forms of contract. At the same time, as in any industry, to draft a good contract one needs to understand the industry in question. Some law firms have specialization in brewing collaboration agreements, and if the trend of brewing collabs continues, we may see an expansion of the number of such firms. Further, it may be noted that there are some drafts contracts available for free online, such as the one published by the Nebraska Craft Brewers Guild.[13]

A 2018 study by academics from Edith Cowan University suggested that the key benefits gained from collaborations amongst craft brewers include quality improvements, increasing knowledge of craft beer recipes and equipment, and strategic knowledge of the industry.[14] A good collaboration agreement is an essential ingredient for obtaining those benefits.

9.3 COMPETITION AND TRADE

The beer market is highly competitive. Here we will first make some observations about the law and competition in domestic beer markets. We then examine vertical relationships between brewers and pubs, and whether some breweries have too much market power.

9.3.1 *Competition in Domestic Beer Markets*

Elsewhere (see Chapter 5), we pointed out that two recent trends dominate the beer market: persistent consolidation on the one hand, and multiplication of breweries on the other. The concentration of market power in the hands of a few breweries has continued almost unabated around the world. A very good example is the Australian market, where two big Japanese corporations (Asahi and Kirin) together have 85 per cent of the market. In the US, AB InBev (which includes the erstwhile Anheuser-Busch company) and Molson Coors have 65 per cent market share; and in Austria, Heineken through its Brau Union subsidiary has 60 per cent of the market (to name

[13] 'Collaborative Brewing Agreement', *Nebraska Liquor Control Commission* (Web Page) https://lcc.nebraska.gov/sites/default/files/COLLABORATIVE%20BREWING%20AGREEMENT%20BLANK.pdf.

[14] Alonso Duarte, Nevil Alexander, and Seamus O'Brien, 'Collaboration and the Emerging Craft Brewing Industry: An Exploratory Study' (2018) 19(3) *Journal of Asia-Pacific Business* 11.

but a few).[15] On the other hand, the number of craft breweries has also continued to grow in the 'partitioned market' for speciality beers.

There have been competition issues because of the cross-over between these two markets. A particular issue in that regard has been the big brewers' attempts to control 'pub taps'. This is their practice to offer pubs incentives to provide their own 'craft brews' on tap and not to offer the brews of independent craft brewers. The latter have complained bitterly about this practice, but seemingly to little effect: an Australian Competition and Consumer Commission (ACCC) report recently recommended against any particular measures to put a stop to these practices.

Another issue is vertical integration – brewers, or more broadly beverage companies moving into distribution and retail. Power over retail means that brewers (let's call them that although they are often integrated (alcoholic) beverage companies) can control how their products will be presented in licensed stores and in supermarkets (where sale is permitted in such stores). In other words, they can ensure that competing brews (often from smaller and weaker brewery actors) are either not carried in stores or are so placed or promoted that the consumer has little chance of seeing them. A further issue is the fact that many supermarket chains now also have their 'home brand' brews – we mentioned Aldi in this regard in (see Chapter 5). This enables them to relegate other brands to lesser store positions and prefer their own, thus increasing their profit margins. Nonetheless, they benefit from all the beer advertising that the actual breweries do.

9.3.2 *Vertical Relationships between Brewers and Pubs*

Of course, a degree of vertical integration was already widespread before brewers moved into the distribution and retail space. That is in particular because brewers have a less than arms-length relationship with pubs. They might either own pubs outright (own the real estate and run the pub with their own personnel); own the pubs but rent them out to 'independent' publicans who acquire their beer on wholesale terms; or the loosest form of relationship known as 'tying'. In return for various forms of support from the brewer, the otherwise independent pub will agree to be contractually bound in various ways. That might be through resale price maintenance (the brewer sets the price at which the pub must sell its beer); exclusive dealing (where the pub can only sell that brewer's products or products that the brewer agrees on); quantity forcing, where a pub is required to purchase a minimum amount of the brewer's product; and tying, where a brewer will only supply a product if the purchaser also acquires (an)other product(s) from the brewer.

Such arrangements are said to have a consumer upside because they will encourage the benefiting brewer's investment in the pub concerned; it is only in return for

[15] Brau Union/Heineken has fallen foul of the competition authority in Austria. See Ina Verstl, 'Trust-Busters: Heineken Unit Brau Union Abuses Market Power', *BRAUWELT International* 2024 (Web Page, 6 July 2024) https://brauwelt.com/en/international-report/europe-russia/647077-trust-busters-heineken-unit-brau-union-abuses-market-power.

these contractual benefits that the brewer will lend money or invest in the refurbishment of the pub. That might be good for the publican but can also provide a more attractive environment for the pub-goer. The downside of such practices, however, is also apparent: the limiting of consumer choice and the maintenance of higher prices on the one hand, and the exclusion of competing (in particular craft) brewers on the other. If the taps of a pub or café are tied to a particular brewer, the pub will likely serve that brewer's national pilsner brand, and also its own 'craft' brew or brews, freezing out independent craft brewers; this is referred to as 'foreclosure' of the entry of new rivals in the brewing sector. Slade talks of this situation in more subtle terms, however: retailers are incentivized to free-ride on the value of a beer brand and not make much of an effort, and will also free-ride on efforts of others at their own level (the promotion of the beer brand by retailers, and perhaps also by other pubs).[16] Tying taps to brewers is a common practice but, perhaps surprisingly, it is not automatically condemned by competition authorities (such as in Australia). There the ACCC reported:

> 'Although some venues had exclusivity arrangements, most pubs and clubs said they did not feel constrained from allocating taps to smaller brewers and could make taps available for craft beer if necessary.' ... Some contracts included minimum volume requirements that could make it harder for craft brewers to gain access to taps in these venues. ... 'While some craft brewers may have been refused access to taps by certain venues, our investigation found that the venues were responding to consumer demand for certain beer brands, rather than restrictions imposed by the big brewers ... In fact, over half of the venues contacted by the ACCC indicated that customer preference was the key factor in determining the brands, types of beer and number of craft beers offered by the venue.'[17].

The ACCC's conclusions about tying thus accord with the higher-level analysis by Slade which tends to identify some positives that balance the downsides of the practice. It is also the case that those who want real craft beers will often attend brewhouses or craft breweries directly; on the other hand, they might want to purchase packaged beer from liquor stores. Which takes us to another aspect of market power – to what extent do brewers have market power in the packaged beer sector?

9.3.3 *Do Some Breweries Have Too Much Market Power?*

We can only answer this question if we adopt certain presumptions, in the first instance about what the market is: for beer; for craft beer or international pilsner beer; for beer and wine as direct rivals; for beverages; for fermented beverages

16 See Margaret Slade, 'Competition Policy towards Brewing: Rational Response to Market Power or Unwarranted Interference in Efficient Markets?' in Johan Swinnen (ed), *The Economics of Beer* (Oxford University Press, 2011) 177.

17 See Australia Competition and Consumer Commission, 'ACCC Releases Findings of Beer Taps Investigation', ACCC (Media Release, 13 July 2017) www.accc.gov.au/media-release/accc-releases-findings-of-beer-taps-investigation.

(including cider and alcoholic ginger beer); and so on. There are of course many different ways to address this question: for instance, there is one market if the goods concerned are usually produced by the same companies (for example, integrated beverage companies might commonly make or supply beer, wine, and spirits, or own multiple brands across that range); how products are retailed (wine, beer, alcoholic cider, and alcopops might be commonly supplied in liquor stores, but not soft drinks); or what are substitute products (do consumers see beer and wine as interchangeable substitutes, or beer and craft beer, or only international pilsner-style beers). Another way is to observe how market actors of a certain size operate and work backwards from that: for instance, if the big multinational beer brands (AB InBev, Heineken, Carlsberg) act to supply the demand for craft beers, establishing that craft and standard beer forms a single market. Then a question might be what volume of supply represents market power, and where and through what channels. There are thus very complex questions to answer before a competition law position can be taken vis-à-vis brewers – in particular in the context of mergers and acquisitions, but also in the context of certain market practices (such as the ones relating to pubs mentioned above). What is also relevant is vertical integration with other stages of the supply chain: a brewer might be of a certain size but also own a fair slice of distribution or of retail spaces; when is that a concern?

Significant is that we are here not dealing with beer-specific issues. As Koltay and colleagues said recently (in 2023): 'Recent empirical evidence suggests that market economies are changing in fundamental ways. There is an increase in firm markups, higher aggregate industry concentration, a decline in the labor share of output, larger firm and income inequality, and a reduction in business dynamism.'[18] The authors are referring to Europe in their article, but the truth of their statement is more universally experienced, as is the fundamental underlying issue; as Slade puts it, 'with both horizontal and vertical cases, the possibility of competitive harm must be balanced against the potential for realizing production, distribution, and organizational efficiencies'.[19] The question no economist seems to be able to answer, but which competition authorities seem to answer by stressing the realization of efficiencies, is how many competitors should there be in a 'market'? Can an oligopoly be good for consumers because of its efficiencies? The crucial follow-on question might then be where the benefit of those efficiencies stick: with the producer in greater profits or the consumer in lower prices, or somehow a bit of both. It is certainly the case that competition authorities have allowed a considerable amount of concentration at the national or EU-wide level in the brewing industry. Interestingly enough, the Big Beer brewing industry is one of dominant

[18] Gábor Koltay, Szabolcs Lorincz, and Tommaso Valletti, 'Concentration and Competition: Evidence from Europe and Implications for Policy' (2023) 19(3) *Journal of Competition Law and Economics* 466.

[19] Slade (n 16) 191.

multinationals – and there is simply no competition authority applying competition law to multinationals.

Of course, it is possible to ignore the question of markets and market power, as competition law does, and simply outlaw certain practices which are presumed to be anti-competitive. That happens in all jurisdictions – but it is not a simple exercise, as we have seen in relation to tap ties between brewers and pubs. The practices may take many different forms: if a large brewer acquires local plots of land which are zoned for light industrial activities (including brewing) so as to foreclose new craft breweries opening up, does this infringe the competition law? If a brewer which has a few brands with a large market share demands from retailers that their packaged beer is displayed more prominently than competing brews, is there a breach of the competition law? If a large supermarket sells an own-label brew, which it does not spend anything on advertising and promoting, and places it above or in a better position than third-party-brand brews in its supermarkets, what then? The dividing line between smart competition and abusive competition is often difficult to draw while allowing for a free and not over-regulated market. Perhaps the average prices of beer compared between nations might give an indication of how competitive in aggregate a national beer market is. In the Asia-Pacific region, Singapore had the highest cost in 2024 with US$13 per unit, China the lowest with about US$3 per unit – that's definitely a big difference; take into account that China is the world's biggest beer market, and Singapore likely one of the smallest.[20]

9.4 INTERNATIONAL TRADE

International trade in beer is limited by the comparatively short shelf life of beer.[21] Beer is also rather heavy and bulky – characteristics that work against international trade. The need for cooling of modern beer is another impediment to long-distance trade. Nevertheless, international trade in beer has a long history and the world market for imported beer continues to increase. As the demand for imported beer increases, countries that export beer must increase production to meet these demands. With the backing of the World Trade Organization (WTO) and its set of agreements, restrictions to the trade of beer continue to decrease, and beer is freely traded across many states.

Initially, Europe was the biggest producer of beer and ,as seen throughout this book, many of the beer traditions around the world still originate in Europe. However, attitudes towards the cross-border trade in beer have varied and are often linked to what suits the state at the time. For example, the importation of beer – and

[20] Statista Research Department, 'Average Price Per Unit of Beer in the Asia-Pacific Region in 2023 with a Forecast for 2024, by Country or Territory', *Statista* (Web Page, 11 September 2024) www.statista.com/forecasts/1420456/apac-average-price-of-beer-by-country.

[21] Henry Thompson, *International Economics: Global Markets and International Competitions* (World Scientific, 2001) 240.

TABLE 9.1 *Tallies in the global beer industry*

Category	Country/Company
Largest beer producer	China – In 2020, China produced 341.1 million hectolitres of beer, which is equivalent to approximately 286 million barrels[a]
Largest beer consumer per capita	Czech Republic – 181.9 litres. Consuming almost twice as much as any other nation, the average Czech gets through 320 pints a year[b]
The largest exporter of beer	Mexico – Mexico is the world's leading beer exporter. The country exported 42 million hectolitres in 2021, 11.5% more than in 2020, according to Cerveceros de México[c]
The largest importer of beer (trade value)	The United States was the world leader in terms of beer imports in 2021, receiving beer valued at over US$6 billion[d]
Largest beer company in the world	Anheuser-Busch InBev was the largest beer company in the world, with a revenue of $57.786 billion in 2023[e]

[a] VinePair Staff, 'Top 20 Beer Producing Countries in the World', *VinePair* (Web Page, 22 July 2024) https://vinepair.com/booze-news/top-20-beer-producing-countries-2024/#:~:text=Today%2C%20China%20produces%20more%20beer,to%20five%20percent%20per%20year.%3C.

[b] Louis Thomas, 'Ten Countries That Drink the Most Beer', *The Drinks Business* (Web Page, 7 November 2022) www.thedrinksbusiness.com/2022/11/top-10-countries-that-drink-the-most-beer-per-capita/.

[c] 'Mexico Is the World's Leading Beer Exporter in the World', *MexicoNow* (Web Page, 15 August 2022) https://mexico-now.com/mexico-is-the-worlds-leading-beer-exporter/#:~:text=MEXICO%20%E2%80%93%20Mexico%20is%20the%20world's,Belgium%2C%20Germany%20and%20the%20Netherlands%3C.

[d] Jan Conway, 'Leading Beer Importing Countries Worldwide in 2022, by Trade Value', *Statista* (Web Page, 22 May 2024) www.statista.com/statistics/1239917/top-beer-importers-worldwide-trade-value/.

[e] Chris Kolmar, 'The 10 Largest Beer Companies in the World', *Zippia* (Web Page, 19 April 2023) www.zippia.com/advice/largest-beer-companies.

a range of over 200 other products including wine, spirits, oranges, and coffee – was banned in Sweden in 1756 due to the poor state of the country's economy.[22]

After the 1950s, however, America and many Asian countries gradually began to catch up with European levels of production.[23] While the 1990s and early 2000s brought significant investment in Central and Eastern Europe, the years since the new millennium have been characterized by huge investments in the Chinese, South American, Latin American, Mexican, and Brazilian markets. This was because internationalizing companies wanted to gain a foothold in regions where beer consumption was rising fast.[24]

In the last two years, the figures for the beer industry have been impressive So far, the updated tallies for beer production, import and export are as shown in Table 9.1.

As we have pointed out repeatedly above, the beer market is marked by global concentration – some multinational behemoths have acquired market power on a

[22] Yppighetsförordningen 1756 (Sweden).

[23] Eva Bieleková, and Ján Pokrivčák, 'Determinants of International Beer Export' (2020) 12(2) *AGRIS on-line Papers in Economics and Informatics* 17.

[24] Ibid 3.

global scale – their brands are common and recognized in many different countries: think Heineken, Stella, Carlsberg's principal brands. To some degree, this globalization has resulted from opportunity and the vision of some brewers – AB InBev went from a national brewer known as Stella Artois to a global mega-brewer in a very short space of time because of the adoption and execution of a deliberate growth strategy. Important for these brewers is that they have outgrown the local, regional, and then national markets, and become players in a global market. This enables fluctuations in domestic demand to be arbitraged by exports (for instance, beer consumption in Belgium has been in steady decline, but this is countered by the enormous export growth of some of its brews); and allows both exports of physical beer and, more importantly in this sector, international licensing of brands and brewing.

Therefore, the big brewers take a significant interest in impediments to international trade, and in this segment the principal ones are tariffs on the one hand, and restrictions on the brewing and selling of beer by virtue of national laws on the other. Beer being an alcoholic beverage, national authorities tend to put all sort of restrictions on its sale, in terms of health, public order, youth protection, and other reasons. This tends to clash with the ambitions of multinational beer brands to open up further markets for their brews, and leverage globally their investments in promotion and advertising (for instance, Heineken sponsoring high-profile football competitions in Europe which are avidly consumed around the world). Various authors have pointed out that, crucially, the WTO takes the approach that alcoholic beverages (including beer of course) are just another product, or are primarily regarded as just another set of items of consumption, subject to trade rules that sought to create an open international market for commodities, free of governmental restrictions, which in this context are conceived as 'barriers to trade'. The authors go on to say that '"public health exceptions" in trade treaties, in principle, offered some protection for measures that controlled and restricted imports in the interest of public health, but justifying exceptions for alcohol on these grounds has proven difficult and uncertain'.[25] They illustrate how certain health-inspired requirements are watered down by international trade agreements.

Global, regional, and bilateral trade agreements, of course, aim to *increase* international trade by removing tariff and quantitative restrictions on imports, and also by addressing domestic regulations that have an adverse effect on inward-traded goods and services. In the sphere of spirits in particular, this has meant a clear clash between domestic policies that aim to limit alcohol sales, and international trade policy that aims to ease access to domestic markets for foreign providers of alcoholic beverages. In other words, there is a clash between health regulation, which is a

[25] Robin Room, Deborah Gleeson, and Mia Miller, 'Alcoholic Beverages in Trade Agreements: Industry Lobbying and the Public Health Interest' (2021) 40(1) *Drug and Alcohol Review* 19, 20.

common reason for limiting alcohol sales, and international trade liberalization as dictated by the WTO and other trade agreements.

However, the main focus of trade agreements has been on the importation of spirits and wine, goods that are physically traded from one country to another. By contrast, beer is more often brewed under licence in destination countries, sometimes to the dismay or confusion of consumers.[26] Those licences are commonly held by the big multinational brewers. Where their interests are affected is often in relation to advertising restrictions, where there can be an argument that the effect of national restrictions is to limit international trade under the General Agreement on Trade in Services (GATS), or where the effect is said to be discriminatory against new entrants from other jurisdictions, since their products are not already known by the domestic public. Government monopolies on the sale of alcoholic beverages (including in Scandinavia and Canada[27]) have also presented problems in relation to international treaty obligations; as measures that limit alcohol supply, by also limiting trading hours or retail outlet numbers, they might amount to quantity-based restrictions as outlawed by GATS. Quantitative restriction considerations were used against Germany in relation to its purity laws for beer.[28] Similarly Technical Barriers to Trade provisions (TBT) might also be used as leverage against certain measures imposed by national governments, such as taxation of certain receptacles (which might favour national providers, depending on their predominant choice of glass vs plastic or aluminium, for instance). National treatment requirements might also mean that differential taxes between alcoholic beverages might be able to be undermined depending on what is deemed to be a 'like' product – since like products from other member states of a trade agreement must get like treatment under national treatment principles.[29]

Thus, multinational brewers, although they tend not to export physical beer much, are in fact impacted or can benefit from international trade agreements, as

[26] See Dan Svantesson, 'With Many "Foreign" Beers Now Brewed in Australia, Is It Time for Clearer Labels?', *ABC News* (Web Page, 11 October 2017) www.abc.net.au/news/2017-10-11/foreign-beers-brewed-in-australia-time-for-better-labels/9035576; Pete Brown, 'Who Really Owns/Brews Your Favourite Beer?', *Pete Brown* (Web Page, 16 December 2022) www.petebrown.net/2022/12/16/is-that-craft-beer-or-mediterranean-lager-really-what-is-claims-to-be/; Pete Drinks, 'Import vs. Brewed under License', *Pete Drinks* (Web Page, 17 October 2014) www.petedrinks.com/beer/import-vs-brewed-under-license/. See also 'Taste Test: Locally Brewed vs Imported', *Choice* (Web Page, 12 August 2014) www.choice.com.au/food-and-drink/drinks/alcohol/articles/imported-vs-locally-brewed-beer-taste-test. For more data about foreign beer brewed under license, see Will Smale, 'Italian Label Maybe but the Beer's British Brewed', *BBC* (Web Page, 15 December 2022) www.bbc.com/news/business-63901215.

[27] See, eg, 'Canada – Tax Exemptions and Reductions for Wine and Beer', *World Trade Organization* (Web Page) www.wto.org/english/tratop_e/dispu_e/cases_e/ds354_e.htm.

[28] See *Re Purity Requirements for Beer: EC Commission v Germany* (Case 178/84) [1988] 1 CMLR 780.

[29] All these various issues are well described and illustrated in Donald W Zeigler, 'The Alcohol Industry and Trade Agreements: A Preliminary Assessment' (2009) 104(1) *Addiction* 13.

these tend to reduce the imposts and limitations on the supply of beer to consumers in domestic markets. Their influence in the treaty-making process is thus significant, and their impact on public health in many jurisdictions is not to be discounted. The clash is somewhat broader because international trade liberalization comes into conflict with the sovereign right of states to tax goods – and beer as an alcoholic beverage has always been a special target of the fiscal managers in government.[30] More generally, local brewers might fear the impact trade liberalization measures have on their local and domestic markets, and therefore lobby against them – and thus against the big beer multinationals.[31] In international trade terms, breweries' international acquisitions are of course subject to investment restrictions, which might on occasion provide (cold) comfort to local brewers.[32] Alternatively, the craft brewers might take some comfort from battles between the big multinationals, such as between AB InBev and Heineken about a novel beer dispenser.[33]

9.4.1 *Cross-Border Internet Sales*

A particular form of international trade can be seen in the increasing trend of beer being ordered online and shipped across borders. This gives rise to a range of legal issues, not least since, as we have discussed in this book, the sale and marketing of beer is associated with particularly strict regulation in many countries. As a consequence, once the sale and marketing of beer enters the online arena – characterized by a certain 'borderlessness' – it is immediately exposed to a particularly complex matrix of overlapping, and in some cases contradictory, legal rules. This makes it important to consider legal risk management in online sales of beer.

So how can those engaging in online sales and marketing of beer cope with this? One obvious option is to include clear statements delineating which markets they service, and to simply not include any delivery mechanisms for other markets. Such structures can be supplemented by technological measures such as geolocation

30 See 'Sovereign Right to Tax Goods in "Taxation"', *World Trade Organization* (Web Page) www.wto.org/english/tratop_e/dispu_e/repertory_e/t3_e.htm.

31 See, eg, Gifford Lee, 'Fears for Aussie Brewers over Euro Free Trade Deal', *Beer & Brewer* (Web Page, 13 October 2022) www.beerandbrewer.com/fears-for-aussie-brewers-over-euro-free-trade-deal/.

See also Kym Anderson, 'Beverage Market Disruptions and Their Trade Consequences', *CEPR* (Web Page, 16 February 2020) https://cepr.org/voxeu/columns/beverage-market-disruptions-and-their-trade-consequences.

32 Damiaan Persyn, Johan Swinnen, and Stijn Vanormelingen, 'Belgian Beers: Where History Meets Globalization' (Discussion Paper No 271, LICOS Centre for Institutions and Economic Performance, October 2010).

33 Mathieu Klos, 'AB InBev and Heineken Settle Global Beer Dispenser Dispute', *JUVE Patent* (Web Page, 5 May 2020) www.juve-patent.com/cases/ab-inbev-and-heineken-settle-global-beer-dispenser-dispute/#:~:text=Last%20week%2C%20Anheuser%20Busch%20InBev,official%20confirmation%20of%20the%20settlement.

technologies that block access to potential consumers from countries to which the seller does not wish to deliver.

However, some sellers seem to intentionally push the boundaries. For example, it has been noted that, while it is illegal to do so, some stores sell alcohol online to people in Iceland, and the government has not enforced the law.[34] Clearly this is not a phenomenon limited to Iceland. Rather it is a common issue. Montonen and Tuominen concludes that:

> Probably the only effective way to prevent cross-border advertising from undermining national restrictions is to follow the model of the Framework Convention on Tobacco Control, that is, having signatories agree to apply the same restrictions to domestic and out-flowing advertising and recognise the right of others to take action to limit in-flowing advertising.[35]

However, they are also realistic about the prospects of this approach and note that '[t]he factual and political "degree of difficulty" for regulating alcohol advertising with an international agreement is apparently higher than for banning tobacco advertising'.[36]

A key issue in this context is, as discussed by the WHO, how far a country's jurisdiction stretches in the online environment. The 2023 report titled 'Restricting Digital Marketing in the Context of Tobacco, Alcohol, Food and Beverages, and Breast-Milk Substitutes: Existing Approaches and Policy Options' notes how, for example, Mexico's relevant advertising law provides that 'advertising aimed at being disseminated in the national territory, independently of its origin, must abide by this law, the regulation and other applicable provisions'.[37] This raises complex jurisdictional issues within both public and private international law. While fascinating, a detailed examination of those topics falls outside the scope of this book.

9.5 BEER LAW AND THE ENVIRONMENT

The topic of beer, law, and environmental considerations deserves a book of its own. Here, our limited aim is to highlight a small selection of issues on an admittedly rather superficial level.

[34] Helga Dís Björgúlfsdóttir, 'Beer in Iceland: A Historical Overview', *Your Friend in Reykjavik* (Web Page, 3 August 2023) https://yourfriendinreykjavik.com/beer-in-iceland-a-historical-overview/.

[35] Marjatta Montonen and Ismo Tuominen, 'Restricting Alcohol Marketing on Social Media in Finland' in Antonia Lyons et al (eds), *Youth Drinking Cultures in a Digital World: Alcohol, Social Media and Cultures of Intoxication* (Routledge, 1st ed, 2017) 213.

[36] Ibid.

[37] 'Restricting Digital Marketing in the Context of Tobacco, Alcohol, Food and Beverages, and Breast-Milk Substitutes: Existing Approaches and Policy Options', *World Health Organization* (Web Page, 2023) 30 https://iris.who.int/bitstream/handle/10665/373130/9789240077249-eng.pdf?sequence=1; 'Reglamento de la Ley General de Salud en Materia de Publicidad [Regulation of the General Law on Health in Matters of Advertising]', (Web Page, 4 May 2000) art 4 www.diputados.gob.mx/LeyesBiblio/regley/Reg_LGS_MP.pdf.

The first point we wish to make is that the brewing industry impacts the environment in a variety of ways.[38] Brewing requires large volumes of water and generates large amounts of solid and liquid waste by-products. The brewing process is energy intensive, and beer uses a large amount of packaging, both glass and aluminium. Getting the beer from brewery to consumer may create transport emissions. Some of these concerns for the environment may be mitigated. For example, many breweries are working hard to cut down on water usage, 'spent grains' can be used as animal feed, and some breweries have made a point of sourcing 'green energy' for the production. Producing an environmentally friendly beer has strong advantages, and we have discussed the issue of 'greenwashing' in Chapter 7 dealing with consumer protection.

We will not go into any details, but simply note that breweries – like any other businesses – may be subject to environmental laws impacting how they operate. Such laws are likely to increase over coming years.

Apart from the need to comply with environmental law, and the desirability of an environmentally sound product, there is at least one additional aspect of the environment that must be mentioned in this context: breweries are obviously strongly impacted by changes in the environment. To see why, we need only consider where beer brewing traditionally has taken place. Access to water is simply a necessity. Furthermore, while barley is a relatively hardy plant, scientists are already pointing to lower yields due to climate change.[39] Hops are more sensitive and are significantly affected by changes in the climate. Yields are lower, and of lower quality.[40] All this amounts to a serious threat to the beer industry, and, of course, the beer drinkers.

9.6 CONCLUDING THOUGHTS

Beer in all its form and elegance continues to be an important commodity that is traded internationally. Trade agreements have played an important role in setting rules to trade and also a dispute mechanism to hear complaints. From the earliest adoption of the General Agreement on Tariffs and Trade (GATT) to the numerous WTO treaties, liberalization has been the main thrust of international trade regulation. The different agreements passed over the years have affected components of the beer industry. More importantly, not just the trading of beer as a product is regulated but so is the service industry associated with beer. Member states have

38 'Contemporary Environmental Challenges and Opportunities within the Brewing Industry', *Donut Waste* (Web Page, 7 February 2023) www.donutwaste.com.au/contemporary-environmental-challenges-and-opportunities-within-the-brewing-industry/.

39 Virgílio A Bento et al, 'The Impact of Climate Change in Wheat and Barley Yields in the Iberian Peninsula' (2021) 11(1) *Scientific Reports* 15484.

40 Martin Mozny et al, 'Climate-Induced Decline in the Quality and Quantity of European Hops Calls for Immediate Adaptation Measures' (2023) 14(1) *Nature Communications* 6028.

FIGURE 9.2 Pale Czech lager.

been quick to present a case to the panel if they consider that domestic regulations were implementing some form of trade barriers. As the beer industry grows rapidly in size and revenue, many administrative and regulatory issues arise. Further, nations are realizing that brands are important and there is a need to protect certain brand names as originating from a specific country and not being associated with a foreign brew. That is where provisions of the Agreement on Trade-Related Aspects of Intellectual Property Rights (TRIPS agreement) come in handy. More importantly, the beer industry is growing in every other continent and many brews that are produced outside of Europe have done well. In accordance with the WTO's push for trade liberalization, the beer industry will continue to improve by leaps and bounds. The industry will always face challenges for health, environment, or even religious reasons, but beer is a resilient product that has stood the test of time. It has been a favourite drink through the ages and will be there deep into the future (Figure 9.2).

10

North America

From Making Love in a Canoe to a Vibrant Craft Brew Scene

10.1 INTRODUCTION

From full-bodied Double-IPAs with big, rich, complex maltiness and intense pine and tropical fruit flavours, to the flavourless and watery American light beers that Monty Python compared to making love in a canoe ('fucking close to water'),[1] the United States of America has given the beer world a highly diverse range of beer experiences. The contributions by its northern neighbour – Canada – are perhaps less well known, but they include, for example, the North American ice beer. And then there is the neighbour to the south – Mexico. Best known for the worldwide success of 'Corona', and, as we illustrated in Chapter 1, a true beer country in that beer amounts to no less than 85.3 per cent of the consumption of alcoholic beverages in the country.

Beer Consumption in North America

The beer consumption varies somewhat between the countries studied here. According to Statista's per capita volume sales in the beer market worldwide by country in 2023, while the consumption in the US and in Canada is almost identical (68.5 and 67.5 litres per capita per year respectively), Mexicans drink 59.5 litres per capita per year.

This chapter seeks to provide a brief overview of beer law and culture in North America (Canada, Mexico, and the USA). Much could be said, but we have opted to pay particular attention to a small selection of particularly interesting illustrations of beer law such as: the famous 'Prohibition' and the equally famous craft beer revolution.

[1] As referred to in 'Monty Python Live at the Hollywood Bowl', *IMDb* (Web Page) www.imdb.com/title/tt0084352/quotes/.

At a first glance, one might assume that these two phenomena are each other's opposite; after all, one is about people not drinking beer at all, and the other is about people drinking a particular 'category' of beers. But while the law during prohibition aimed to eradicate drinking, it may perhaps not be any great stretch to imagined that it sparked human creativity in those who still wanted a beer – or beer-like drink – and that this creativity may have carried over into the craft beer revolution.

So far so good. But as highlighted below, there is a missing step between prohibition and the craft beer revolution and that step is law related. What we are referring to is nothing less than what may be argued to be the second most important beer law in history (so far) after the much better-known German *Reinheitsgebot* – the catchily named 'HR Bill 1337 – An Act to amend the Internal Revenue Code of 1954 with respect to excise tax on certain trucks, buses, tractors, et cetera, home production of beer and wine, refunds of the taxes on gasoline and special fuels to aerial applicators, and partial rollovers of lump sum distributions'! But more about that later.

So let's begin.

10.2 BEER DRINKING IN NORTH AMERICA

The native population of what is now Canada, Mexico, and the United States of America produced fermented drinks – some of them beer-like – also prior to the arrival of Europeans. However, beer in a modern sense was introduced by European settlers and the beer culture has ever since been largely shaped by immigration.

Casey masterfully describes the development:

> For much of the first century after our founding, beer as an alcoholic beverage was a relatively minor player, with distilled liquors and hard ciders being our predominant beverages of choice. During this first century, 'American beer' overwhelmingly meant English-style ales, porters, stouts, pale ales, and India pale ales. But all that started to change when, beginning in the 1840s, lager beer was first brewed in the United States. Originally a beer produced by and for German immigrants from the 1840s through 1860s, this lager was the darker, sweeter, maltier, reddish-brown, all-malt Munich Dunkel style of beer. But then something profound took place when Pilsner-style lager beer was first brewed in the United States beginning the 1870s. This pale and translucent style of lager beer captured the imagination of the nation, so much so that by the 1890s it was routinely referred to in the press as the nation's 'national beverage'.[2]

Interestingly, a uniquely American style of lager soon developed that still dominates in North America today; that is, the American lager beer containing adjuncts such as rice and corn, creating a lighter beer with comparatively greater clarity (especially when served really cold, which was appreciated in the US). In fact, sources have

[2] Gregory Paul Casey, 'The Inspiring and Surprising History and Legacy of American Lager Beer' (2020) 57(1) *Master Brewers Association of the Americas Technical Quarterly* 9, 9.

FIGURE 10.1 Bavarian beer culture in Newport, Kentucky.

been found showcasing that already by 1912, 95 per cent of the beer sold contained unmalted cereals in varying proportions and other substitutions for malt, in addition to the malt.[3] And this market dominance must be viewed in the light of the half-century-long, maltster-driven assault on the adjunct lager industry between the 1870s and 1910s to impose an 'American Reinheitsgebot' requiring all-malt brewing (Figure 10.1).[4]

Given our focus on the interaction between beer and law, we may here pause and consider the fight for and against an 'American Reinheitsgebot' in some more detail. Doing so is especially enlightening in what it tells us about how lawmakers are being lobbied:

> a Washington D.C., lawyer and lobbyist by the name of H. W. Brelsford had sent letters to a selection of the larger, more prominent malting companies in the United States offering his services, for a mere $250 per firm, to 'agitate' on their behalf for

[3] Ibid 10.
[4] Ibid.

> the very legislation eventually drafted by Senator Wolcott and Representative Turner [what may be described as an 'American Reinheitsgebot']. Unfortunately for Brelsford, one of these firms, the Charles Ehlerman Hop & Malting Company of Saint Louis, conveniently forwarded their letter to the attention of the UBSA and President Miles, which Miles read verbatim to McKinley's committee. Included in this letter were nuggets like this one: 'In order to keep the matter entirely confidential, only a few leading maltsters, like your house, have been communicated with. If you will give $250, and the others in the same proportion, it will, together with what is already subscribed, give us a fund which, it is thought, will be sufficient.' The letter continues: 'The agitation in the press is already commenced, and we think public opinion will force it to a successful issue, and that, beyond the necessary counsel fees, expert testimony, printers' ink, etc., very little money will be required. You will appreciate the business reasons which make it inadvisable for the maltsters interested in this bill to meet and confer together.'

This was of course a big scandal, and the bill failed. In a way, the win against the 'American Reinheitsgebot' bill was only a temporary win for the brewing industry of that time, since Prohibition started only a few years later. However, the current market share of American adjunct lager beer is a direct result of that win.

The Volstead Act, or National Prohibition Act, came into force in 1920, marking the start of a period commonly referred to as the Prohibition era. Lobbying for the law had been underway for a long time, driven by the Women's Christian Temperance Union and the Anti-Saloon League. President Woodrow Wilson had vetoed the Act, but his veto was overridden by the Senate. The Volstead Act made it illegal to 'manufacture, sell, barter, transport, import, export, deliver, furnish, or possess' intoxicating beverages, defined as anything that contained more than 0.5 per cent alcohol (Canadian prohibition laws set the limit at 2.5 per cent).[5]

The impact on the brewing industry was felt long-term. Before Prohibition, there were about 1,500 breweries in the US.[6] While the Volstead Act was repealed in 1933, in the 1960s there were still fewer than 50 breweries in the US.[7] However, for lawyers interested in evaluating the efficiency of the Volstead Act, it may be noted that in New York, 'before Prohibition, there were 15,000 bars. After Prohibition, there were 32,000 speakeasies'.[8]

5 'The Senate Overrides the President's Veto of the Volstead Act', *United States Senate* (Web Page, 28 October 1919) www.senate.gov/artandhistory/history/minute/Volstead_Act.htm.

6 Emily Standlee, 'A Brewery without Booze: How Anheuser-Busch Pivoted to Survive Prohibition', *Feast Magazine* (Web Page, 31 May 2023) www.feastmagazine.com/bars/a-brewery-without-booze-how-anheuser-busch-pivoted-to-survive-prohibition/article_00cfc35e-fef2-11ed-9dd7-03c38231f703.html (not accessible in the EU area).

7 Charles W Bamforth, *Grape vs. Grain: A Historical, Technological, and Social Comparison of Wine and Beer* (Cambridge University Press, 2008) 54.

8 Ibid 53.

Before leaving the topic of Prohibition, it should be noted that even after the end of Prohibition in 1933, it remained illegal to allow Native Americans to purchase alcohol. That discrimination did not end until 1953.[9]

10.3 THE BEER MARKET AND STYLES OF NORTH AMERICA

According to statistics from April 2024, it is now a Mexican beer that is the best-selling beer in the United States. Modelo Especial tops the list, before Bud Light, Michelob Ultra, and Coors Light.[10] Nevertheless, the 'light/lite' segment clearly dominates, with six out of the top ten best-selling beers being light beers (Figure 10.2). So, what is a 'light beer', or 'lite beer' as some producers prefer to call it?

The problem is that there is no universally accepted definition. But put simply, light, or lite, beer is beer that is lower in calories than usual for a 'regular' beer. Consequently, any style of beer – dark or pale, ale or lager – can have a light version. Often, light beers are also lower in alcohol, but that is not a necessity. Like many other inventions, it has a complex and interesting history involving commercial failures and legal aspects.

Bamforth explains that a brewmaster (and biochemist) – Joseph L. Owades – at Rheingold breweries realized in the mid-1960s that people hesitated to drink beer out of a fear of gaining weight. To make a product that might be appealing to people with such concerns, he added an extra enzyme (amyloglucosidase) during the beer production. This led to all the starches being converted into ethanol during fermentation. The resulting stronger beer was then brought down to a lower alcohol level by adding water, and '[t]he result was a beer within the typical alcohol range, but possessing less residual starchy material and therefore lower calories'.[11] Starting in 1967, this beer was sold as 'Gablinger's Beer' and Owades was later crowned 'the Father of Light Beer'.[12] However, the beer itself was a flop and it has been noted that perhaps Gablinger's television advertisement 'showing a man with the girth of a sumo wrestler shoveling spaghetti into his mouth and downing a Gablinger's did little to help the cause'.[13] As noted by Dr Owades: 'Not only did no one want to try the beer, ... they couldn't even stand to look at this guy!'[14]

[9] Grace Lee-Weitz, '7 Indigenous Breweries to Support during Native American Heritage Month (and Forever)', *Hop Culture* (Web Page, 16 November 2021) www.hopculture.com/native-american-breweries-native-american-heritage-month/.

[10] Mike Snider, 'On National Beer Day 2024, the US is Drinking More Modelo than Bud Light as NA Brews Rise', *USA Today* (Web Page, 6 April 2024) www.usatoday.com/story/money/2024/04/06/national-beer-day-2024-history-facts-sales/73225409007/.

[11] Bamforth (n 7) 155.

[12] Adam Bernstein, 'Joseph Owades Dies at 86; The Father of Light Beer', *The Washington Post* (Web Page, 21 December 2005) https://truthinadvertising.org/wp-content/uploads/2014/10/Joseph-Owades-Dies-at-86-The-Father-of-Light-Beer.pdf.

[13] Ibid.

[14] Ibid.

FIGURE 10.2 Super Bowl beer advertisement.

Following the commercial failure of the Gablinger's Beer, Dr Owades obtained approval to share his formula with a friend at a Chicago brewery (Meister Brau brewery). The process for producing the resulting 'Meister Brau Lite' later ended up at Miller Brewing Company when it acquired Meister Brau in the early 1970s. The Miller Brewing Company first produced the well-known Miller Lite in 1975 and promoted it with the 'tastes great, less filling' marketing strategy, and the beer was a success.

The process Owades adopted was based on a patent filed by a Swiss scientist named Hersch Gablinger. Filed in the US in 1965 and published in 1968, that patent was for a method primarily aimed at producing a beer which would remain clear and free of haze for exceptionally long periods. The patent, however, noted that '[a]nother part of the invention is the resulting beer which along with that property has a significantly lower content of dextrins and other calories-providing substances in its real extract, in proportion to its alcohol content'.[15] It seems

[15] See United States Patent Office, 'Preparation of a Low Dextrin Beer by Using Amyloglucosidase' (Web Page) https://patentimages.storage.googleapis.com/b1/1d/aa/27af4dcab157c0/US3379534.pdf.

appropriate that Hersch Gablinger's image formed part of the design of the Gablinger's Beers.

The Canadian beer market is dominated by lagers such as Molson Canadian (part of Molson Coors), Labatt Blue (part of Belgian AB InBev), and Moosehead Lager (Canada's oldest independent brewery). However, one beer style is arguably Canadian – so-called ice beer. Put simply, ice beer is a beer that has undergone some degree of freezing after the fermentation. This process produces a potentially smoother, high-alcohol beer, since excess water is captured as ice and can be removed. The problem with calling this a Canadian style is of course that German brewers have a long history of producing 'ice beer' – most famously the 'Eisbock' (a style recognized in the Beer Judge Certification Program style guide).

Anyhow, Canadian ice beer is interesting not least due to the legal issues it sparked. To cut a long (and complex) story[16] short, in the early 1990s, both Labatt and Molson were working on ice beers. Labatt gained a patent for the production method for its Labatt Ice, but Molson Canadian Ice only just beat it to the market.

The race then began to launch ice beer on the US market. Labatt reached out to US brewing powerhouse Anheuser-Busch to negotiate a licensing agreement. However, Anheuser-Busch carefully considered both the option of licensing and the option of producing its own ice beer. In the end, Anheuser-Busch favoured the latter option and started selling its Ice Draft from Budweiser in October 1993, and soon after Labatt placed Labatt Ice on the US market. By then Molson's ice beer had already been on the US market since a few months earlier.

At the end of November 1993, Labatt sent a letter to Anheuser-Busch accusing them of trademark infringement and, in response, Anheuser-Busch started a legal process against Labatt. A jury found that the relevant terms ice, ice brewing, ice brewed, and ice beer are not trademarks. On appeal, the Eight Circuit commented that:

> the result of the nineteen-day battle between these beer-garden goliaths [in the District Court litigation] is this: Labatt has no trademarks in the ice terms, and A-B [Anheuser-Busch] recovered, in addition to its costs, one dollar (with interest accruing at a rate of 7.03% per annum) for Labatt's publication of injurious falsehood.[17]

So let us now look at the American styles included in the BJCP style guide. These span across all alcohol levels and all colours. From the American light lager to the heavy and strong American barley wine, and from American pale ale to the dark American stout. From modern styles such as hazy IPA to historic beers such as Kentucky Common. In fact, more than twenty-five American beer styles are

[16] Paul Kix, 'How David Fincher, Sharon Stone and a Bunch of Scheming Canadians Conspired to Create Ice Beer', *Thrillist* (Web Page, 23 July 2015) www.thrillist.com/drink/nation/the-insane-improbable-unbelievable-history-of-ice-beer.

[17] *Anheuser-Busch, Inc v John Labatt Limited*, 89 F 3d 1339 (8th Cir, 1996) 1343.

included in the BJCP style guide. In sharp contrast, the BJCP style guide does not include any distinct Canadian or Mexican beer styles.

But before leaving the topic of Mexican beer styles, there is a question that we cannot ignore – what is the connection between the beer style 'Vienna Lager' and Mexico? What makes this question so interesting is the fact that, while Vienna Lager was virtually dead in Europe, including in Austria, it was nevertheless blossoming in Mexico. Why is that? The most common answer to this has been to point to the fact that an Austrian – Maximilian I – was Emperor of the Second Mexican Empire from 1864 to 1867, and that he promoted the brewing of Vienna Lager.[18] However, that story has come under increasing scrutiny; after all, how do you brew a lager beer in a country with Mexico's weather conditions without refrigeration? The reality seems to be that the large-scale brewing of Vienna Lager-style beers came to Mexico via the US in the late 1800s, well after the execution of Maximilian I on 19 June 1867. And in fact, it has rightly been noted that the Mexican version seemingly devoid of the Vienna malt used for the original, and brewed with different water, different yeast, and with adjuncts such as rice and corn, has so little in common with the Austrian original that it should not be called Vienna Lager.[19]

10.4 THE CRAFT BREW REVOLUTION: BORN IN THE USA

If you look at the craft brew scene anywhere in the world, the strong US influence is both obvious and indisputable. This should not be dismissed by reference to the fact that many of the most well-known current craft breweries are US-based. The real reason is deeper and is found in the fact that it was the US that drove the craft beer revolution (Figure 10.3).

It is commonly noted that the craft beer industry originated in the United States in the 1960s, specifically when Fritz Maytag acquired the Anchor Steam Beer Company in 1965.[20] Maytag's achievements included things like reviving the classic American 'steam beer' style associated with Anchor Steam, brewing the first American India Pale Ale, bringing back traditional porter, reviving the custom of a spiced holiday beer, and creating the first American barley wine, and brewing the first American wheat beer since Prohibition:

> Maytag also recognized at the outset that his small operation could never match the cost efficiencies of modern, large-scale brewing facilities. To cover high per-unit production and packaging costs, he knew that his beer would have to sell at retail

[18] See, eg, Adrian Tierney-Jones (ed), *1001 Beers You Must Try before You Die* (Cassell, 2013) 194.

[19] Kevin Kain, 'Rethinking Vienna Lager in Mexico', *Casket Beer* (Web Page, 11 November 2020) www.casketbeer.com/home/2020/11/9/rethinking-vienna-lager-in-mexico.

[20] Sara R Jaeger et al, 'Preference Segments among Declared Craft Beer Drinkers: Perceptual, Attitudinal and Behavioral Responses Underlying Craft-Style vs. Traditional-Style Flavor Preferences' (2020) 82 *Food Quality and Preference* 103884.

FIGURE 10.3 Eliot Ness Amber Lager by Great Lakes Brewing Co.

> prices matching those of expensive imported brands. The task was to brew beer that would be worth the candle.[21]

And maybe this is exactly the essence of the craft brew scene – the small-scale production of a beer that stands out sufficiently to justify the higher retail price that comes with small-scale production. At any rate, what Maytag started, others soon followed. To give a few examples, McAuliffe created the New Albion Brewing Company in 1976, Grossman and Camusi founded the iconic Sierra Nevada Brewing Company in Chico, California, which opened its doors in 1981, and Koch started the Boston Beer Company with the Samuel Adams brand portfolio becoming the best-selling craft beer in the United States.[22]

Authors describing the history of the craft brew revolution also correctly point to the strong influence of the early promotors of craft beer such as Fred Eckhardt, Charles Papazian, and Michael Jackson:

> The stimulation of demand for craft brewing was achieved through the dissemination of information about (1) home brewing, which weaned many beer consumers

[21] Kenneth G Elzinga, Carol Horton Tremblay, and Victor J Tremblay, 'Craft Beer in the United States: History, Numbers, and Geography' (2015) 10(3) *Journal of Wine Economics* 242, at 246.

[22] Ibid 246–7.

> away from the lager products of Big Beer; (2) craft beer production; and (3) beer as a serious consumption good to be paired with food, rather than as a liquid that quenched thirst on a hot day or offered an inexpensive buzz.[23]

In addition, historians point to the beer innovators – the brewmasters – such as Professor Lewis, and the previously mentioned brewer-consultant Owades (who in addition to his pioneering work on light beers also made many contributions in the craft beer sector). Furthermore, it is commonly noted that brewing equipment, and for example bottling and canning equipment, in the early days of the craft brew revolution were aimed to meet the very different demand of the big beer brands, leaving the early craft brewers to 'build or cobble together equipment to brew in small batches'.[24] It is consequently no coincidence that many of the early craft brewers were skilled welders.

Perhaps then it may be said that, just as there are four key ingredients in beer, there were four main ingredient in the craft brew revolution: (1) brewery operators willing to risk going for a small-scale expensive product; (2) promoters raising the public's understanding and appreciation of beer beyond the big brands; (3) brewmasters with the skills to truly innovate; and (4) creative constructors of brewing equipment suitable for small-scale production.

However, the picture painted so far is incomplete. As so often is the case when it comes to beer, the law has also played a crucial role. First, one of the innovations of the craft brew industry was the creation of new beer styles often using – at the time – unconventional raw materials such as fruits and spices.[25] This would not have been possible had the 'American Reinheitsgebot' won the day some 100 years earlier.

Second, some commentators have noted that the craft beer industry was spurred by HR Bill 1337,[26] signed by President Jimmy Carter in 1978, to allow home brewing in the United States.[27] This hypothesis may be defended by reference to the fact that approximately 90 per cent of craft beer producers started their business at home.[28] Consequently, it seems that while the craft beer industry originated in the creativity

[23] Ibid 248.

[24] Ibid 251.

[25] Jaeger et al (n 20).

[26] HR1337 – An Act to amend the Internal Revenue Code of 1954 with respect to excise tax on certain trucks, buses, tractors, et cetera, home production of beer and wine, refunds of the taxes on gasoline and special fuels to aerial applicators, and partial rollovers of lump sum distributions. 95th Congress (1977–1978).

[27] See, eg, Julia Herz, 'The Roots of American Craft Brewing', *CraftBeer.com* (Web Page, 15 May 2014) www.craftbeer.com/craft-beer-muses/the-roots-of-american-craft-brewing; Ben Keene, 'The Oxford Companion to Beer Definition of Carter, James Earl, Jr', *Craft Beer & Brewing* (Web Page) https://beerandbrewing.com/dictionary/3WZc5lsyPY.

[28] See Travis Milburn and Favian Alejandro Guertin-Martín, 'Tapping into Environmental Harm in Brewing: An Exploration of Pollution and Waste in Beer Production' (2020) 28(3) *Critical Criminology* 407. See also Charlie Papazian, *The Complete Joy of Home Brewing* (William Morrow & Company, 3rd ed, 2014).

of certain brewers in the 1960s, the reason that it could develop into a craft brew revolution is found in the following legislative amendment from 1978:

> (c) BEER FOR PERSONAL OR FAMILY USE. – Subject to regulation prescribed by the Secretary, any adult may, without payment of tax, produce beer for personal or family use and not for sale. The aggregate amount of beer exempt from tax under this subsection with respect to any household shall not exceed –
>
> (1) 200 gallons per calendar year if there are 2 or more adults in such household, or
>
> (2) 100 gallons per calendar year if there is only 1 adult in such household.[29]

To fully understand this key provision, it should be noted that the Bill made clear that '"adult" means an individual who has attained 18 years of age, or the minimum age (if any) established by law applicable in the locality in which the household is situated at which beer may be sold to individuals, whichever is greater'.

At any rate, here we again see with great clarity the important role that the law has played in driving the direction of beer.

[29] An Act to Amend the Internal Revenue Code of 1954 with Respect to Excise Tax on Certain Trucks, Buses, Tractors, et Cetera, Home Production of Beer and Wine, Refunds of the Taxes on Gasoline and Special Fuels to Aerial Applicators, and Partial Rollovers of Lump Sum Distributions, Pub L No 95-458, 92 Stat 1255.

11

Why Tax Beer

What Has It Achieved?

11.1 INTRODUCTION

As it turns out taxing beer has achieved much more than you might think.

Beer has been taxed for almost as long as it has existed. There is evidence of beer being taxed or used to pay taxes from around 3000 BCE.[1] Early paintings, poems, and myths from ancient Mesopotamia show that beer was consumed regularly, almost as a daily dietary staple.[2] It was considered a 'democratic drink', since most people could afford it.[3] Beer was also easy to make, so there was lots of it. Consequently, it was an obvious target for taxation. Put simply, beer was likely to provide an adequate and reliable revenue source.

Clay tablets were used to record beer receipts and taxes paid. These taxes predated even coins and money and were paid in kind, including with beer. While only the beer was taxed in those very early days (rather than the ingredients or even the straws through which the beer was consumed), different parts of the brewing, distribution, and selling process became subject to tax over time. This chapter will begin by considering those taxes and how they were collected in Europe and England.

> The tax payable for burying a body in Mesopotamia was 'seven kegs of beer, 420 loaves, two bushels of barley, a wool cloak, a goat, and a bed presumably for the corpse' according to Oklahoma State University historian, Tania Sherlach.[4]

1 'Beers of Old', *Central European University* (Web Page, 16 June 2014) www.ceu.edu/article/2014-06-16/beers-old.

2 Joshua Mark, 'Beer in the Ancient World', *World History Encyclopedia* (Web Page, 2 March 2011) www.worldhistory.org/article/223/beer-in-the-ancient-world/.

3 Beers of Old (n 1).

4 Tonia Sherlach, 'How Old Are Taxes? Older than You Think', *National Geographic* (Web Page, 11 April 2024) www.nationalgeographic.com/history/article/160414-history-bad-taxes-tax-day.

Having collected all this money, how did the relevant authorities spend the taxes, and what did they achieve? Was it purely revenue raising to fund wars or gain power, or were there other reasons, such as behavioural regulation and health considerations? This chapter will also consider the impact of taxes on these topics before concluding with some current trends in taxing beer, including non-alcoholic beer.

11.2 TYPES OF BEER TAXES

Since brewing and selling beer is a multistage process, it allows the taxing of anything from the ingredients to production and selling, or all of these, but hopefully not all at the same time! While the most common tax is an excise tax (a tax on the sale of beer), other taxes have been imposed relating to beer.

11.2.1 *Licence Fees*

One of the early taxes was a 'flavouring licence' or 'Grutrecht' introduced in northern Europe in the Middle Ages.[5] The term comes from the word 'grut' (or 'gruit'), which, as we have discussed elsewhere, was a mixture of herbs used to flavour beer and to help preserve it. In other words, this was a tax on one of the ingredients that went into brewing beer. The amount of the tax was determined by the local authorities and imposed on brewers. Tax evasion was avoided as the exact formula for the grut was known only to the local authorities, and the brewers, mainly town brewers, were protected from competition as it was unlawful to brew beer without grut.[6]

A licence fee, while not strictly a tax, operated effectively as a tax since brewers could not produce and sell their beer without paying the licence fee and were subject to fines if they were caught selling without it.[7]

Later, when brewers began using hops instead of grut to brew beer, this revenue source was threatened, causing many local authorities in England and Europe to forbid the use of hops.[8] When it was finally accepted that hops were superior, the Grutrecht was abolished in favour of a general tax (or excise) on beer payable by all commercial brewers, regardless of the ingredients used.[9]

5 Eline Poelmans and Johan Swinnen, 'A Brief Economic History of Beer' in Johan Swinnen (ed), *The Economics of Beer* (Oxford University Press, 2011); Diana W Thomas, 'Deregulation despite Transitional Gains: The Brewers Guild of Cologne 1461' (2009) 140(3/4) *Public Choice* 329.

6 Poelmans and Swinnen (n 5).

7 Richard W Unger, *Beer in the Middle Ages and the Renaissance* (University of Pennsylvania Press, 2004) ch 12.

8 Ibid.

9 Diana W Thomas and Peter T Leeson, 'The Brewer, the Baker, and the Monopoly Maker' (2012) 1(1) *Journal of Entrepreneurship and Public Policy* 84.

11.2.2 *Taxes on Production (the Precursor to Excise Taxes)*

Another form of early taxation was a production tax. For example, in England, the Anglo-Saxon lords charged their tenants a small amount, known as a 'tolcester', for each jug or brewing vat (known as a 'sester', hence the name of the tax[10]) they brewed. By taxing production instead of consumption, the authorities were more likely to remain popular since the tax was 'hidden' and not objected to by consumers to the same extent.

Production taxes were also easier to police since there were fewer brewers, especially after the commercialization of brewing in the seventeenth and eighteenth centuries. Also, brewers received the protection of the authorities, so they were more cooperative than might be the case today. The tax impact of the protection afforded brewers is discussed later in this chapter.

11.2.3 *Fines That May as Well Be Taxes*

Since the production and sale of beer were always highly regulated, it was easy and very common to impose fines for non-compliance. By the thirteenth century, enforcement officers in England, known as 'aletasters', used to check each barrel of beer being brewed and 'enforcers' would bring offending brewers to court to be punished. Since virtually everyone who brewed beer was charged and fined, these fines were effectively a tax.[11] Similar systems were in use in many European towns during the Middle Ages.

11.2.4 *Import Duties*

Other taxes imposed by authorities were import duties on foreign beers. For example, in Leuven in the province of Brabant in 1547, imported beer was taxed at double the tax imposed on locally brewed beer. It was argued that since local brewers had already paid tax on production, this was merely to level the playing field.[12] However, it was also more noticeable to consumers, suggesting that even in the sixteenth century, governments preferred the 'locally made' approach.

Another more indirect effect of import duties occurs when, for example, in England, high import duties were imposed on French wine after the Nine Years' War.[13] This led to beer being considerably cheaper than wine in England, driving

[10] Mary Elizabeth Scott, 'A Herefordshire Nunnery, A Calendar, with Introduction, of the Aconbury Cartulary' (MPhil thesis, University of Southampton, 2001).

[11] Unger (n 7).

[12] Ibid.

[13] John Nye, 'Brewing Nation: War, Taxes, and the Growth of the British beer Industry in the Eighteenth and Nineteenth Centuries' in Johan Swinnen (ed), *The Economics of Beer* (Oxford University Press, 2011) ch 4.

up demand for beer. Although, at that time, wine imports from Portugal were allowed at considerably reduced wine tariffs, the lower quality of their wines did not win over the English; beer was still their preferred drink.[14] Obviously, the greater the demand, the greater the revenue obtained from beer taxes.

11.2.5 *Excise Taxes*

The beer industry was revolutionized when hops were introduced on a wide scale. Hops were easily obtainable, gave a better and more consistent flavour, and allowed beer to stay fresh for longer, enabling brewers to transport their beer to markets further afield. This resulted in the commercialization of brewing, thereby expanding the tax base and reducing the importance of monastic brewing.[15]

Excise taxes were already in place in the Netherlands (imposed in 1616),[16] and although they had been tried unsuccessfully in France, they were not widespread by the time excise taxes were introduced in England.[17] Despite being warned that introducing an excise tax on beer was 'the Devil's remedy', the Long Parliament introduced the first excise duties on beer in 1643.[18]

Earliest Excise Tax in Britian: Excise Ordinance 202-14 (22 July 1643)

The excise rates introduced were:

- Two shillings for every barrel of strong beer and ale sold for eight shillings or more, to be paid by the first retailer
- One shilling for every barrel of strong beer and ale sold for eight shillings or more for private use, to be paid by the first buyer (the same applied to private house-keepers who brewed their own beer and kept it for themselves)
- Two shillings for every barrel of ale or beer brewed and sold by any Alehouse-keeper to be paid by that Alehouse-keeper
- Six pence for [cheaper] beer sold for six shillings and consumed in private houses to be paid by the common brewer.

Excise taxes are considered to have a regulatory function as opposed to a production tax, but the effect can be the same.

As with any taxes, they are never simple or straightforward. The 'devil is in the detail'. This was true even when the first excise taxes were imposed. There were

[14] Ibid.

[15] Ibid.

[16] Unger (n 7).

[17] Henry Yeomans, 'Taxation, State Formation, and Governmentality: The Historical Development of Alcohol Excise Duties in England and Wales' (2018) 42(2) *Social Science History* 269.

[18] William J Ashworth, *Customs and Excise: Trade, Production, and Consumption in England, 1640–1845* (Oxford University Press, 2003) ch 6.

variations in the rates of tax payable depending on the quality of the beer or some other criteria (see the British Ordinance referred to in the box).[19]

Earlier variations can also be seen, for example in Holland in 1582, when the tax rates varied between 20 per cent on cheap beer and 100 per cent on expensive beer, where 'cheap' and 'expensive' referred to the quality of the beer rather than the price. Taxes on foreign beer were even higher, and some beer was exempt altogether for being of extremely low quality – 'thin' beer or 'scharbier'.[20]

It is not possible to correlate rates of excise tax on beer from medieval times with current values due to too many variables, but it is impressive to see what percentage of overall revenue they comprised. Between the mid fifteenth century and the early seventeenth century, reliance on taxes from beer in England and Europe was strong, if not critical, to the functioning of some towns.[21] In what is now Belgium, for example, it started from a relatively low 5 per cent of net income to as much as 70 per cent by the seventeenth century, while in the Netherlands, it started at 13 per cent, increased to 89 per cent, and then decreased back to just under 30 per cent. In Hamburg, Germany, the reliance on beer tax was much less – 4.6 per cent to almost 12 per cent, but no higher.[22] By 1780, beer taxes comprised about 40 per cent of government revenue in England.[23]

By comparison, direct taxes such as income tax superseded indirect taxes in importance from as early as the twentieth century and are far more important today;[24] only a very small percentage of the overall revenue generated was from beer excise taxes. For example, in Germany in 2022, beer excises raised only 0.07 per cent of total revenue; in England, in 2023, it was 0.44 per cent.[25]

11.2.6 *Exemptions*

Another common phenomenon with taxation is the exceptions and exemptions – there are always some. Interestingly, until the late fourteenth century, many of the brewers in Europe and England were monasteries which were not subject to any tax. They brewed their beer for their own consumption and for visiting pilgrims and the poor.[26] Beer was preferred over water as the water was frequently polluted, and the

[19] Charles Harding Firth and Robert Sangster Rait (eds), *Acts and Ordinances of the Interregnum, 1642–1660* (His Majesty's Stationery Office, 1911).

[20] Koen Deconinck, Eline Poelmans, and Johan Swinnen 'How Beer Created Belgium (and the Netherlands): The Contribution of Beer Taxes to War Finance during the Dutch Revolt' (2016) 58(5) *Business History* 694.

[21] Ibid.

[22] Ibid.

[23] Nye (n 13).

[24] Yeomans (n 17).

[25] Jan Conway, 'Annual Revenue from Beer Excise Duty in Germany from 2008 to 2022', *Statista* (Web Page, 2 May 2024) www.statista.com/statistics/447866/beer-excise-duty-revenue-germany/; D Clark, 'Tax Receipts in the United Kingdom from 2000/01 to 2023/24', *Statista* (Web Page, 3 July 2024) www.statista.com/statistics/284298/total-united-kingdom-hmrc-tax-receipts/.

[26] Poelmans and Swinnen (n 5).

beer complemented the monks' meagre diets while also being allowed to be consumed during fasting periods.[27]

Other examples of exemptions can be found in the Netherlands during the Middle Ages and the Renaissance. Decreased taxes were allowed so that sailors about to leave for overseas would buy the local beer rather than beer produced at the ports they visited.[28]

Today, we see exemptions for non-alcoholic beers, so the tradition lives on.

11.3 COLLECTION OF BEER TAXES

One of the reasons beer taxes have been so successful in Europe and England is due to the effective tax collection systems. Some of the earlier collection systems would be frowned upon today, but were probably effective at the time, such as the brewers having their right hands cut off if they didn't pay their taxes in Aix-la-Chapelle in France in the thirteenth century.[29] Later, more civilized methods were used to collect taxes. Comprehensive regulation of brewing, exemplified by the *Reinheitsgebot* or Purity Law in 1516, allowed local authorities to impose taxes and track beer production and distribution to safeguard their revenue source.

An example of the system that developed at the beginning of 1542 in Ghent began with a brewer having to request a 'ticket' from a tax collector before starting the brewing process. The ticket specified how much and what kind of beer would be brewed and when.[30] In 1543, tax collectors demanded weekly updates from each brewer so they could check if that brewer was complying with their allocated tickets. Buyers were also required to issue receipts and report quarterly so tax collectors could compare and check that sellers and buyers were telling the truth. Even the porters who delivered the barrels of beer from the brewers to the buyers had to have documentation that corresponded with the tickets and receipts. There was checking and double checking and plenty of fines for non-compliance or cheating.[31]

Not surprisingly, loopholes were found, and new regulations were passed to close them.[32] By the seventeenth century, tax regulation was incredibly complex, with every step of the production, selling and consumption of beer carefully monitored by tax officials (strict separation of beer making, beer transportation, and beer selling was one of the most effective devices to combat fraud).

In England, tax collection was made easy, too. When the first excise taxes were introduced in 1643, the legislation simultaneously introduced an administration

[27] Ibid.

[28] Deconinck, Poelmans, and Swinnen (n 20).

[29] Candida Moss, 'How Beer Ruled the Ancient World', *Daily Beast* (Web Page, 6 March 2021) www.thedailybeast.com/how-beer-ruled-the-ancient-world/.

[30] Unger (n 7).

[31] Ibid.

[32] Ibid.

system that would last over 200 years.[33] A Committee for Regulating the Excise was formed and was responsible for administering the system.

The Committee appointed and dismissed the excise officers (who were called sub-commissioners or farmers). They also acted as courts of appeal for taxpayers against fines and seizures and ensured the system functioned efficiently. It was a relatively stable system with a sense of continuity among the staff. For example, more than half of the clerks and accountants in the London Office in 1658 were still employed in 1661. Unlike in Europe, brewers in England were not required to use specific porters, but the Committee employed gaugers or tasters to taste the beer to determine the level of taxes required to be paid. Just as today, the excise officers had unprecedented powers to enter premises, question people under oath, and demand documentation.[34] While it was supposed to be a temporary tax, most taxes are not usually withdrawn once imposed.

Of course, with the invention of computers and data-matching, the process of collecting excise taxes today in Europe and England is one that early local authorities could only dream of, but the mechanics of recording, reporting, and paying tax have not really changed.

11.4 WHAT DID BEER TAXES ACHIEVE?

It is argued that beer taxes achieved several different goals over the centuries. Initially, the revenue raised from beer taxes was used to fund wars and secure power, but it has also been said to help the development of the nation-state and, more recently, to try and influence the moral and health behaviour of society.

11.4.1 *Revenue-Raising to Fund Wars*

The earliest reference to using beer taxes to fund wars seems to be from ancient Egypt. Cleopatra imposed taxes on beer, which she used to fund her wars with Rome.[35] The use of beer taxes to fund wars continued in a rather haphazard way during the Middle Ages. Taxes were raised by specific rulers for each battle. Rates varied depending on how much revenue was required.

During the fifteenth and sixteenth centuries, the nature and scale of warfare changed. Technical changes and innovations (such as cannons) led to different tactics. Armies had to surround cities and starve them into submission instead of quickly overrunning them as they had done in the past. This new approach took

33 D'Maris Coffman, 'Towards a New Jerusalem: The Committee for Regulating the Excise, 1649–1653' (2013) 128(535) *English Historical Review* 1418.

34 Ashworth (n 18).

35 Kelly Phillips Erb, '13 Quirky Beer and Tax Facts on National Beer Day', *Forbes* (Web Page, 7 April 2015) www.forbes.com/sites/kellyphillipserb/2015/04/07/13-quirky-beer-tax-facts-on-national-beer-day/?sh=61b1e10d4631.

much longer and therefore required more soldiers. Which, of course, resulted in higher costs that needed funding.[36] This was the start of a more structured system of beer taxes, which would provide that funding.

A good example can be seen in the Dutch Revolt. In the early years of the Dutch uprising in 1574, they faced a Spanish empire with a large and well-trained army financed by wealthy colonies in America. As the war continued, income from the colonies became unreliable, leading to sometimes long periods when Spanish soldiers went unpaid. This resulted in widespread discontent and many mutinies (on average, more than one per year). The confusion and chaos this caused was in complete contrast to the more disciplined Dutch. They recognized early on that they needed to secure finance for the war and developed an efficient taxation system to achieve this.[37]

The Dutch managed to increase their war budgets by 8.3 per cent per year between 1586 and 1600, thanks largely to taxes on beer. This enabled the Dutch to maintain a regularly paid and well-trained army. They did not suffer from the mutinies endured by the Spanish; in fact, the steady wages played a major role in maintaining soldiers' morale.[38] Their secret was their reliance on excise duties, primarily on beer. Ultimately, the Dutch defeated the Spanish, in no small part thanks to beer taxes.

Similarly, the first excise taxes in England were specifically justified by reference to the Civil War and the need to maintain the 'Forces raised for Defence', as referred to in the preamble of the 1643 Ordinance.[39] In fact, all the early increases in excise taxes in Britain correlated with its major military conflicts. For example, the introduction of hops duties in 1711 coincided with the War of the Spanish Succession, and a sharp increase in duties on beer, malt, and hops took place during the wars with Revolutionary and Napoleonic France (1792–1815).[40] Many have attributed Britain's success in these wars to the extra revenue generated by the excise tax on beer.[41]

The technical improvements and transformation from small-scale home brewers to a concentrated large-scale industry in the seventeenth and eighteenth centuries made the task of collecting beer taxes much easier.[42] For example – the number of brewers registered by the authorities in England was about 160–190 from 1684 to 1708, but by 1830 there were fewer than 100.[43]

36 Deconinck, Poelmans, and Swinnen (n 20).
37 Ibid.
38 Ibid.
39 Firth and Rait (n 19).
40 Yeomans (n 17).
41 Ibid.
42 Ibid.
43 Nye (n 13).

This resulted in such an increase in reliable revenue for the government that Britain was able to develop and maintain its army, and therefore its worldwide dominance, during the eighteenth and early nineteenth centuries.[44]

Even in the US, Congress imposed an excise tax on 'all beer, lager beer, ale, porter, and other similar fermented liquors' through the Revenue Act of 1862. It was signed into law by President Abraham Lincoln and used to help pay for the American Civil War.[45]

11.4.2 *Recognition of the State as a Governing Body through Protectionist Policies Granted in Exchange for Payment of Beer Taxes*

Another possible impact of beer taxes is to cement the strength of the state (or local authorities) as a ruling body.

In the Middle Ages and Renaissance periods, there was a clear overlap between local authorities and brewers in Europe. Since local authorities only controlled what happened in their towns, they could only impose taxes on beer produced and consumed within the town walls.[46] Country brewers escaped these taxes, but since, for a long time, beer brewed in the country was generally inferior, no one complained. However, after the introduction of hops into brewing, country beer improved and provided real competition for town brewers.[47] It was then that the symbiotic relationship between large town brewers and local authorities was realized. Local authorities wanted to minimize tax evasion and ensure their revenue streams, and the town brewers wanted to continue to be profitable without the competition from country brewers. To achieve this, local authorities often imposed restrictions on purchasing and consuming country-brewed beer. In some cases, consuming country-brewed beer was even prohibited.[48]

Realizing the importance of this relationship, many brewers became powerful members of local authorities. For example, between the fifteenth and eighteenth centuries, large brewers were members of town councils in Germany, Holland, and Scandinavia, such as the mayor of Leiden, who was a brewer in the mid fifteenth century.[49]

With the cooperation of the brewers in collecting and paying tax, large revenues were generated for local authorities, enabling them to protect their townsfolk and provide services. This provided the local authorities with the power to remain in

[44] Ibid.

[45] Kelly Phillips Erb, '15 Fun Facts about Beer and Taxes on National Beer Day', *Forbes* (Web Page, 7 April 2023) www.forbes.com/sites/kellyphillipserb/2023/04/07/15-fun-facts-about-beer-and-taxes-on-national-beer-day/.

[46] Unger (n 7).

[47] Ibid.

[48] Richard W Unger, 'Beer Production, Profits, and Public Authorities in the Renaissance' in Johan Swinnen (ed), *The Economics of Beer* (Oxford University Press, 2011) ch 2.

[49] Ibid.

charge. In other words, the concept of the state or local government may be traced, in part, to beer taxes.

In England, protection took a slightly different form. No attempt was made to protect urban brewers from their country colleagues. While in Europe, all the different local governments were responsible for imposing their own taxes, it was far more uniform in England. Taxation was considered a royal matter, and the Crown applied taxes which were applied to everyone, regardless of their location.[50]

Instead, the brewers united with the tax collectors, often buying the rights to collect the taxes on behalf of the government. For example, between 1665 and 1668, the trustees of the London Brewers' Company were responsible for collecting taxes in the greater London area.[51] Later, after the industrialization of the brewing industry and a further concentration of brewers, the government realized that it only had to negotiate with a few large brewers. It did this very successfully, granting protection in return for payment of taxes. Soon, the beer producers were so dependent on protection (in the form of higher taxes on wine and spirits and the prohibition of imported beer) that their cooperation in paying whatever tax was imposed was secured.[52] The beer producers received substantial profits in return for the payment of tax. This allowed for a stable and consistent increase in government revenues in England, allowing it to build its military power, expand and strengthen the Empire, and gain it recognition.[53]

While it is not possible to estimate the exact influence of beer taxes on the recognition of the state as a governing body, it may certainly be argued that there was a relationship between brewers paying taxes and the recognition or power of governments.

Given the democracies in place in Europe and England today, governments are unlikely to be so dependent on the revenue support of a particular industry to ensure their existence. Protectionist policies are more likely to target the safeguarding of local industry. For example, after joining the EU, Sweden was warned that it had to change its excise duties because wine was taxed more heavily than beer. The unsubtle reason was that beer was locally produced, and wine was largely imported, mostly from countries within the EU. This was considered discriminatory and contrary to the principles of the EU.[54]

11.4.3 *Beer Taxes' Influence on Behaviour and Health*

Historically, the major purpose of beer taxes was revenue-raising to fund wars and secure the power of governments, as discussed. While the behavioural impact of

50 Unger (n 7).
51 Ashworth (n 18).
52 Nye (n 13).
53 Ibid.
54 'Excise Duties: Commission Moves against Sweden over Tax Discrimination against Wine', *European Commission* (Press Release, IP/01/819, 12 June 2001).

beer has always been in the background, it is only relatively recently that beer taxes have been specifically used to try and influence peoples' behaviour and consequently their health.

As early as in ancient Egypt, Cleopatra recognized that beer caused 'public drunkenness'. Early communities also recognized that drinking too much beer led to general debauchery, adultery, and other undesirable behaviours.[55] For this reason and the need for governments to raise funds to protect their communities, a certain level of taxation was tolerated.

It appears that it was only after the need for war financing declined and societies prospered that the focus turned to more healthy living. Before the eighteenth century, the government's attitude in England had clearly been 'the more the merrier', with policies designed to promote licences for new pubs and beer houses, thereby increasing government revenue.[56] From the 1730s, the now-established government began restricting licences[57] and in 1830 the Beer Act abolished excise taxes on beer altogether.[58] Taxes on spirits increased in an effort to encourage Britons to drink more beer and avoid drinking spirits. It was thought that all bad behaviour from drinking came from spirits, not beer. Beer was thought to have beneficial properties that would improve the 'strength, health, and general behaviour of the population'.[59] With hindsight, and not unexpectedly, the poor behaviour continued, and beer taxes were reintroduced in 1880. However, for much of the nineteenth and twentieth centuries excise duties continued to be used to try and influence people's drinking behaviour.[60] By the twentieth century, the health issues became so obvious that they began to dominate over the need to raise revenue.

Clearly, beer taxes had not been successful in altering consumption in the nineteenth century. It was widely recognized, especially in the Nordic countries in the early twentieth century, that there was still a severe drinking problem. To combat these problems, governments in Scandinavia and the US took the extraordinary step of introducing prohibitions on some or all alcoholic drinks. Governments were prepared to completely forgo their tax revenue to try and improve their people's health and well-being. Finland, for instance, had prohibitions for as long as fifteen years, ending in 1932. The US imposed prohibition from 1920 to 1933. Norway had a partial prohibition, and Sweden narrowly avoided prohibition in 1922.[61] Although reductions in consumption during prohibitions suggested a possible health benefit, there were increases in other crimes, such as

55 Mark (n 2).

56 Nye (n 13).

57 Ibid.

58 Yeomans (n 17).

59 Ibid.

60 Ibid.

61 Robin Room (ed), *The Effects of Nordic Alcohol Policies: What Happens to Drinking and Harm When Alcohol Controls Change* (Nordic Alcohol and Drug Council No 42, 2002).

TABLE 11.1 *Comparison of taxes on alcoholic beverages in the Nordic countries, February/March 2000*

	Denmark	Finland	Norway	Sweden
Beer	0.47	1.46	2.33	0.87
Wine	0.97	2.40	5.13	3.22
Liquor	15.10	20.60	35.97	23.75

*Euros per litre of beverage with alcohol content of 5% for beer, 11% for wine and 40% for liquors. Extracted from Robin Room, 'The Effects of Nordic Alcohol Policies: What Happens to Drinking and Harm When Alcohol Controls Change', 2002 (Web Page) www.infocenters.co.il/ada/multimedia/full-pdf/nordic%20alcohol%20policies-2002-nad42.pdf.
Source: European Commission, Taxation and Customs Union, Excise Duty Tables, February/March 2000, quoted in CAN Report 2001. Converted into euros using the mean of the Swedish Bank's exchange rate for February/March 2000, 1 EUR = 8.4531 SEK.

smuggling and organized crime, which led to different health and behavioural problems.[62] It appears prohibition merely swapped one evil for another, making the loss of revenue not worthwhile.

When prohibitions were lifted in the Nordic countries, strict government controls were introduced, including price regulation and excise taxes. However, as beer was seen as the lesser evil of the other alcoholic drinks, lower taxes were imposed on beer compared with spirits and wine, and, in Finland and Sweden, beer could be purchased in supermarkets.[63] History repeated itself, and Sweden, once again, became a country of beer-drinkers. Table 11.1 makes it easy to understand why.

As we discuss elsewhere, Iceland went in the opposite direction, allowing wine and spirits but maintaining the ban on beer. At any rate, by the late twentieth century, it was accepted that beer taxes, when imposed, always raised revenue. In the past, this revenue achieved successes such as funding wars and strengthening governments. The lower rates of tax on beer compared with other alcoholic drinks, however, meant that the health and behavioural impacts of beer, which always simmered in the background, continued.

11.5 CURRENT TRENDS IN BEER TAXES

11.5.1 *Standardizing the Basis of Calculating Excise Taxes on Beer*

Huge changes in beer taxes took place in Europe with the formation of the European Union in 1992. No longer could countries rely on state-owned

62 Per Ole Johansen, 'The Norwegian Alcohol Prohibition: A Failure' (2013) 14(1) *Journal of Scandinavian Studies in Criminology and Crime Prevention* 46.

63 Room (n 61).

monopolies to regulate sales prices and high rates of taxes on wines to protect their locally brewed beer. Directive 92/84/EEC was issued with the aim of harmonizing, among other things, the excise duties on beer throughout the EU. Although initially wanting to have a standard tax rate common to all EU member states, this proved too difficult to reach a consensus on, and the Directive ended up requiring only a minimum rate of excise on beer. It was '€1.87 per hectolitre/degree of alcohol of finished product'[64] and it has not changed since then. This equates to about €0.03 per 330ml (11.2 oz) bottle of beer with a 5 per cent alcohol content.[65]

As you can see from Table 11.2,[66] very few member states charge the minimum. In fact, most countries, including the UK, levy much higher excise taxes on beer.

Further, excise duties are generally much higher in Europe and the UK than in the US, where the median US state rate of excise on beer in 2023 was $0.02 per 11.2oz bottle of beer with 5 per cent alcohol content.[67] For interest, the cheapest beer may be found in Wyoming and the most expensive in Tennessee.[68]

Excise duties are imposed in the US at both the federal and state levels and by some local cities or counties. In general, the duties are not imposed on the basis of alcoholic strength but rather on a categorical approach.[69] Beer, wine, and spirits are taxed differently. The rate is calculated based on ingredients and how the drink is produced. While this differentiation originally correlated roughly to alcohol by volume (on average, beers contained 5 per cent alcohol, wine 11 per cent, and spirits 40 per cent), due to recent innovations in the alcohol industry, with some beers having low or no alcohol, this way of imposing taxes seems limited.[70] While there have been suggestions that the US overhaul and simplify its tax system to bring it in line with Europe and the UK, this seems a faraway dream at present, despite the changes made by the Craft Beverage Modernization Act of 2020.[71]

The US could learn from the UK government. After the troubles caused by COVID-19, the Russian war on Ukraine, and a poor economic outlook, the UK government agreed in August 2023 to standardize the rates of excise duties on all alcoholic drinks to make them based on alcoholic strength only. There are still differing rates of excise on beer corresponding to increases in alcoholic strength, but these rates are the same for wine or spirits with the same alcohol content. This

[64] *Council Directive 92/84/EEC of 19 October 1992 on the Approximation of the Rates of Excise Duty on Alcohol and Alcoholic Beverages* [1992] OJ L 316/29, art 6.

[65] Adam Hoffer, 'Beer Taxes in Europe, 2023', *Tax Foundation* (Web Page, 19 September 2023) https://taxfoundation.org/data/all/eu/beer-taxes-in-europe-2023/#:~:text=EU%20law%20requires%20every%20EU,with%205%20percent%20alcohol%20content.

[66] Ibid.

[67] Ibid.

[68] Adam Hoffer, 'Beer Taxes by State, 2024', *Tax Foundation* (Web Page, 11 June 2024) https://taxfoundation.org/data/all/state/state-beer-taxes-2024/.

[69] Adam Hoffer, 'Modernization of the Alcohol Tax', *Tax Foundation* (Web Page, December 2023) https://taxfoundation.org/wp-content/uploads/2023/12/FF826.pdf.

[70] Ibid.

[71] Ibid.

TABLE 11.2 *Beer taxes in Europe and the UK, July 2023*

Ranking	Country	Excise duty per 330ml (11.2oz) beer bottle at 5% abv.	
		€	**US$**
1	Finland	0.63	0.66
2	United Kingdom	0.40	0.42
3	Ireland	0.37	0.39
4	Sweden	0.32	0.34
5	Estonia	0.21	0.22
6	Greece	0.21	0.22
7	Slovenia	0.20	0.21
8	Lithuania	0.14	0.15
9	Latvia	0.14	0.14
10	France	0.13	0.13
11	Netherlands	0.13	0.13
12	Italy	0.12	0.13
13	Denmark	0.11	0.11
14	Cyprus	0.10	0.10
15	Portugal	0.09	0.09
16	Croatia	0.09	0.09
17	Poland	0.08	0.09
18	Belgium	0.08	0.09
19	Austria	0.08	0.09
20	Malta	0.08	0.08
21	Hungary	0.07	0.07
22	Slovakia	0.06	0.06
23	Czech Republic	0.05	0.05
24	Romania	0.04	0.04
25	Spain	0.03	0.03
26	Luxembourg	0.03	0.03
27	Germany	0.03	0.03
28	Bulgaria	0.03	0.03

Note: Some countries levy reduced excise duties for independent small breweries. The excise duties were converted into USD using the average 2022 USD–EUR exchange rate (0.951), see IRS, 'Yearly Average Currency Exchange Rates' (Web Page) www.irs.gov/individuals/international-taxpayers/yearly-average-currency-exchange-rates. See also Adam Hoffer, 'Beer Taxes in Europe, 2023', *Tax Foundation* (Web Page, 19 September 2023) https://taxfoundation.org/data/all/eu/beer-taxes-in-europe-2023/#:~:text=EU%20law%20requires%20every%20EU,with%205%20percent%20alcohol%20content. See also 'Taxes in Europe Database v4', *European Commission* (Web Page) https://ec.europa.eu/taxation_customs/tedb/#/home; 'Tax on Shopping and Services', *Gov.UK* (Web Page) www.gov.uk/tax-on-shopping/alcohol-tobacco.

correlates with the perceived increases in harm and cost of mitigation caused by increases in alcohol levels.[72]

While harmonization is impossible across the EU, revenue is skewed by the differing excise rates. With the ease of free movement within the EU and lack of

[72] Ibid.

import duties, people can source cheaper beer in other member states, thereby reducing the revenue that goes to their home country.[73] This has led to a somewhat comical situation in which, for example, it is common for Norwegians to go to Sweden to buy beer, Swedes travel to Denmark to buy cheaper beer, Danes get beers from Germany, Germans from Poland, and so on. Or take, for example, the differences in excise duties on beer in Ireland and Germany. The excise duties imposed on beer in Ireland are 11.4 times higher than those in Germany. This would translate into a pint of stout purchased at a bar or pub being 60 cents cheaper in Ireland if German excise and VAT rates were applied compared to Irish rates. Assume a price of €5.77 (May 2024); this would make the stout 10.4 per cent cheaper at €5.17. A similar result applies to lager purchased in a bar or pub.[74]

There are obviously other variables affecting government revenue from excise duties, such as overall consumption and economic prosperity, but it may be suggested that some harmonization and simplification of excise duties in Europe and the US, respectively, are goals that should be at the forefront of tax policy in the future.

11.5.2 *Variation of Excise Rates*

So far, much of this analysis has relied on traditional beer containing 5 per cent alcohol content by volume (abv) and sold in bottles or cans. However, there have been, and still are, significant variations in the alcohol content of different beers and between draught vs bottled beer and differences arising from craft beer. These differences have also played out in the imposition of excise taxes.

11.5.2.1 Draught Beer

Draught beer is defined as beer served on tap in pubs and alehouses. Of course, all beer was originally sold in draught. While glass bottles began being used in the seventeenth century, the commercialization and widespread use of glass bottles and cans for beer did not begin until much later. This means that early excise taxes on beer were, in effect, on draught beer. It was only in the early twentieth century that the demand for bottled beer increased. It is speculated that as more and more factories developed, their workers preferred bottled beer as it was considered too difficult to bring jugs or glasses of beer from nearby inns to the factories. Building workers also realized their thirst could be quenched regularly by a bottle of beer kept in their pockets.[75]

[73] Anthony Foley, *International Comparisons of Irish Alcohol Excise Taxation in the European Union and the UK in 2024* (Research Report, July 2024).

[74] Ibid.

[75] Mikuláš Teich, 'The Mass Production of Draught and bottled beer in Germany 1880–1914' in Terry Gourvish and Richard Wilson (eds), *The Dynamics of the Modern Brewing Industry* (Taylor & Francis, 2003) 75.

It is not known what exactly the cause was, whether it was the change in drinking habits or the fact that excise duties were imposed on factors other than alcohol content, but there was certainly a difference in excise taxes on draught beer from very early on. It may have been cheaper to serve draught beer as there was less processing required and little packaging (casks or barrels were used to store the beer before selling as opposed to lots of glass bottles or cans).[76] Whatever the reason, it has been a feature of excise taxes on beer for much of the last century that lower rates applied to draught beer. Even the most recent major change in England in August 2023 to how excise taxes are imposed contained a retention of the 'Draught Relief'. Draught beer was previously taxed at 5 per cent less than other beer and, if eligible, draught beer will now be taxed at 9.2 per cent less than the tax on other beer. This should result in a pint of beer becoming cheaper by up to 11 pence (or 14 cents) if the full benefit is passed on to consumers.[77]

11.5.2.2 Craft-Brewed Beer

During the Middle Ages, the country-brewed beer would probably be the equivalent of today's craft-brewed beer. At that time, due to a lack of jurisdiction and probably also the small size of the country brewing industry, taxes were not imposed on country brewers in Europe, although some taxes were still imposed in England. With the industrialization and commercialization of the brewing industry in the nineteenth century, as already mentioned, these smaller country brewers were commonly pushed out of the market in favour of monopolies and oligopolies.

With the encouragement of governments in England and Europe, especially northern Europe, beer production and consumption increased throughout the seventeenth and eighteenth centuries. It is believed that beer consumption peaked globally in the mid 1970s, although it has since decreased.[78] While consumption may have declined in the last fifty years, societies in Europe, the UK, and the US have become wealthier and more concerned with living a healthier life. There has been a shift in the ambitions of beer drinkers from quantity to quality, leading to a revival of the craft brewing industry.[79] This has been made worthwhile for craft brewers since the excise taxes on craft-brewed beer are up to 50 per cent less than on regular beer. EU Directive 92/83/EEC allowed member states to group beer into

[76] See 'What Is Draught or Draft Beer? Everything You Need to Know', *Beer & Wine Guide* (Web Page, 18 April 2023) https://beerandwine.guide/beer/what-is-draught-or-draft-beer-everything-you-need-to-know/.

[77] HM Treasury, 'Chancellor Unveils a Budget for Growth', *Gov.UK* (Web Page, 15 March 2023) www.gov.uk/government/news/chancellor-unveils-a-budget-for-growth.

[78] Kym Anderson, 'The Emergence of Lower-Alcohol Beverages: The Case of Beer' (2023) 18(1) *Journal of Wine Economics* 66.

[79] Ibid; Dimiter Toshkov, '30 Years of Socio-Economic Developments in Central and Eastern Europe', *Dimiter Toshkov* (Web Page, November 2019) www.dimiter.eu/Visualizations_files/CEE.html.

categories and apply different rates of excise tax for each category. Reduced rates below the minimum rate could be applied to small craft breweries which produced less than 200,000 hectolitres of beer per year, provided similar concessions applied to small craft wine and spirit makers.[80]

In EU Directive 92/84/EEC, craft brewers or independent small breweries were defined as 'a brewery which is legally and economically independent of any other brewery, which uses premises situated physically apart from those of any other brewery and does not operate under licence'.[81] A similar regime applies at the federal level in the US. Small domestic brewers who produce less than 2 million gallons of beer a year are entitled to reduced rates of excise on the first 60,000 gallons of beer they produce.[82]

Despite the recent increase in craft beer consumption, there does not appear to be any appetite for increasing excise taxes on this type of beer. Perhaps tax policymakers believe they have the correct balance between raising revenue and controlling consumption to reduce harm to health and behaviour.

11.5.2.3 Low- or No-Alcohol Beer

Another area that has developed, almost as an extension of the craft-brewing industry (and probably for similar reasons), is the development of the low- and no-alcohol sector.[83] Ever since excise duties were imposed on alcohol content, these beers have attracted little or no tax, making them cheaper and more attractive, not just for health reasons. As with prohibition, governments are prepared to forgo revenue on these products in return for the reduced costs from all forms of harm that would hopefully follow.

In Europe, Directive (EU) 2020/1151 amends Directive (EU) 92/83/EEC in a significant way. It was noted in the preamble of Directive (EU) 2020/1151 that the permitted reduced rates for low-strength beer were insufficient to provide any 'tangible incentive' for brewers to be innovative and create new low-strength products. Additional encouragement was needed, so the threshold for applying reduced rates was raised from the previously set 2.8 per cent maximum alcohol by volume to 3.5 per cent from 1 January 2022.[84]

The brewing industry appears to have embraced these incentives as new technologies have been developed to allow lower-alcohol beers to still have the same

80 *Council Directive 92/83/EEC of 19 October 1992 on the Harmonization of the Structures of Excise Duties on Alcohol and Alcoholic Beverages* [1992] OJ L 316/21, art 4.1.

81 Ibid art 4.2.

82 *Craft Beverage Modernization Act (CBMA).*

83 Anderson (n 79).

84 Council Directive (EU) 2020/1151 of 29 July 2020 Amending Directive 92/83/EEC on the Harmonization of the Structures of Excise Duties on Alcohol and Alcoholic Beverages [2020] OJ L 256/1, art 1.2.

flavours as regular strength beers.[85] This is providing new markets for beer producers, which had seen declines in demand for their full-strength beers, and with cheaper prices due to lower excise taxes, it is a win–win for both producers and consumers.

11.6 OTHER TAXES: VAT

In addition, all European countries and the UK also levy a value-added tax (VAT). However, this tax is imposed on a value or price basis per product, regardless of what it is. Since VAT is mostly uniform across all alcoholic beverages, this does not impact beer other than an overall price increase, which is the same for all wine and spirits. There are some variations; for example, lower VAT rates are imposed on draught beer in the Czech Republic (10% instead of the standard rate of 21%) and Romania (5% instead of the standard rate of 19%).[86] Beer sold in bars and restaurants can also sometimes be subject to reduced VAT rates. In Italy and Spain, a 10 per cent VAT rate is applied instead of their standard rates of 22 and 21 per cent, respectively.[87] In the US, there is no federal VAT because each state imposes its own.

11.7 CONCLUSION

Taxes on beer have been around forever and are here to stay, but at least now they are no longer the dominant income source for governments, nor are they being relied upon to fund war efforts. Thanks to innovation in the industry, wealthier societies, and concern for healthy living, beer taxes are now imposed in a far more nuanced way compared to 1643. As craft brewing re-establishes itself around the world, and high-quality low- and no-alcohol beers are developed, beer taxes will continue to be tweaked to strike a balance between health and welfare, revenue-raising, and a free market.

Interestingly, it may be speculated that social media, for all its faults, may be achieving something positive. Firstly, since meeting others is commonly conducted over various social media platforms in a virtual context (as opposed to in person), young people do not need alcohol to relax or boost their courage to converse.[88] Secondly, since it is so easy to be photographed or videoed behaving badly when drunk and to have those photos or videos uploaded for future employers, the media, the public, or even prospective partners (or indeed prospective mothers-in-law!) to see, the younger generation is turning to lower- and non-alcoholic drinks to avoid

[85] Anderson (n 79).
[86] Foley (n 74).
[87] Ibid.
[88] Jari Luomanen and Pertti Alasuutari, 'The Rising Social Media and Declining Alcohol Use: The Case of Finnish Teenagers' (2022) 49(2) *Contemporary Drug Problems* 213.

this and secure their futures.[89] This, of course, will reduce government revenues but, as suggested earlier, will hopefully also reduce healthcare costs, so overall there may be a net gain – one can only hope.

To come back to the question posed in the title of this chapter – why tax beer? – the answer is simple: it provided large amounts of revenue, which helped establish the dominance of certain rulers and governments in the early years, and more recently has been used to fund health care to cover some of the adverse costs of over-drinking. Most importantly, current excise taxes on beer are not motivated by revenue raising as much as they are about attempting to influence people's behaviour towards a more peaceful and healthy society.

[89] Robin Room et al, 'Supranational Changes in Drinking Patterns: Factors in Explanatory Models of Substantial and Parallel Social Change' (2020) 28(6) *Addiction Research & Theory* 467.

12

British and Irish Beer Traditions

12.1 INTRODUCTION

Britain and Ireland are nations of beer drinkers, both historically and today. Many traditions have been built over the centuries and will be discussed here.

Beer has been described in Britain both positively and negatively, but overwhelmingly positively. Phrases such as beer being 'a necessity', 'a dietary staple[1]', 'an essential commodity' and 'a moral species of beverage'[2] are all attributed to beer in Britain, while sometimes beer is described negatively as the 'root cause of multiple social problems'[3] such as drunkenness and debauchery.[4] Regardless, beer has always been a part of the national identity of Britain and Ireland.

Beer Consumption in Britain and Ireland

According to Statista's per capita volume sales in the beer market worldwide, by country in 2023, the beer consumption in Ireland is 66 litres per capita per year. The equivalent figure for the United Kingdom is 56 litres per capita per year.

While governments have regulated brewing, banned hops, imposed taxation, protected the industry, and promoted it, the good people of Britain and Ireland have continued to drink beer. Despite declining consumption since 1980, it was still

[1] Henry Yeomans, 'Taxation, State Formation, and Governmentality: The Historical Development of Alcohol Excise Duties in England and Wales' (2018) 42(2) *Social Science History* 269.

[2] Lord Brougham famously described beer in this way in the House of Commons during the debate on the Beer Act 1830 (ibid).

[3] Yeomans (n 1).

[4] Nicholas Mason, '"The Sovereign People in a Beastly State": The Beer Act of 1830 and Victorian Discourse on Working-Class Drunkenness' (2001) 29(1) *Victorian Literature and Culture* 109.

the number one drink in Britain in 2023 with 36.1 per cent of beer drinkers compared to 33.7 per cent of wine drinkers.[5]

12.2 GOVERNMENT INTERFERENCE: THE BEER ACT OF 1830 AND BEYOND

Historically, governments have always regulated the beer and malt industries, but the Beer Act of 1830 is regarded as the single most dramatic change in the beer industry. The Wellington government abolished excise taxes on beer but retained them on malt and hops. The legislation also opened up the licensing regime, allowing anyone to apply for a selling licence (on or off premises) provided they paid the requisite fee.[6] The cost of this change was a whopping £3 million a year (in 1830).[7]

The problem was that there had been a slump in beer consumption with a commensurate increase in consumption of spirits. There was also an impending election for the Wellington government and the deterioration of the health of George IV, so they took a popular decision to reform the beer industry and free up trade in beer.[8]

The 'beer-is-best; best-for-health, best-for-Britain' campaign had gained momentum in the decade prior to the passing of the Beer Act of 1830.[9] Despite all the criticism, such as from the Chief Constable of Lancashire in 1849, who referred to the beer houses (pubs) as 'the most serious social evil of the day',[10] the expected debauchery and crime did not eventuate (at least not after the first few weeks of drunken celebrations). The small brewers and beer house owners did not have the resources to purchase licences and produce large enough quantities of beer to sustain a business or provide any real competition to the large commercial brewers. Instead of a revolution in the beer industry, the larger commercial brewers were provided with opportunities to acquire the more successful smaller breweries.[11] The status quo returned when beer excises were reintroduced in 1880, with taxes on malts and hops being abolished instead.

During the nineteenth century, there was strong and continuous growth in the beer industry. This was partly due to the Beer Act of 1830 but also because of all the

5 James Evison, 'Drinking Habits Shift as UK Changes from Beer to Wine', *The Drinks Business* (Web Page, 27 November 2023) www.thedrinksbusiness.com/2023/11/drinking-habits-shift-as-uk-changes-to-wine-from-beer/.

6 TR Gourvish and RG Wilson, *The British Brewing Industry 1830–1980* (Cambridge University Press, 2008).

7 Yeomans (n 1).

8 Gourvish and Wilson (n 6).

9 Ibid.

10 Ibid.

11 Mason (n 4).

innovations such as lagering, isolating different strains of yeast, refrigeration, the use of glass bottles, and the ability to control the stability of beer once bottled.[12]

This was followed by a decline in the first half of the twentieth century – due to World War I and World War II. There was a growth period between 1950 and 1980 – 1980 being regarded as the high point of the beer industry. Consumption declined again from 1980 and has really only picked up with the new low- and no-alcohol beers and the growing craft beer industry.[13]

12.3 BEER TODAY

Today, Britain still has a thriving beer industry. In 2023, the beer and pub industry employed over 900,000 people and contributed £34 billion to the UK economy.[14] This highlights the importance of brewers and pubs to the British economy. The beer industry provides substantial employment especially to young people, contributes to economic growth, and improves the health and well-being of society by creating friendly environments for all communities to come together and socialize.[15]

British beer styles such as bitter and porter are well-known around the world. The same is true for Irish stout – not least due to the remarkable success of Guinness. Scottish beer styles are commonly 'weaker, sweeter, darker, lower in attenuation, and less highly hopped compared to equivalent modern English beers',[16] and are less known internationally. As might be expected, beer styles from Britain and Ireland featured prominently in the 2021 Beer Judge Certification Program style guide. In fact, there are no fewer than twenty-three beer styles from Britain and Ireland; British, Scottish, and Irish styles even have their own categories.

So how did we develop all these different beers?

12.4 THE COLOUR OF BEER (THE SPECTRUM AS DETERMINED BY THE MALTING INDUSTRY)

Beers may be differentiated based on their colour. The various colours of beer, from light to dark, are determined by the malting process. As is commonly the case internationally, brewing and malting have been separate industries in Britain for

[12] Eline Poelmans and Johan Swinnen, 'A Brief Economic History of Beer' in Johan Swinnen (ed), *The Economics of Beer* (Oxford University Press, 2011).

[13] Ibid.

[14] British Beer and Pub Association, 'Written Evidence Submitted by the British Beer and Pub Association', *UK Parliament* (Web Page, October 2022) https://committees.parliament.uk/writtenevidence/112003/pdf/.

[15] 'The Beer and Pub Manifesto 2024', *British Beer and Pub Association* (Web Page) https://beerandpub.com/policy-campaigns/manifesto-2024/.

[16] 'BJCP Style Guidelines', *Beer Judge Certification Program* (Web Page, 18 May 2023) www.bjcp.org/bjcp-style-guidelines/.

centuries, although they are symbiotic. Beer and malt have been produced in Britain, it is thought, since Neolithic times and definitely since Roman times.[17]

Malting began with small farmers steeping sacks of barley in streams to allow germination. Although barley was the most common grain used, other cereals were also used across Britain.[18]

After steeping or soaking, barley was then dried in small kilns over a stove.[19] Of course, this was a rather 'hit and miss' affair regarding the quality of the beer made using these malts. However, by the mid fourteenth century, the malting process had been refined, and malt could be graded as high or regular. It was only by the mid eighteenth century that malt was classified according to pale, amber, and brown. Pale and amber malt was made using coke in the drying process, whereas brown malt was dried using wood, straw, or ferns. It was these different types of malt that gave rise to the different colours of the beer. For example, a lightly roasted malt will produce a pale beer, whereas a deep or heavily roasted malt (that is, at higher temperatures or for longer) will produce a darker beer.[20] The English revolution of the malting process had impacts globally, making possible the lighter beers famously created by Josef Groll (the Czech Pilsner Urquell) and Anton Dreher (Austria's Vienna-style lager).

Later, as malthouses developed, floor malting was used to malt larger quantities of barley. This required a heavily labour-intensive process of turning the barley manually to reduce heat buildup and aerate the grain. Repeal of the malt tax in 1880 (when beer taxes were reintroduced – see Chapter 11) also included deregulation of the malting process. Couching was no longer required, and different methods of steeping were permitted.[21] With the consolidation of brewers in the nineteenth century, the malting industry was industrialized, and the process known as 'pneumatic malting' was developed.[22]

These days the malting process is much better understood, and the equipment available more sophisticated, allowing a nuanced approach to malting to reach the required colour for the particular beer being produced.

12.5 WHAT'S IN A NAME? ALES VS BITTERS VS LAGERS VS BEER

There appears to have been much confusion over the nomenclature of beers. Should they be called 'ales' or 'bitter' or just plain 'beer'?

[17] Amber Patrick, *The Buildings of the Malting Industry: The Production of Malt from Pre-history to the 21st Century* (Liverpool University Press, 2023).

[18] 'History of the Malting Process', *Great Western Malting* (Web Page) www.greatwesternmalting.com/process/history-of-the-malting-process/#:~:text=Great%20Western%20Malting%20-%20Read%20about.

[19] Ibid.

[20] 'Malt', *All About Beer* (Web Page) https://allaboutbeer.com/learn/beer/malt/.

[21] Patrick (n 17) 2.

[22] See History of the Malting Process (n 18), which notes that pneumatic malting was made possible by two Belgian inventions – the aerated rectangular box by Galland and the turning machine by Saladin.

One possible answer comes from the ingredients used to make beer. Ale (or 'old beer') used to be flavoured with a range of herbs and spices but not hops. Ale was made this way until after the Hundred Years War between France and England (1337–1453)[23] when hops were finally allowed to be used. Initially hops were imported until, in about 1520, they began being cultivated in Kent.[24] Beer made with hops was considered 'beer' or 'hopped beer' (ale was 'unhopped'). Both types of beer continued to be brewed and consumed in Britian. It is not known exactly when unhopped ales became unpopular, but it is thought to have been in the eighteenth century. It is also not clear when hopped beer started to be called 'ale'.[25] What is clear is that 'bitter' is an English style of pale ale that varies in colour from gold to dark amber and is the beer most likely to be served in pubs when a customer asks for a 'pint'.

As noted in Chapter 1, a clearer distinction is made between 'ale' and 'lager' because of the differences in the fermentation process. Beer produced using the 'lager' method was referred to as the 'new' beer or cold lager, whereas the ale retained its name or was referred to as bitter.

This was another confusion in the terminology. What was the difference between 'ale' and 'bitter'? It is suggested that this was purely a matter of language usage. Customers in pubs used to refer to 'ale' as 'bitter' because they could not tell the difference between the different taps of beer on offer. At that time, all beer was sold as draught (or on tap), but there were no labels back then. Instead, customers differentiated the 'taps' by reference to the taste of the beers – bitter for ale and sweet for lager.[26]

Brewers still referred to them as pale ales but as customers continued to call them 'bitters', the term caught on and most brewers now include at least one bitter among their collection. The terms 'ales' and 'bitters' are now interchangeable, although the British public seems to have referred to pale ales as 'bitter' since early in the nineteenth century.[27]

12.6 WARM OR COLD BEERS? WHAT IS THE CORRECT TEMPERATURE TO SERVE A BEER?

Well, the answer depends on the type of beer.

Since bitters or ales are brewed using the top, warmer and faster, fermentation process, they should be drunk fresh, preferably by the pint (not sipped). They are,

[23] Poelmans and Swinnen (n 12).

[24] 'British Beer History', *Beer Day Britain* (Web Page) www.beerdaybritain.co.uk/history/#:~:text=The%20earliest%20mention%20of%20beer%20being.

[25] Ibid.

[26] 'Search the Oxford Companion to Beer', *Craft Beer & Brewing* (Web Page) https://beerandbrewing.com/dictionary/.

[27] 'British Beer History' (n 24).

therefore, best served at cellar temperature, 11–14°C (50–55°F).[28] This does not make them 'warm and flat', as some foreigners who prefer ice-cold beers would suggest, but is a product of their brewing process.

In contrast, since lagers use a cold, bottom fermentation process, they should arguably be served colder so as not to spoil the beer.

12.7 BUYING A ROUND: GENEROUS OR JUST EFFICIENT?

Another tradition that seems to be prevalent in British pubs is the concept of 'buying a round'.[29] Since there is rarely table service in pubs, and pubs are often small and can easily become crowded, it is easier if only one member of a group goes to the counter to order drinks. This is a great custom that ensures everyone is paying roughly the same amount and is seen as being friendly and generous. It is not essential that you have the same number of rounds as there are people in your group; this custom of buying a round can take place over several visits to the pub. There are also exceptions; for example, if the boss is paying, then it is acceptable to let them pay.[30]

12.8 GUINNESS: A REMARKABLE SUCCESS STORY

Ireland, like Britain, has a long history of brewing. It began with the Celtic tribes making mead and, as in Europe, was continued by the monks in their monasteries during the Middle Ages. Its most famous beer is, of course, the delicious, dark Guinness.

Arthur Guinness, the remarkable brewer behind this renowned beer, began his career in 1759 when, at the age of thirty-four, he used an inheritance to buy a 9,000-year lease of a disused brewery, St James's Gate, in Dublin for an annual rent of £45. From there, Arthur Guinness went on to build the global brand that we know as Guinness.[31]

Initially, Arthur Guinness began making ale and table beer and then, sometime in the 1770s, he began brewing a new type of English beer – called porter.[32] By 1796 the records show that Guinness was brewing both porter and an ale which used less malt and hops and was considered a weaker beer.[33] However the brewery went through hard times, and when Arthur Guinness II took over after the death of his father in

28 'Search the Oxford Companion to Beer' (n 26).

29 'The Custom of Buying a Round', *Britain Explained* (Web Page) https://britainexplained.com/the-custom-of-buying-a-round/.

30 Ibid.

31 'Guinness through the Ages: The Story of Guinness', *Guinness Storehouse* (Web Page) www.guinness-storehouse.com/en/discover/story-of-guinness.

32 Ibid.

33 Patrick Lynch and John Vaizey, *Guinness's Brewery in the Irish Economy 1759–1876* (Cambridge University Press, 1960) ch 4.

1803, he changed the famous recipe to include unmalted roasted barley instead, as it was not subject to malt tax.[34] This gave the porter or stout a unique taste which the brewery exploited, resulting in Guinness becoming the largest brewery in Europe by the end of the nineteenth century.[35] In fact, due to the success of Arthur's porter, they stopped producing ale in 1799 and concentrated on developing their porter range or dark stout.[36]

Interestingly, researchers have since discovered that it was not only the use of unmalted roasted barley that made the difference. Since at least 1903, the yeast used to make the stout, known as Guinness, is genetically different from that used in other Irish beers, where the yeast is closer to that used in Britian.[37]

Another little-known fact about Guinness, which demonstrates its superiority as a brewery, is that it was the first brewery to employ scientists in all aspects of its beer production. In particular, they wanted to verify the quality of their beer. As mentioned in Chapter 5, William Sealy Gosset, a keen statistician, was employed in 1899 and developed ways of accounting for the uncertainty that arises around the small sample sizes involved in beer testing.[38] The test developed by Gosset is known as the 't-test' and is still used in all scientific fields today, from biology and physics to psychology, economics, and medicine.[39]

Arthur Guinness was a good businessman; apart from employing scientists to ensure objectivity in beer testing, he was also concerned with the marketing of his product and designed his labels astutely. There were three components to the Guinness label that was trademarked in 1876 – his signature, the harp, and the Guinness wordmark.[40]

The harp was chosen as it was a distinctive Irish symbol that had been used in Ireland since the thirteenth century. The particular Guinness harp emblem was based on the famous fourteenth-century Trinity College harp, the original of which is still on display in the long room at Trinity College Dublin today.

In 1922, when Ireland separated from the United Kingdom, the Irish government wanted to use the same harp as its emblem. However, the government had to face

34 Ibid 158.

35 Kelly Phillips Erb, '13 Quirky Beer and Tax Facts on National Beer Day', *Forbes* (Web Page, 7 April 2015) www.forbes.com/sites/kellyphillipserb/2015/04/07/13-quirky-beer-tax-facts-on-national-beer-day/?sh=61b1e10d4631.

36 'Guiness through the Ages' (n 31).

37 Chen Ly, 'Guinness Yeasts Are Genetically Unique among Irish Beers', *New Scientist* (Web Page, 12 January 2024) www.newscientist.com/article/2412033-guinness-yeasts-are-genetically-unique-among-irish-beers/.

38 Karen Lamb and David Farmer, 'The Genius at Guinness and His Statistical Legacy', *The Conversation* (Web Page, 16 March 2018) https://theconversation.com/the-genius-at-guinness-and-his-statistical-legacy-93134#:~:text=The%20first%20scientific%20brewer%2C%20Thomas,in%20particular%20crops%20of%20hops.

39 Ibid.

40 'The Story of Guinness', *Guinness* (Web Page) www.guinness.com/en-gb/our-craft/guinness-story.

the harp in the other direction to avoid infringing the Guinness trademark. The Guinness harp is still proudly displayed on all Guinness labels.

The Guinness brewery continues to innovate and improve production methods. In the mid twentieth century, a mathematician turned brewer, Michael Ash, created today's Guinness Draught by using nitrogen in the brewing process.[41]

Some of the success of the Guinness pint, it has been said, is due to the myths and traditions behind the name. Wherever you are in the world, the Irish people continue to identify themselves with the Guinness name and feel compelled to drink their 'national' drink.[42]

However, Ireland is not just the home of its most famous export, Guinness. It also hosts a variety of crisp lagers, malty red ales, and many other varieties of stout. In recent years, as in many places in the world, there has been a surge in craft brewing in Ireland. Perhaps here we see the influence of the EU as some of these craft beers include the complex Belgian-style ales.[43]

12.9 CONCLUSION: SUMMARY OF INFLUENCE OF BRITISH TRADITIONS

Finally, while speaking about British influence on brewing traditions, there are certain places in Britain and Ireland that are worth noting for their unique and long-lasting contributions to the brewing industry.

Dublin, and specifically St James's Gate, has already been identified and continues to be influential for the particular brand of world-renowned beer, Guinness stout.

Burton-upon-Trent, known as the capital of brewing, was famous for the quality of its water, which was derived from the Trent River since the nineteenth century. The water was 'hard' and contained calcium sulphate, which helped enhance the hop bitterness in beer and also improved its clarity. The British Brewing Museum is located in Burton-upon-Trent.[44]

Other regions are Kent, Herefordshire, Worcestershire, and Oxfordshire, where the traditional hops have been and are grown, such as East Kent Goldings and Fuggle.[45] These varietals of hops are still used widely in brewing around the world.

Lastly, and probably the most important, of course, is the traditional British and Irish pubs (from the name 'public house'). They are part of the history and heritage

[41] 'Guinness through the Ages' (n 31).

[42] Brenda Murphy, 'Pure Genius: Guinness Consumption and Irish Identity' (2003) 7(4) *New Hibernia Review* 50.

[43] 'What Makes Irish Beer Special [2024]', *Best in Ireland* (Web Page, 14 November 2024) www.bestinireland.com/what-makes-irish-beer-special/.

[44] Ryane, 'English Pale Ale: Exploring Its Unique Taste and History', *Brewers Union* (Web Page) www.brewersunion.com/english-pale-ale/.

[45] 'Search the Oxford Companion to Beer' (n 26).

of every town, village or city, and play a key role in local communities. They are a place for friends and family to socialize, relax, and have a drink, even if today it might be a no- or low-alcohol beer! Pubs are also continuing to adapt, including being at the forefront of the thriving craft brewing sector.

Pubs not only have beer traditions but also food traditions. The 'pub lunch' is a simple menu strengthened by the traditional 'Sunday roast lunch'. Long may these traditions continue to be part of the pubs across Britain and Ireland.

13

Broader Lessons from the Regulation of Beer

As we near the end of this book, we will summarize the broad lessons from the previous chapters. We will also take a deep dive into some more philosophical aspects of beer law before making some concluding remarks.

13.1 REGULATORY IMPACTS ON BEER AND BEER MARKETS

Having read this far, there can be no remaining doubt that the law has played a tremendous role in shaping beer and the brewing industry. Laws have influenced what beers are brewed, what beers we drink, how much of them we drink, and, perhaps, how we think and feel about them. But we have also seen the resilience of beer and its production. Even when the law has sought to prevent brewing and drinking, it has failed to do so.

The book has also demonstrated that beer regulation has a long history, and that the societal goals the law has pursued in relation to beer have varied considerably over time.

Examples have highlighted that regulators in other legal fields may learn from the successes and failures of those who have sought to regulate beer and brewing. For example, in the discussion of the German *Reinheitsgebot*, we have seen the importance of lawmakers understanding the technology they are regulating – an unsurprising observation, perhaps, but clearly a major issue in modern attempts at regulating fast-moving technologies.

We have seen how the relationship between health and beer has shaped the law, and how some beer-related laws have tightened over the years while others have become more relaxed. Take, for example, the 2003 decision by the Swedish government not to standardize the size of beer ordered as *en stor stark* versus the fact that the Babylonian Code of Hammurabi required tavern keepers who poured 'short measures' of beer to be drowned. Those were the good old days when consumer protection was taken seriously!

We have seen how the law has banned some ingredients and mandated others, and how this has both impacted and stemmed from international trade considerations. The immense role of tax law has been highlighted, as has the effect of beer and ingredient taxes on world history.

We have seen how beer, culture, and law interact, and how intellectual property law and competition law have impacted beer (and vice versa). We have learned that how beer competes with other drinks has much to do with the images it projects, which in turn are regulated by laws on advertising, unfair competition, and trademarks.

In fact, we can almost conclude that regulation does not just impact beer, it constitutes beer. There are many reasons for governments to interfere with beer: health, tax, public order, religion, culture, honest trading, and heritage, to name a few. That leaves aside the fact that beer's competitors benefit from its stricter regulation; the market-distorting effect of differential excise regimes for beer and wine is obvious. Because beer has been so intensely scrutinized by regulators, it is a great model for considering how regulation impacts consumption and society.

Taking into account all the above, we have no doubt that beer law will continue to be relevant and important. And, with cases such as the one we are about to introduce you to, we also think that beer law can continue to be rather entertaining.

13.1.1 *'Fucking Hell'*

'Fucking Hell' is a beer brand that, seemingly, is especially popular with heavy metal fans. It started as the idea of three German businessmen who wanted to bring a new beer to market. One of them lived close to Fucking, a small Austrian village with ninety-three inhabitants. They combined 'Fucking' with the German word for pale lager, 'Hell'. A beer war had begun brewing in Germany.

The application for a community trademark was first rejected by the examiner in the Harmonisation Office for the EU and then permitted by the Board of Appeals of the Office.[1] The Board found that 'Fucking Hell' contained no semantic indication that could refer to a certain person or group of persons, stating: 'It cannot even be understood as an instruction that the reader should go to hell.' The Board also found combining place names to *not* be reprehensible, even if that combination had different meanings in other languages. Surely, the inhabitants of Fucking were not aware of their village name's English meaning. However, when the village sign was stolen a couple of times, they changed the name to 'Fugging'. The beer went on sale in Europe, Asia and Australia in 2011. In 2020, a trademark was granted in the US.

The trademark was later extended to be used as a brand name for food and clothing. An initial rejection by the German Patent and Trade Mark Office was overturned by the German Patent Court, which stated that the combination formed a surprising and imaginative play on words. The Court also noted that assessing good

[1] Decision of the Fourth Board of Appeal of 21 January 2010 (Case R 385/2008-4) OHIM.

taste would not be part of the application procedure. In a later case, a different chamber refused to register 'Fucking Hell' on the basis of it being against public morals. No objection was made to this decision, leaving the issue open at a general level.

13.2 LEGAL METHOD AND SOME BEER LAW PHILOSOPHY

Brewing recipes have the same impact on beer as regulatory methods and particular rules do on law. Just as a beer recipe dictates the character of the resulting beverage, the regulatory method dictates how the law operates. So, in this chapter, we will use what we earlier learned about beer law and discuss possible methodological approaches to the study of beer. We will also pick the method that seems right for beer law, defining a 'main purpose' that will serve as a guiding principle. Finally, we will take a closer look at the institutions that proved to be most important for the development of beer technology, markets, and laws.

13.2.1 *Pragmatic Method in Beer Law*

In Chapter 1, we argued that beer law may well be regarded as a distinct legal field. Some will find that controversial. However, beer law would not be the first field of law met with resistance. For instance, wine law was once a new and controversial field; today, it is well-accepted.[2] Similarly, IT law is now a well-established field of law, but, initially, many refused to view it as a distinct legal field.

At first glance, beer does not seem to have much in common with information technology. However, there are some interesting similarities between beer law and IT law. Interpreting legal rules that regulate beer production and distribution requires knowledge of relevant technologies and market mechanisms. The same applies to IT law that is strongly influenced by technological and economic determinants.

We have seen that beer-making very significantly relies on a *technology*. Some aspects may be relatively simple and based on trial and error, but, more recently, much of it is also scientific and based on a substantial knowledge base. Brewers deploy technical and technological knowledge and they use instruments to brew, package, transport, and serve beer. Their technological prowess plays a crucial role in their success, and therefore in the consumer's tendency to drink beer over other beverages.

Besides their technological natures, beer law and IT law also share key development factors such as invention, creativity, labour, branding, and security, which are

[2] See, eg, Matt Harvey and Vicki Waye, *Global Wine Regulation* (Thomson Reuters, 2013); Julien Chaisse, Fernando Dias Simões, and Danny Friedmann (eds), *Wine Law and Policy: From National Terroirs to a Global Market* (Brill, 2021); Carol Robertson, *The Little Red Book of Wine Law: A Case of Legal Issues* (American Bar Association, 2008).

covered by similar legal tools (ranging from intellectual property to market regulations to security compliance). Commercially, the global beer market is valued at US$900 billion and the IT market at US$1,400 billion – both are massive.

Another quite interesting similarity between beer law and IT law is that they both work with virtuality and virtualization. Virtuality is talked about mostly in connection with computers, but the concept and method of virtualization are much older, and its basics have been described even by ancient philosophers. And, however surprising it may sound, beer has historically been an enabler of virtualization for much longer than computers have.

In a nutshell, virtualization means taking something and changing its form while preserving its substance.[3] Computers do that job brilliantly because they can virtualize phenomena ranging from friendship to education and assets.

Beer does not disembody phenomena – it can virtualize them while keeping their physical bodies untouched. For example, an ancient Egyptian legend holds that when Hathor, the goddess of inebriation, invented beer, 'she was turned from a wild lioness into an amiable, fun-loving lady'.[4]

But beer can do far more than just softening or sharpening various rough or edgy forms like lionesses. In beer places (such as alehouses, cafés, pubs, hotels, *Biergartens*, and craft breweries), social interactions gain specific dynamics, regardless of whether or what respective participants drink, and 'going for one' virtualizes everything from business to romantic relationships.

When two lawyers 'go for one' (see Chapter 8) to discuss their clients' mutual dispute, the merits of the dispute do not change, but a different stage can impact the exchange of opinions and arguments. Such staging can show, for example, the will of the parties to settle, which could be difficult to communicate otherwise. And it may not be too far from the truth to state that if a dispute cannot be settled over a beer, then it is genuinely serious.

Beer production, distribution, and consumption also played crucial roles in virtualizing communities, economies, and even societies around Europe throughout the past millennium. Beer did not change their *nature*, but helped transform how they operated and enabled their further development. For example, beer brewing let monasteries dramatically improve their economic performance and establish new forms of communication with the general public via the sale of beer.[5] Gaining beer brewing rights also helped cities and burghers to become economically and politically competitive with the nobility. In both cases, brewing and distributing beer virtualized formal properties of both groups (monasteries and burghers), which led to better economic performance and societal status.

3 See Pierre Lévy, *Becoming Virtual: Reality in the Digital Age* (Plenum Trade, 1998) 23.

4 See Ian Hornsey, *A History of Beer and Brewing* (Royal Society of Chemistry, 2003) 111.

5 See Richard W Unger, *Beer in the Middle Ages and the Renaissance* (University of Pennsylvania Press, 2004) 27.

The presence of a beer place[6] always changes its host area or community[7] – not always for the better, of course, but virtualization is not always positive or progressive.[8] Even when phenomena are virtualized with IT, the results are not always better compared to their prior – offline, analogue, physical – states.

Beer, of course, has incomparably less virtualizing potential than IT. That is also the reason we have relatively few beer-specific laws; most beer law consists of general legal rules applied to beer. In comparison, IT law, although it also works with general legal rules, has specific laws for many virtualized phenomena.

Despite that difference, IT law and beer law have the same main method of interpretation and application: pragmatism. Traditionally, there are three well-established methodologies in law, which are the positivist, naturalist, and pragmatic methods. How are they different? Radbruch's trinity of defining purposes in law would categorize them as certainty, justice, and practicality.[9]

Positivism aims for certainty (which may sometimes be unjust), while naturalism focuses on justice (whatever that may mean). Pragmatism[10] aims to develop immediately functioning realist solutions that practically work for given circumstances but may be neither perfectly just nor stable over time.

A pragmatic approach to lawmaking and legal interpretation is beautifully pictured in *The Little Prince* in the conversation between the little prince and the king. It reads:

> 'If I ordered a general to fly from one flower to another like a butterfly, or to write a tragic drama, or to change himself into a sea bird, and if the general did not carry out the order that he had received, which one of us would be in the wrong?' the king demanded. 'The general, or myself?'
>
> 'You', said the little prince firmly.
>
> 'Exactly. One must require from each one the duty which each one can perform', the king went on. 'Accepted authority rests first of all on reason. If you ordered your

[6] For a more detailed explanation of the phenomenon of a public house or a pub, see David Preece, 'Turbulence in UK Public House Retailing: Ramifications and Responses' in Ignazio Cabras, David Higgins, and David Preece (eds) *Brewing, Beer and Pubs: A Global Perspective* (Palgrave Macmillan, 1st ed, 2016) 247.

[7] See Claire Markham and Gary Bosworth, 'The Village Pub in the Twenty-First Century: Embeddedness and the "Local"' in Ignazio Cabras, David Higgins, and David Preece (eds) *Brewing, Beer and Pubs: A Global Perspective* (Palgrave Macmillan, 1st ed, 2016) 266. See also Ignazio Cabras, '"Pillars of the Community": Pubs and Publicans in Rural Ireland' in Ignazio Cabras, David Higgins, and David Preece (eds) *Brewing, Beer and Pubs: A Global Perspective* (Palgrave Macmillan, 1st ed, 2016) 282.

[8] Many recent examples of beer changing communities or acting as an indicator of complex societal situations in Africa are analysed, together with sociological and philosophical explanations. See Steven van Wolputte and Mattia Fumanti (eds) *Beer in Africa: Drinking Spaces, States and Selves* (LIT Verlag, 2010).

[9] See Aernout Schmidt, 'Radbruch in Cyberspace: About Law-System Quality and ICT Innovation' (2009) 3(2) *Masaryk University Journal of Law and Technology* 195.

[10] The Greek word πρᾶγμα (pragma) means a fact or something that actually happens.

people to go and throw themselves into the sea, they would rise in revolution. I have the right to require obedience because my orders are reasonable.'[11]

Legal rules are rules. They do not name or describe reality but prescribe obligations. Consequently, the making and interpretation of legal rules should not just consist of naming and describing natural happenings. At the same time, governing, or rule-making, must reflect on reality to prevent unreasonable conclusions. Reason, as used by the king, should limit rulemaking and interpretation of rules to the extent of practical (pragmatic) possibility. That pragmatic approach should apply across all technology-related fields of law, and it should not be limited to extreme regimes like writing a tragic drama or throwing oneself into the sea.

One aspect of pragmatism is practical possibility – that is, how realistically possible is something? For example, a law requiring businesses to use a specific technology is 'possible' under legal positivism if that technology is objectively available, regardless of price or operating difficulty. Pragmatism, though, considers other practical aspects of that law's application, such as its economic viability, operational limitations, moral acceptability, and societal acceptance. Pragmatism also tends to promote shaping products and interaction through regulation, rather than regulating an already 'complete' product or interaction that has a defined character.

Let us look at pragmatism in the context of beer. If brewing and selling beer is generally permitted in a specific country, the pragmatic approach means making and interpreting beer-related rules so brewing and distributing beer is not only theoretically possible but also practically doable. For example, if health laws allow, in general, for beer to be brewed and distributed, they should not contain auxiliary rules and restrictions that would deter reasonable institutions from brewing or distributing beer, or reasonable people from drinking it.

An interesting example of a pragmatic legal argument involved the 'Clean Water Act Case' in the US Supreme Court.[12] The Court was to consider whether the federal Clean Water Act overprotected water sources and gave the Environmental Protection Agency too much power. While the case was mainly about landowners arguing against ecologists, nearly sixty craft breweries also stepped in.[13] They argued that leaving water sources unregulated or locally regulated would make brewing beer economically impossible, because the quality of local water sources[14] could

[11] Antoine de Saint Exupéry, *Le Petit Prince [The Little Prince]* (Reynal and Hitchcock, 1943).

[12] See *Sackett v Environmental Protection Agency*, 598 US 651 (2023).

[13] See the Brief of Amici Curiae Craft Brewers in Support of Respondents in an amicus brief to the US Supreme Court No 18-260.

[14] For a detailed description of specific beer-related properties of US water sources, see David J Nemeth and Charles, 'Sweetwater, Mountain Springs and Great Lakes: A Hydro-Geography of Beer Brands' in Mark Patterson and Nancy Hoalst-Pullen (eds) *The Geography of Beer* (Springer, 2014) 98.

decline to the extent that brewers will either have to acquire water treatment equipment they cannot afford or brew beer that would taste awful.[15]

Another example of the pragmatic approach is blood alcohol content (BAC) drink-driving limits. There is no empirical proof that drinking alcohol before driving has any benefits, but it *has* been proven that a single beer or glass of wine does not significantly decrease driving ability. As such, many countries allow a BAC of 0.02–0.05 grams per 100 millilitres,[16] because they pragmatically acknowledge that people may fancy having a light drink before travelling from a dinner or some other occasion.

An even more interesting situation exists in countries with BAC limits of 0.0 – that is, a total ban on drinking before driving. In the Czech Republic, which is one of four EU members with a 0.0 BAC limit,[17] there is an official interpretive guideline that acknowledges the possibility of divergent measuring equipment and the natural presence of alcohol in the human body. Consequently, police officers are pragmatically guided to *not* sanction measurements of BAC under 0.024 grams per 100 millilitres, provided that the driver does not admit to drinking before driving or seem intoxicated.[18] While BAC limits of 0.02–0.05 are a pragmatic approach to legislation, the guidelines for BAC limits of 0.0 show pragmatism in the interpretation and application of legal rules.

13.2.2 *Institutions and Performance-Based Beer Regulation*

Institutions are crucial for the development of beer culture and beer law. Their importance is illustrated by the case of beer prohibition in Iceland (see Chapter 4). A referendum in 1908, which led to the full prohibition of alcohol in 1915, reflected a national desire to be politically and culturally independent from Denmark.[19] Alcohol became a defining element of the independence movement because drinking was considered a cultural feature of Denmark, but not of Iceland.[20]

[15] See Tucker Higgins, 'Brewers Warn Supreme Court: Back the Clean Water Act, or Beer Will Taste Like Medicine', *CNBC* (Web Page, 15 October 2019) www.cnbc.com/2019/10/15/brewers-beer-will-taste-like-medicine-if-supreme-court-doesnt-back-clean-water-act.html.

[16] For a complete list of BAC for EU countries, see, for example, the web of the NGO European Transport Safety Council.

[17] The other three countries are currently Hungary, Romania, and Slovakia.

[18] See the response upon a freedom of information petition, 'Hladina alkoholu v krvi řidiče vozidla do 0,2% [The Level of Alcohol in the Blood of the Driver of the Vehicle up to 0.2%]', *Policie České republiky* (Web Page, 2016) www.policie.cz/clanek/hladina-alkoholu-v-krvi-ridice-vozidla-do-0-2.aspx.

[19] It may be of note that women did not have voting rights back then in Iceland.

[20] See 'Why Iceland Banned Beer', *BBC* (Web Page, 1 March 2015) www.bbc.com/news/magazine-31622038 referring to one of the most visually appealing books about beer ever made, Höskuld Sæmundsson, Robbery of Flygenring, and Stefan Pálsson, *Bjór – Umhverfis heiminn á 120 glösum [Beer – Around the World in 120 Types]* (Crymogea, 2014).

Institutional backing of the prohibition first took a heavy hit when Spain threatened to limit the import of Icelandic fish unless Spanish wine was allowed in Iceland. Consequently, wine was swiftly exempted from the alcohol ban. Even before 1933, when the ban was lifted for spirits, institutional enforcement of the prohibition was not strong. Besides smuggling and moonshine production, drinkable alcohol for industrial and medical purposes was legally imported, thanks to the supportive attitude of institutions such as the health service. It was not uncommon for alcohols such as cognac to be officially prescribed by medical practitioners.

Beer, however, was a different story. For a long time, there was no significant institutional pressure to lift the ban on beer. Stefán Pálsson, author of *Beer: Around the World in 120 Pints*, writes that Icelandic practitioners frequently prescribed wine or spirits for heart disease or bad nerves, but 'the head doctor put his foot down and said beer did not qualify as a medicine under any circumstances'.[21] This was despite beer having certain medicinal properties that could plausibly have been used to prescribe it – for, say, digestive conditions or kidney malfunctions.[22]

Lack of pro-beer pressure from institutions meant that the beer prohibition was only partially lifted in 1980 after an individual discrimination case brought by a local lawyer led to a change in the law. (Previously, only foreigners and flight crew were allowed to import duty-free beer into Iceland.) Legislation then granted the same right to travelling Icelanders, before the ban on beer was completely lifted on 1 March 1989.

The Iceland case shows that a lack of enforcement activity can mitigate or even nullify legal rules. It also demonstrates that, on the other hand, changing established laws can be very hard if the movement in question lacks institutional support.

One could argue that, in Iceland, there may not have been a proper societal or economic case for allowing beer alongside other alcoholic drinks, and that institutional backing was absent because the movement lacked political merit – whether that stemmed from health concerns, nationalist sentiment, or the mere fact that Iceland is a cold place and people prefer stronger alcohol.

However, if that was the case, beer would hardly have become so popular so quickly after the prohibition ended. Sixty per cent of total alcohol consumed in Iceland is beer – much more than traditionally beer-oriented countries like the Czech Republic, Germany (both slightly over 50 per cent), and the UK (under 40 per cent).[23] It is more likely that this example shows the difference between institutionalized demand for wine and spirits and non-institutionalized demand for beer.

Contrasts to Iceland's lack of institutional backing for beer can be found in medieval Belgium, the Netherlands, Germany, and Bohemia. In those countries,

[21] Ibid.

[22] For a detailed explanation of various health implications of beer, positive and negative, see Rajkumar Rajendram and Victor R Preedy, 'Part 2: General Effects on Metabolism and Body Systems' in Victor R Preedy (ed) *Beer in Health and Disease Prevention* (Elsevier Science & Technology, 1st ed, 2009).

[23] See 'Why Iceland Banned Beer' (n 20).

brewers gained such prominence, mostly thanks to their tax contributions,[24] that the lines between the beer brewing industry and politics practically disappeared. Historian Richard Unger noted that '[t]he cooperation between government and brewers to increase public income, even as early as the fifteenth century, led to a merging of the profession and public power',[25] pointing to the city of Wismar, where 'twenty-one of the twenty-four members of the town council came from among the 182 brewers in the town'.

How institutions translate rules into reality was investigated in the second half of the twentieth century by Otto Weinberger, who was considered the last true follower of the famous legal philosopher Hans Kelsen.[26] Weinberger suggested that a rule is not valid if it was just adopted and published by a lawmaking body (that is, it has positivist formal properties) – it also needs to be backed by relevant institutional activity.[27]

It may seem like there is nothing new in Weinberger's teaching. Obviously, legal rules barely exist if they are not backed by society and enforced by the state. Weinberger, however, understood institutions and institutional activities as much broader than just state authorities and enforcement actions. Besides motivating legislative changes or modulating the enforcement of laws, Weinbergerian institutions may also play an active role in autonomous rulemaking – that is, independently creating, implementing, and enforcing their own internal rules and procedures. The contrast between these institutions' size, economic and societal strength, and technical competence on one side, and the lack of technical capabilities and competences of states on the other, are reflected in technology-oriented fields of law by the growing use of performance-based rules.

In comparison to standard behavioural rules, performance-based rules do not define particular obligations. Instead, they set basic standards and desired outcomes and let the regulated subjects develop their own internal rules and technological solutions.[28] A good example of the use of performance-based rules is fire safety, where legal rules only define minimum technological standards and then let, for example, operators of large buildings develop their own internal rules for preventive measures, training, and evacuation.[29]

[24] The share of town income from taxes on beer between the fifteenth and seventeenth centuries rose to a believable 55 per cent in Amsterdam (1552), 70 per cent in Hasselt (1622), 78 per cent in Leiden (1449), and 88.5 per cent in Haarlem (1437). See Unger (n 5) 197.

[25] Ibid 181.

[26] Hans Kelsen, *Reine Rechtslehre [Pure Theory of Law]* (Mohr Siebeck, 1934).

[27] Weinberger explains his institutional normative theory in Ota Weinberger, *Law, Institutions and Legal Politics: Fundamental Problems of Legal Theory and Social Philosophy* (Kluwer Academic Publishers, 1st ed, 1991).

[28] See Cary Coglianese, 'The Limits of Performance-Based Regulation' (2017) 50(3) *University of Michigan Journal of Law Reform* 525.

[29] See, eg, Graham Spinardi, 'Performance-Based Design, Expertise Asymmetry, and Professionalism: Fire Safety Regulation in the Neoliberal Era' (2019) 13(4) *Regulation & Governance* 520.

Other examples of performance-based regulatory models include personal data protection and cybersecurity. In these areas, it turned out that a one-size-fits-all behavioural model was not functional and that regulated subjects can autonomously create efficient, functioning regulatory and technological solutions under generalized performance-based obligations.

As we've implied in previous chapters, the performance-based regulatory method has not been commonly used in beer law. Regulation tends to be detailed and prescriptive. One reason is that trade regulations, protection of indications, and health regulations are not a natural fit for performance-based rules. A performance-based regulatory model is also not suitable when the purpose of regulation does not align with the economic or cultural interests of institutions. For example, breweries want to sell more beer, while public health institutions want to keep alcoholism and other alcohol-induced issues under control.

Despite that, there may be a good case for performance-based regulation in beer law. Laws regulating production processes, phytosanitary standards, and quality assurance could benefit from being performance-based. Beer institutions such as breweries, brew cooperatives, beer tap chains, and professional guilds also seem capable, thanks to their immersion in all pragmatic aspects of beer production and distribution (see Chapter 13, Section 13.2.1), of creating and implementing rules more efficiently than public authorities.

Imagine, for example, rules regarding the amount of water allowed to be used for the production per litre of beer. Under a performance-based approach, it would be left to each brewery to comply with that limit however they saw fit.

Consequently, using performance-based rules over behavioural rules could help develop autonomous regulatory frameworks that are technologically and economically sound, more flexible and efficient, and more open to creativity and invention. Those rules may also be more practically enforceable compared to standard legal rules that simply prescribe or prohibit some specifically defined behaviour. Performance-based rules may also help the beer industry react to future challenges such as automation or the use of gene technology.[30] If there is one thing that we have made clear in this book, it is that, although beer is ancient, its production, character, and consumption have never ceased to change and likely never will.

13.2.3 *Teleology in Beer Law*

It is almost impossible to define the purpose of beer, beer brewing, or beer culture. But questioning the purpose of beer law *does* make sense, because purpose directly affects how beer law is interpreted.

[30] See Charles W Bamforth, *Beer: Tap into the Art and Science of Brewing* (Oxford University Press, 2nd ed, 2003) 188.

The role of purpose in legal interpretation was hugely debated around the end of the nineteenth century and the beginning of the twentieth century. Hans Kelsen (mentioned above), whose positivist doctrine is still the basis of legal methodology in the Alpine countries, strictly refused to use the purpose of legal rules (norms) as a factor in the interpretation of the law. Contrastingly, legal philosophers such as Radbruch, Engliš, and Jhering argued that purpose represents an integral part of the material substance of legal rules, so interpretation should always contain some teleology.[31] In other words, anybody who interprets laws should actively consider the purpose for which those laws were made or, at a minimum, refrain from interpretations that conflict with that purpose. One example is how the purpose of old constitutional laws affects their modern application.

The teleological approach clearly won in international and EU law.[32] EU directives and regulations normally start by outlining the reasons for legal rules and how they should be interpreted. But, as we've seen in previous chapters, the teleology of some generic legal instruments, such as intellectual property laws, may become tricky when applied to beer. A good example is trademarks and their use in labelling beer. Trademark law serves many different purposes and interests – the consumer who does not want to be misled, the owner who does not want competitors diluting their mark, and the general value of advertising (which can be affected by parasitic misuse by competitors).

Most classical commercial trade marks date back to the rise of industrialized society during the eighteenth century. Beer trademarks, though, are often much older – Stella Artois and Löwenbrau originated in the fourteenth century. These trademarks, quite notably, refer to a brand and brewing institution respectively, not to places or products. Their original purpose was to protect the investments and reputation of breweries.

In contrast, some later trademarks and other legally protected beer indications had different purposes, such as protecting consumer expectations of quality, highlighting unique properties of particular beer types, and protecting the integrity of regional beer production. Some of these purposes were so important that they led to new, more targeted forms of protection such as the protected geographical indications (PGIs) and traditional specialities guaranteed (TSGs) in the EU.

The multitude of purposes of trademarks may represent a problem when interpreting trademark law for beer trademarks. It may then matter a lot whether a court

[31] For a complex work on the role of purpose in law, see Rudolf Von Jhering, *Law as a Means to an End* (Boston Book Company, 1913); Gustav Radbruch, *Grundzüge der Rechtsphilosophie* (Quelle & Meyer, 1914). Karel Engliš was a noted economic theorist and was also the first rector of Mazaryk University and author of works including on teleology and economic theory.

[32] One of the reasons is the multilingual nature of the EU law. If EU laws were interpreted only upon their normative codifications, it would be impossible to apply them uniformly around the EU. That is why EU directives and regulations contain lengthy recitals that mostly contain detailed explanations of the purposes of respective provisions.

would hold that the purpose of some beer trademark is protecting the integrity of the brand, such as the origin of the product, some traditional rights, consumer expectations, or something else.

Even the Court of Justice of the European Union (CJEU) has stated that the primary purpose of a trademark is to 'guarantee the identity of the origin of the goods'.[33] But this teleological interpretation varies across decisions. In some cases, the Court emphasizes the general guaranteeing function of a trademark,[34] while elsewhere it stresses the guarantee is 'to consumers'.[35] In other decisions, the Court added purposes, stating that trademarks 'guarantee that all the goods bearing the mark have been manufactured or supplied under the control of a single undertaking which is responsible for their quality'[36] or directly guarantee 'the quality of the goods or services in question'.[37] This illustrates that adopting a teleological approach requires examining what a regulation's purpose might be, and how different purposes should be prioritized – something about which reasonable minds might easily differ.

When teleology is applied to beer, the results are unclear. Is the purpose of trademark law to just protect the branding (regardless of the quality control or even the mere quality of the product) or protect the branding because it signifies something else – like quality control or the quality of the beer? The second option opens an interesting interpretive possibility. Beer brand trademarks could be protected only when the trademark owner can prove that the infringing beer has brand-identical quality. The Court would first have to examine the historical qualitative identity of the brand protected by a trademark and compare it with the recent quality of the product.

Imagine that a traditional brand with a strong product identity is taken over by a new owner, after which the quality of beer sharply declines. A third party then starts brewing beer under the original brand's trademark, which meets consumers' expectations of the original brand. The Court, when assessing possible trademark violation, might then find the purpose of the trademark is to guarantee 'the quality of the goods in question'.

Under that finding, the third party's use of the trademark would not violate the rights of the trademark owner, as long as the trademark owner did not meet the original quality expectations but the alleged trademark violator did. In short, a court could then decline a trademark action solely on the basis that the beer brewed by the

[33] See, eg, *PrenzMarien GmbH v European Union Intellectual Property Office* (T-766/20) [2022] CJEU 123, [37].

[34] Ibid.

[35] See, eg, *Google France SARL and Google Inc v Louis Vuitton Malletier SA* (C-236/08), *Google France SARL v Viaticum SA and Luteciel SARL* (C-237/08) and *Google France SARL v Centre national de recherche en relations humaines (CNRRH) SARL and Others* (C-238/08) [2010] CJEU 159, [77] ('*Joined Cases C-236/08 to C-238/08*').

[36] See *L'Oréal SA and Others v eBay International AG and Others* (C-324/09) [2011] 474, [80].

[37] See *Joined Cases C-236/08 to C-238/08* (36) [77].

owner of the trademark is not as good as it used to be. This might, in fact, accord with consumer interests, which, when it comes to beer, are closely aligned with the product's inherent characteristics (as opposed to its image or perception, as might be the case with a high-class clothing or jewellery brand). It all depends on what the consumer wants – a product, an image, a 'virtualization' of a product, or a bit of all three.

While it is not always possible to use teleological interpretation in beer law, we can define one universal purpose that can be used for both beer-specific laws and general laws that apply to beer. Since pragmatism should be the dominant method of beer law, that universal purpose should simply be the practical availability of beer.

Teleology should be centred around relevant institutions (such as breweries, pubs, and guilds), so the question of beer availability should rest on the ability of those institutions to produce and distribute beer. Consequently, there should be, in a country that generally allows beer, no rule made or interpreted in a way that would practically prevent relevant institutions from brewing and distributing beer.

13.3 TO CONCLUDE

Beer is not only a drink, but a complex cultural phenomenon that, over the millennia, has become hugely significant for many nations. Brewing and serving beer has always been a matter of agriculture, technology, and logistics – and one of rules and laws. Beer continues to evolve and the attitudes of the law, the goals of regulators, and consumers' expectations of the law constantly impact its reality and virtualization.

There is no such thing as beer law, in the sense of a separate set of rules solely dedicated to beer. Instead, we have discussed beer law as a combination of (a few but important) specifically dedicated laws and (a few more and equally important) beer-related applications of general laws, from health and trade to intellectual property and consumer protection.

When beer is allowed in a jurisdiction, the ultimate purpose guiding the interpretation of beer law should be the pragmatic (or practical) availability of beer. It should, primarily, consider the perspective of relevant beer institutions, from farmers to breweries to consumers. However, that does not mean that legal rules should be made and interpreted to serve the interests of institutions. Practical aspects of beer brewing, and distribution should not shape beer law itself but should only act as a *factor* in its interpretation.

It is a general indicator of culture that order is established by rules, and that legitimate rules are superior to any sort of raw power. It may, then, become a matter of serious conflict if order based on rules collides with order based on blatant factual force. Beer culture, so unprecedentedly rich, inspiring, and orderly, can prevail and develop only if legitimate rules of beer law keep ruling it. This also represents the realities of the market – power and concentration seem to rule, but beer and beer law also show how they can suddenly and unexpectedly be subverted, such as by the emergence of craft brewing and consumption.

Finally, we can see that the law has divided society – or at least the beer-drinking public and brewing community – into two factions. The first is the 'beer purists'. Beer purists view the *Reinheitsgebot* as something positive, even as a 'holy commandment'. It is a guide to what is acceptable as beer, and anything going outside that regulatory framework is inferior (or at least not deserving of the prestigious label of 'beer'). The other faction is the 'beer libertarians'. They embrace the proverb '*de gustibus non est disputandum*' (in matters of taste, there can be no disputes) and view the *Reinheitsgebot* as a barrier to creativity, imagination, and innovation. So, to which of these factions do you belong? The answer may tell you as much about your views on the law as your stance on beer.

Postscript

14.1 FROM 'BEER LAW' TO A 'LAW BEER'

So, what do you do when the 'Beer Law' book is written and sent to the wonderful people at Cambridge University Press? Well, it feels like a time to celebrate and what could be more appropriate than to celebrate with a beer, and why not then a 'Law Beer'?

What we will do here is describe the beer we brewed to celebrate the book. We wanted this beer to represent something from each of the countries in which the six authors live; that is, Australia, Belgium, Czech Republic, and Germany.

Each of these countries has made significant contributions to the world of beer and we could have opted for a great range of different influences from each country. In the end, we chose malt from Germany, yeast from Belgium, hot side hops from the Czech Republic, and cold side hops from Australia.

But even after this decision had been made, there were countless options when it came to all the ingredients. The first question we had to confront was whether to aim for an established 'style' or not. As we wanted a beer that is 'unique' (if such a goal still is ascertainable and achievable), we chose not to commit to an established style. But we still needed to choose amongst the basic options of light or dark beer, and we opted for something in between – namely an amber. In more detail, we chose to base our malt bill on the German Märzen style since its history is so entwined with the law.

The History of Märzen

The history of Märzen can be traced to the 1553 decree by Duke Albrecht V of Bavaria we mentioned in Chapter 1. That decree prohibited summer brewing. As we noted in Chapter 1, this caused brewers to unknowingly select cold-tolerant yeasts, driving the evolution of lager yeasts. But it also resulted in the Märzen beer style, and the word 'Märzen' stems from the German word for the month of March: März.

The 2021 the Beer Judge Certification Program style guide notes that:

> Modern versions trace back to the lager developed by Spaten in 1841, contemporaneous to the development of Vienna lager. However, the Märzen name is much older than 1841 – the early ones were dark brown, and the name implied a strength band (14 °P) rather than a style. The amber lager style served at Oktoberfest from 1872 until 1990 when the golden Festbier was adopted as the standard festival beer.

In other words, while its history is much longer, the modern Märzen style that we are working from is closely connected to the Oktoberfest.

A key feature of the BJCP style guide is that it provides 'vital statistics' for each style. These statistics can be seen to set the parameters for a brewer aiming to brew a particular style. The vital statistics for a Märzen are included in the text box.

Vital statistics: OG: 1.054–1.060
IBUs: 18–24 FG: 1.010–1.014
SRM: 8–17 ABV: 5.6–6.3%

The International Bitterness Units refers to the bitterness and the range of 18–24 IBU can be seen to represent a moderate hop bitterness. The Standard Reference Method value describes the colour of the final beer, and an SRM of 8–17 provides scope for a relatively wide range of colours from amber orange to deep reddish copper. The ABV of 5.6–6.3 per cent means that a Märzen is a relatively strong beer. Finally, the original gravity and the final gravity refer to the density of the wort before and after fermentation, respectively.

More generally, the BJCP style guide describes a Märzen as: 'An amber, malty German lager with a clean, rich, toasty, bready malt flavor, restrained bitterness, and a well-attenuated finish. The overall malt impression is soft, elegant, and complex, with a rich malty aftertaste that is never cloying or heavy.' Of course, since we are only taking inspiration from the Märzen style, we do not need to feel constrained by this description. Nevertheless, it may always be useful to have some style in mind as a starting point when designing a beer recipe.

14.2 THE 'LAW BEER' INGREDIENTS

Now that we have described roughly what we were aiming for, it is time to look more closely at the ingredients. We stuck to the 'famous four': barley malt, yeast, hops, and water.

Ok, so to the malt we go. Germany has several world-leading maltsters. We chose to use malt from Weyermann – a major maltster based in

Bamberg[1] (Germany) founded in the late 1800s. With the aim of achieving a beer with the characteristics of a Märzen, as far as the malt profile is concerned, we put together the following malt bill:

Isaria 1924 (66%) – 'Made from the oldest German malting barley variety Isaria, which was officially approved for the beer production in 1924. Brewers used Isaria to brew traditional, unfiltered and flavorful traditional German Lagers. Sensory: malty-sweet taste and soft biscuit like aroma; soft mouthfeel.'[2]

Munich II (26%) – Munich II malt is often used to add rich malt aroma and colour for malt-forward and deeper colour beer styles. 'Sensory: pronounced malt aroma with notes of caramel, honey and bread.'[3]

Carahell (5%) – Specially manufactured to achieve almost complete caramelization of the grain, this malt type 'helps to improve foam and its stability, and helps improve the mouthfeel of any beer. Sensory: malty-sweet; fine caramel notes'.[4]

Acidulated (3%) – Acidulated malt contains natural lactic acid and is used to adjust the pH of the mash. This impacts several factors, including the mash conversion and the pH of the wort that then is fermented. Using this malt, rather than simply adding lactic acid to adjust the pH, keeps us within the German Purity Law. 'Sensory: fruity-acidic, universally applicable.'[5]

Of these malt types, the Isaria 1924 malt is particularly interesting. It will certainly help us achieve the particular malt flavours we are after, but in addition to this, Isaria 1924 is interesting because it is indicative of a relatively recent phenomenon in the brewing industry. When brewers – and this is of course especially the case with craft brewers – have sought to 'tell a story' about their products, focus has typically been placed on the hops, with the malt getting much less attention beyond perhaps a note about the grain bill as such.

But with heirloom malts, the malts too are equipped to 'tell a story', and it will be interesting to see if this impacts the beer styles favoured in the craft beer industry. Perhaps a product such as Isaria 1924 signals that we will enter a new golden era for lagers – lagers brewed with interesting heirloom malts combined either with the traditional novel hops associated with the best traditional lagers, or perhaps utilizing the ever-expanding range of hops.

1 A city famous for the 'Rauchbier' style.

2 'Weyermann® Isaria 1924®', *Weyermann* (Web Page) www.weyermann.de/en-us/product/weyermann-isaria-1924-3/.

3 'Weyermann® Munich Malt Type 2', *Weyermann* (Web Page) www.weyermann.de/en-us/product/weyermann-munich-malt-type-2-2/?cat = specialty-brew-malt-en-us.

4 'Weyermann® Carahell®', *Weyermann* (Web Page) www.weyermann.de/en-us/product/weyermann-carahell-4/?cat = caramel-malt-en-us.

5 'Weyermann® Acidulated Malt', *Weyermann* (Web Page) www.weyermann.de/en-us/product/weyermann-acidulated-malt-4/?cat = specialty-malt-en-us.

While Belgium produces reputable malts, and while Belgian beer is characterized by the use of adjuncts (in the form of fruits, spices, and candi sugar), arguably the ingredient that most clearly sets Belgian beer apart is the yeast. This is why we chose to use Belgian yeast, something that would not be done in a Märzen (that instead uses German lager yeast).

But there are of course several different Belgian yeast strains. One example is the yeast associated with the Belgian Saison style; another is the strains used for traditional Belgian wit beer.

We decided on a yeast strain associated with Abbey and Trappist beers as it delivers 'the signature fruity esters and spicy phenols that characterize what most beer drinkers instantly recognize as "Belgian"'.[6]

Belgian yeast, such as the LalBrew Abbaye we used, result in these classic Belgian characteristics. According to Lallemand – the manufacturer – LalBrew Abbaye:

> Produces the spiciness and fruitiness typical of Belgian and Trappist style ales. When fermented at higher temperatures, typical flavors and aromas include tropical, spicy and banana. At lower temperatures, LalBrew Abbaye™ produces darker fruit aromas and flavors of raisin, date, and fig. Traditional styles brewed with this yeast include but are not limited to Belgian White, Belgian Blonde, Belgian Golden, Dubbel, Tripel, and Quad.[7]

This type of information is of course essential for the brewer. Not only does it highlight what flavour profile may be expected, it also emphasizes that one and the same yeast can be used for different results depending on the fermentation temperature. We chose to ferment at the higher end of the suggested temperature range with the aim of bringing out the tropical, spicy, and banana flavours. These flavours are hopefully a good match with the flavours we will derive from the selected hops.

So, to the hops. The worldwide fame of Czech Saaz hops is such that we simply could not pass on it as our hot side hops. This national treasure, grown in the region around Žatec, provides a noble, herbal character. Its status, and the status of the hop-growing tradition of the area around Žatec, has been recognized in the form of 'Žatec and the Landscape of Saaz Hops' being included on the UNESCO World Heritage List.[8]

While other Nobel hops such as Tettnanger and Hallertau may also be used in a classic Märzen, the choice of Saaz is in line with what one would expect in such a beer. But then our decision to add hops during fermentation – cold side or dry hopping – is a complete break with tradition had we been aiming for a classic Märzen.

6 Dave Carpenter, 'Ask the Experts: Belgian Yeast Strains', *Craft Beer & Brewing* (Web Page, 13 March 206) https://beerandbrewing.com/ask-the-experts-belgian-yeast-strains/.

7 'LalBrew Abbaye™', *Lallemand Brewing* (Web Page) www.lallemandbrewing.com/en/united-states/products/abbaye-belgian-ale-yeast/.

8 'Žatec and the Landscape of Saaz Hops', *UNESCO* (Web Page) https://whc.unesco.org/en/list/1558.

We decided to dry hop our 'Law Beer' with Australia's Galaxy hops, developed by Hop Products Australia (HPA). This was an easy decision since no other Australian hops have gained the same level of international reputation as Galaxy has. As noted by the producer, Galaxy is the: 'most recognised Aussie hop around the world due to its distinctively punchy passionfruit, juicy peach and tangy citrus characteristics'.[9] But as if that was not enough, the Galaxy hops is the most distinctive ingredient in an Australian beer called Stone & Wood Pacific Ale, and this beer was in the centre of one of Australia's leading beer law cases. So there is an interesting legal angle to this remarkable hops.

As we brewed the beer in Australia, the main ingredient – water – was unavoidably Australian. The water character for a traditional Märzen is soft water and by using rainwater we ensured compliance with this characteristic.

The 'Pacific Ale Case'

The case of *Stone & Wood Group Pty Ltd v Intellectual Property Development Corporation Pty Ltd* [2016] FCA 820 (the 'Pacific Ale case') resulted from the enormous success of a beer – *Stone & Wood Pacific Ale* – brewed by a (at the time) small brewery in Northern New South Wales, Australia. When other breweries started producing 'Pacific Ale' with similar characteristics, the question arose whether Stone & Wood enjoyed any protection for its creation. Complex litigation ensued relating to several legal areas including trademarks, the tort of 'passing off', and the Australian consumer law. Important observations were made in the case about what makes a 'beer style'.

For our purposes here, the most interesting part is, however, the description in the case of the beer's flavour profile:

> The Stone & Wood Pacific Ale incorporated a bursting hop aroma of tropical fruit more commonly experienced in beer styles such as American Pale Ale or India Pale Ale, but over a much lighter, crisper body more closely associated with an Australian Pale Ale. The hop aroma was very distinctive, showcasing the signature passionfruit and lychee notes of Galaxy hops but in a much bolder manner than other beers that had used that variety of hops. (para. 70)

It is those 'signature passionfruit and lychee notes of Galaxy hops' that we are seeking to incorporate into the 'Law Beer'.

14.3 THE 'LAW BEER' BREWING PROCESS

So now we have presented all the ingredients. But even when adhering to this one set of ingredients, you could produce beers with different characters based on the process you use. Here is how we did it for our small 'pilot brew' of the 'Law Beer'.

9 'Galaxy', *Hop Products Australia* (Web Page) www.hops.com.au/galaxy/.

We milled the malt while heating the water to a temperature of 63°C. Once the water had reached this temperature we poured in the malt and stirred so as to make sure there were no clumps. We left the mash at this temperature for sixty minutes with the water recirculating through the grains. After sixty minutes, we raised the temperature to 68°C and let it sit there for ten minutes. The next step in this 'step mash' was to raise the temperature to 72°C and leave it there for fifteen minutes. Finally, we did a 'mash out' at 78°C for ten minutes.

We 'sparged' and then disposed of the malt (the 'spent grains'). We boiled the 'wort' for sixty minutes, adding Saaz hop (27 IBU) at sixty minutes (i.e. at the start), 4.4 IBU at five minutes before the end, and 1.3 IBU in the whirlpool (whirlpool for ten minutes).

Having cooled the wort to 20°C, we poured it into the fermenter, adding the yeast. We fermented (initially at 24°C) for a total of nine days, with the temperature dropping to 20–21°C after the intensive fermentation had finished. During the fermentation we added Galaxy hops both six days before bottling and one day before bottling, leaving the hops in for just one day on each occasion. Then we 'cold crashed' (i.e. brought the temperature down close to 0°C) and finally we bottled the beer.

So, what did it taste like? Well, unless we manage to get this one to market somehow, there is only one way to find out. Make it!

Law Beer: The Recipe

Summarizing the above in a manner that makes sense to a brewer, the 'Law Beer' recipe can be described in the following:

OG: 1.053 FG: 1.006 ABV: 6.6% (with bottle fermentation)
IBUs: 32.7 Bitter Ratio: 0.610 SRM: 8

Malt bill: Isaria 1924 (66%), Munich II (26%), Carahell (5%), Acidulated (3%)

Step mash: Mash in at 63°C and rest for 60 min, increase to 68°C and rest for 10 min, increase to 72°C and rest for 15 min, mash out at 78°C for 15 minutes.

Sparge, then 60-minute boil adding Saaz (27.0 IBU) at 60 minutes, and Saaz (4.4 IBU) at 5 minutes. Whirlpool for 10 minutes with Saaz (1.3 IBU).

Cool and add to fermenter. Pitch LalBrew Abbaye yeast at 0.5g/litre.

Start ferment at 20°C and let free rise to 24°C. Dry-hopped with Galaxy 6 days and 1 day before bottling. Ferment until completion, cold crash, then bottle.

Bibliography

BOOKS

Alemanno, Alberto, and Anne-Lise Sibony (eds), *Nudge and the Law: A European Perspective* (Hart, 1st ed, 2015)

Ashworth, William J, *Customs and Excise: Trade, Production, and Consumption in England, 1640–1845* (Oxford University Press, 2003)

Bamforth, Charles W, *Beer: Tap into the Art and Science of Brewing* (Oxford University Press, 2nd ed, 2003)

Grape vs. Grain: A Historical, Technological, and Social Comparison of Wine and Beer (Cambridge University Press, 2008)

Both, Frank, *Gerstensaft und Hirsebier – 5000 Jahre Biergenuss [Barley Juice and Millet Beer – 5000 Years of Beer Enjoyment]* (Verlag Isensee, 1998)

Buck, Holger, '§ 6 France' in Frauke Henning-Bodewig (ed), *International Handbook on Unfair Competition Law* (CH Beck, 1st ed, 2013)

Cabras, Ignazio, '"Pillars of the Community": Pubs and Publicans in Rural Ireland' in Ignazio Cabras, David Higgins and David Preece (eds) *Brewing, Beer and Pubs: A Global Perspective* (Palgrave Macmillan, 1st ed, 2016)

Chaisse, Julien, Fernando Dias Simões and Danny Friedmann (eds), *Wine Law and Policy: From National Terroirs to a Global Market* (Brill, 2021)

Corgill, Dennis, '§ 26 United States' in Frauke Henning-Bodewig (ed), *International Handbook on Unfair Competition Law* (CH Beck, 1st ed, 2013)

Deconinck, Koen, and Johan Swinnen, 'Tied Houses: Why They Are So Common and Why Breweries Charge Them High Prices for Their Beer' in Ignazio Cabras, David Higgins and David Preece (eds) *Brewing, Beer and Pubs: A Global Perspective* (Palgrave Macmillan, 1st ed, 2016)

Dredge, Mark, *A Brief History of Lager: 500 Years of the World's Favourite Beer* (Kyle Books, 1st ed, 2019)

Dunbar, Robin, 'The Social Function of Alcohol from an Evolutionary Perspective' in Riadh Abed and Paul St John-Smith (eds), *Evolutionary Psychiatry Current Perspectives on Mental Health* (Cambridge University Press, 2022)

Exupéry, Antoine de Saint, *Le Petit Prince [The Little Prince]* (Reynal and Hitchcock, 1943)

Firth, Charles Harding, and Robert Sangster Rait (eds), *Acts and Ordinances of the Interregnum, 1642–1660* (His Majesty's Stationery Office, 1911)

Galbraith, John Kenneth, *The New Industrial State* (Houghton Mifflin, 1967)

George, Lisa M, 'The Growth of Television and the Decline of Local Beer' in Johan Swinnen (ed), *The Economics of Beer* (Oxford University Press, 2011)

Gourvish, Terence, and Richard Wilson, *The British Brewing Industry, 1830–1980* (Cambridge University Press, 1994)

Hales, Steven D (ed), *Beer and Philosophy: The Unexamined Beer Isn't Worth Drinking* (Blackwell Publishing, 1st ed, 2007)

Harvey, Matt, and Vicki Waye, *Global Wine Regulation* (Thomson Reuters, 2013)

Hauge, Ragnar, *Lover om alkohol i Norge: fra landskapslovene til 1814 [Laws on Alcohol in Norway: From the Provincial Laws to 1814]* (Rusmiddeldirektoratet, 1998)

Heath, Christopher, 'The Budweiser cases: Geographical Indications v Trade Marks' in Dev S Gangjee (ed), *Research Handbook on Intellectual Property and Geographical Indications* (Edward Elgar, 2016)

Henning-Bodewig, Frauke, 'Unfair Competition Law – An Introduction to a Complex Topic' in Frauke Henning-Bodewig (ed), *International Handbook on Unfair Competition Law* (CH Beck, 1st ed, 2013)

Hernon, Peter, and Terry Ganey, *Under the Influence: The Unauthorized Story of the Anheuser-Busch Dynasty* (Simon & Schuster, 1991)

Hornsey, Ian, *A History of Beer and Brewing* (Royal Society of Chemistry, 2003)

Hough, James S, *The Biotechnology of Malting and Brewing* (Cambridge University Press, 1985)

Jackson, Michael, *Great Beers of Belgium* (Brewers Publications, 6th ed, 2008)

Jacquette, Dale, 'Thirst for Authenticity: An Aesthetics of the Brewer's Art' in Steven D Hales (ed), *Beer and Philosophy: The Unexamined Beer Isn't Worth Drinking* (Blackwell, 1st ed, 2007)

Jhering, Rudolf von, *Law as a Means to an End* (Boston Book Company, 1913)

Kelsen, Hans, *Reine Rechtslehre [Pure Theory of Law]* (Mohr Siebeck, 1934)

Krueger, Ann, *International Trade: What Everyone Needs to Know* (Oxford University Press USA, 2020)

Lévy, Pierre, *Becoming Virtual: Reality in the Digital Age* (Plenum Trade, 1998)

Lucas, André, Agnès Lucas-Scloetter and Carine Bernault, *Traité de la propriété littéraire et artistique* (LexisNexis, 5th ed, 2017)

Lynch, Patrick, and John Vaizey, *Guinness's Brewery in the Irish Economy 1759–1876* (Cambridge University Press, 1960)

MacIntosh, Julie, *Dethroning the King: The Hostile Takeover of Anheuser-Busch, an American Idol* (John Wiley, 1st ed, 2011)

Markham, Claire, and Gary Bosworth, 'The Village Pub in the Twenty-First Century: Embeddedness and the "Local"' in Ignazio Cabras, David Higgins and David Preece (eds), *Brewing, Beer and Pubs: A Global Perspective* (Palgrave Macmillan, 1st ed, 2016)

McGovern, Patrick E, *Uncorking the Past: The Quest for Wine, Beer, and Other Alcoholic Beverages* (University of California Press, 1st ed, 2009)

Meussdoerffer, Franz G, and Hans Michael Eßlinger, 'A Comprehensive History of Beer Brewing' in Hans Michael Eßlinger (ed), *Handbook of Brewing: Processes, Technology, Markets* (Wiley-VCH, 1st ed, 2009)

Mittag, Roger, 'Geographic Appellations of Beer' in Mark Patterson and Nancy Hoalst-Pullen (eds), *The Geography of Beer* (Springer Dordrecht, 1st ed, 2014)

Montonen, Marjatta, and Ismo Tuominen, 'Restricting Alcohol Marketing on Social Media in Finland' in Antonia Lyons et al (eds), *Youth Drinking Cultures in a Digital World: Alcohol, Social Media and Cultures of Intoxication* (Routledge, 1st ed, 2017)

Mosher, Randy, 'Anheuser-Busch' in Garrett Oliver (ed), *The Oxford Companion to Beer* (Oxford University Press, 1st ed, 2012)

Nemeth, David J, and Charles, 'Sweetwater, Mountain Springs and Great Lakes: A Hydro-Geography of Beer Brands' in Mark Patterson and Nancy Hoalst-Pullen (eds), *The Geography of Beer* (Springer, 2014)

Nye, John, 'Brewing Nation: War, Taxes, and the Growth of the British beer Industry in the Eighteenth and Nineteenth Centuries' in Johan Swinnen (ed), *The Economics of Beer* (Oxford University Press, 2011)

Oliver, Garrett (ed), *The Oxford Companion to Beer* (Oxford University Press, 2011)

Papazian, Charlie, *The Complete Joy of Home Brewing* (William Morrow & Company, 3rd ed, 2014)

Patrick, Amber, *The Buildings of the Malting Industry, The Production of Malt from Pre-history to the 21st Century* (Liverpool University Press, 2023)

Poelmans, Eline, and Johan Swinnen, 'A Brief Economic History of Beer' in Johan Swinnen (ed), *The Economics of Beer* (Oxford University Press, 2011)

Preece, David, 'Turbulence in UK Public House Retailing: Ramifications and Responses' in Ignazio Cabras, David Higgins and David Preece (eds), *Brewing, Beer and Pubs: A Global Perspective* (Palgrave Macmillan, 1st ed, 2016)

Radbruch, Gustav, *Grundzüge der Rechtsphilosophie* (Quelle & Meyer, 1914)

Rajendram, Rajkumar, and Victor R Preedy, 'Part 2: General Effects on Metabolism and Body Systems' in Victor R Preedy (ed), *Beer in Health and Disease Prevention* (Elsevier Science & Technology, 1st ed, 2009)

Riepl, Wolfgang, *The Story behind Anheuser-Busch InBev* (Roeselar Trends, 1st ed, 2009)

Robertson, Carol, *The Little Red Book of Wine Law: A Case of Legal Issues* (American Bar Association, 2008)

Sæmundsson, Höskuld, Robbery of Flygenring and Stefan Pálsson, *Bjór – Umhverfis heiminn á 120 glösum [Beer – Around the World in 120 Types]* (Crymogea, 2014)

Slade, Margaret, 'Competition Policy towards Brewing: Rational Response to Market Power or Unwarranted Interference in Efficient Markets?' in Johan Swinnen (ed), *The Economics of Beer* (Oxford University Press, 2011)

Swinnen, Johan (ed), *The Economics of Beer* (Oxford University Press, 2011)

Swinnen, Johan, and Devin Briski, *Beeronomics: How Beer Explains the World* (Oxford University Press, 2017)

Swinnen, Johan, and Thijs Vandemoortele, 'Beeronomics: The Economics of Beer and Brewing' in Johan Swinnen (ed), *The Economics of Beer* (Oxford University Press, 2011)

Tacitus, Cornelius, *Germany and Its Tribes*, trans Alfred John Church, William Jackson Brodribb and Lisa Cerrato (Perseus Books, 1942)

Teich, Mikuláš, 'The Mass Production of Draught and Bottled Beer in Germany 1880–1914' in Terry Gourvish and Richard Wilson (eds), *The Dynamics of the Modern Brewing Industry* (Taylor & Francis, 2003)

Thompson, Henry, *International Economics: Global Markets and International Competitions* (World Scientific, 2001)

Tierney-Jones, Adrian, (ed), *1001 Beers You Must Try before You Die* (Cassell, 2013)

Unger, Richard W, *Beer in the Middle Ages and the Renaissance* (University of Pennsylvania Press, 2004)

Unger, Richard W, 'Beer Production, Profits, and Public Authorities in the Renaissance' in Johan Swinnen (ed), *The Economics of Beer* (Oxford University Press, 2011)

Večerníček, Jaroslav Novák, *Historie piva – od zrození až po konec středověku [History of Beer – From the Origins to the End of Medieval Age]* (Computer Press, 2009)

Wallace, Caroline, Sarah Wood and Jessica Deahl, *Trappist Beer Travels, Second Edition: Inside the Breweries of the Monasteries* (Schiffer Publishing, 2nd ed, 2023)

Weinberger, Ota, *Law, Institutions and Legal Politics: Fundamental Problems of Legal Theory and Social Philosophy* (Kluwer Academic, 1st ed, 1991)

Wolputte, Steven van, and Mattia Fumanti (eds), *Beer in Africa: Drinking Spaces, States and Selves* (LIT Verlag, 2010)

JOURNAL ARTICLES

Amsterdam, Jan Van, et al, 'European Rating of Drug Harms' (2015) 29(6) *Journal of Psychopharmacology (Oxford)* 655

Anderson, Benjamin O, et al, 'Health and Cancer Risks Associated with Low Levels of Alcohol Consumption' (2023) 8(1) *The Lancet Public Health* 6

Anderson, Kym, 'The Emergence of Lower-Alcohol Beverages: The Case of Beer' (2023) 18(1) *Journal of Wine Economics* 66

Antman, Francisca M, and James M. Flynn, 'When Beer Is Safer than Water: Beer Availability and Mortality from Waterborne Illnesses' (2024) 171 *Journal of Development Economics* 103343

Bento, Virgílio A, et al, 'The Impact of Climate Change in Wheat and Barley Yields in the Iberian Peninsula' (2021) 11(1) *Scientific Reports* 15484

Bieleková, Eva, and Ján Pokrivčák, 'Determinants of International Beer Export' (2020) 12(2) *AGRIS on-line Papers in Economics and Informatics* 17

Bonnet, Udo, et al, 'Ranking the Harm of Psychoactive Drugs Including Prescription Analgesics to Users and Others – A Perspective of German Addiction Medicine Experts' (2020) 11 *Frontiers in Psychiatry* 592199

Bonomo, Yvonne, et al, 'The Australian Drug Harms Ranking Study' (2019) 33(7) *Journal of Psychopharmacology (Oxford)* 759

Bowen, Robert, and Maggie Miller, 'Provenance Representations in Craft Beer' (2022) 57(10) *Regional Studies* 1995

Braidwood, Robert J et al, 'Symposium: Did Man Once Live by Beer Alone?' (1953) 55(4) *American Anthropologist* 515

Cabras, Ignazio, and David M Higgins, 'Beer, Brewing and Business History' (2016) 58(5) *Business History* 609

Casey, Gregory Paul, 'The Inspiring and Surprising History and Legacy of American Lager Beer' (2020) 57(1) *Master Brewers Association of the Americas Technical Quarterly* 9

Castro, Pedro, Eduardo Luz and Gladston Moreira, 'Dataset for Hop Varieties Classification' (2021) 38 *Data in Brief* 107312

Coffman, D'Maris, 'Towards a New Jerusalem: The Committee for Regulating the Excise, 1649–1653' (2013) 128(535) *English Historical Review* 1418

Coglianese, Cary, 'The Limits of Performance-Based Regulation' (2017) 50(3) *University of Michigan Journal of Law Reform* 525

Colón, Israel, and Henry SG Cutter, 'The Relationship of Beer Consumption and State Alcohol and Motor Vehicle Policies to Fatal Accidents' (1983) 14(2) *Journal of Safety Research* 83

Deconinck, Koen, Eline Poelmans and Johan Swinnen 'How Beer Created Belgium (and the Netherlands): The Contribution of Beer Taxes to War Finance during the Dutch Revolt' (2016) 58(5) *Business History* 694

Duarte, Alonso, Nevil Alexander and Seamus O'Brien, 'Collaboration and the Emerging Craft Brewing Industry: An Exploratory Study' (2018) 19(3) *Journal of Asia-Pacific Business* 11

Duffy, Martyn H, 'Advertising and the Inter-product Distribution of Demand' (1987) 31(5) *European Economic Review* 1051

Dunbar, RIM, et al, 'Functional Benefits of (Modest) Alcohol Consumption' (2017) 3(2) *Adaptive Human Behavior and Physiology* 118

Elzinga, Kenneth G, Carol Horton Tremblay and Victor J Tremblay, 'Craft Beer in the United States: History, Numbers, and Geography' (2015) 10(3) *Journal of Wine Economics* 242

Gaetano, G de, et al, 'Effects of Moderate Beer Consumption on Health and Disease: A Consensus Document. Nutrition, Metabolism and Cardiovascular Diseases' (2016) 26(6) *Nutrition, Metabolism, and Cardiovascular Diseases* 443

Garavaglia, Christian, 'Industry Evolution: Evidence from the Italian Brewing Industry' (2022) 26(1) *Competition and Change* 75

Garavaglia, Christian, and Johan Swinnen, 'The Craft Beer Revolution: An International Perspective' (2017) 32(3) *Choices* 1

Hafsten, Ult, 'Jordbrukskulturens historie i Oslo of Mjøstrakten belyst ved pollenalytiske undersøkelser [The History of Agricultural Culture in Oslo of the Mjøstrakten Illuminated by Pollen Analysis]' (1958) 21 *Viking (Oslo)* 51

Hockin, Sara, Meghan L Rogers and William Alex Pridemore, 'Population-Level Alcohol Consumption and National Homicide Rates' (2017) 15(2) *European Journal of Criminology* 235

Hruška, Libor, 'Bohemian Breweries Limited – Zlatý důl nebo past? [Bohemian Breweries Limited – Gold Mine or Trap? Part 1: The Founding of Bohemian Breweries in 1889]' (2013) 59(5) *Kvasný Průmysl* 134

Hutzler, Mathias, et al, 'A New Hypothesis for the Origin of the Lager Yeast Saccharomyces Pastorianus' (2023) 23 *FEMS Yeast Research* 1

Jaeger, Sara R, et al, 'Preference Segments among Declared Craft Beer Drinkers: Perceptual, Attitudinal and Behavioral Responses Underlying Craft-Style vs. Traditional-Style Flavor Preferences' (2020) 82 *Food Quality and Preference* 103884

Jarl, Matilda, 'Tobaks- och alkoholkonsumtion ombord på flottans fartyg under 1600- och 1700-talen [Tobacco and Alcohol Consumption On Board Ships of the Fleet in the 17th and 18th Centuries]' (2022) 79 *Forum Navale* 170

Jin, Zhichao, et al, 'Alcohol Consumption as a Preventive Factor for Developing Rheumatoid Arthritis: A Dose-Response Meta-analysis of Prospective Studies' (2014) 73(11) *Annals of the Rheumatic Diseases* 1962

Johansen, Per Ole, 'The Norwegian Alcohol Prohibition; A Failure' (2013) 14(1) *Journal of Scandinavian Studies in Criminology and Crime Prevention* 46

Kniep, Jurgen 'Im Interesse des Renommees und der Exportfähigkeit unseres heimischen Braugewerbes [In the Interest of the Reputation and Export Capability of Our Domestic Brewing Industry]' (2016) 67(2) *Schwäbische Heimat* 157

Koltay, Gábor, Szabolcs Lorincz and Tommaso Valletti, 'Concentration and Competition: Evidence from Europe and Implications for Policy' (2023) 19(3) *Journal of Competition Law and Economics* 466

König, Doris, 'Das Problem der Inländerdiskriminierung – Abschied von Reinheitsgebot, Nachtbackverbot und Meisterprüfung? [The Problem of Discrimination against Nationals – Farewell to the Purity Law, the Ban on Night Baking and the Master Craftsman's Examination]' (1993) 118(4) *Archiv des öffentlichen Rechts* 591

Korpelainen, Helena, and Maria Pietiläinen, 'Hop (Humulus lupulus L.): Traditional and Present Use, and Future Potential' (2021) 75 (3) *Economic Botany* 302

Lane, Melissa M, et al, 'Ultra-processed Food Exposure and Adverse Health Outcomes: Umbrella Review of Epidemiological Meta-analyses' (2024) 384 *British Medical Journal Publishing Group* 077310

Larsson, Lars, 'Från tundra till skog. Miljöförändringar i norra Skåne under jägarstenåldern [From Tundra to Forest. Environmental Changes in Northern Scania During the Hunterian Stone Age]' (2009) 2 *Royal Vitterhets Academy of History and Antiquities* 146

Liu, Li et al, 'Fermented Beverage and Food Storage in 13,000 y-old Stone Mortars at Raqefet Cave, Israel: Investigating Natufian Ritual Feasting' (2018) 21 *Journal of Archaeological Science* 783

López-Olmedo, Nancy, et al, 'Warning Labels on Alcoholic Beverage Containers: A Pilot Randomized Experiment among Young Adults in Mexico' (2023) 23(1) *BMC Public Health* 1156

Luomanen, Jari, and Pertti Alasuutari, 'The Rising Social Media and Declining Alcohol Use: The Case of Finnish Teenagers' (2022) 49(2) *Contemporary Drug Problems* 213

Marcos, Ascensión et al, 'Moderate Consumption of Beer and Its Effects on Cardiovascular and Metabolic Health: An Updated Review of Recent Scientific Evidence' (2021) 13(3) *Nutrients* 879

Martin, Susan E, 'The Links between Alcohol, Crime and the Criminal Justice System: Explanations, Evidence and Interventions' (2001) 10(2) *American Journal on Addictions* 136

Mason, Nicholas, '"The Sovereign People in a Beastly State": The Beer Act of 1830 and Victorian Discourse on Working-Class Drunkenness' (2001) 29 (1) *Victorian Literature and Culture* 109

McGovern, Patrick E, Gretchen R Hall and Armen Mirzoian, 'A Biomolecular Archaeological Approach to "Nordic Grog"' (2013) 2(2) *Danish Journal of Archaeology* 112

Milburn, Travis, and Favian Alejandro Guertin-Martín, 'Tapping into Environmental Harm in Brewing: An Exploration of Pollution and Waste in Beer Production' (2020) 28(3) *Critical Criminology* 407

Moir, Michael, 'Hops – A Millennium Review' (2000) 58(4) *Journal of the American Society of Brewing Chemists* 131

Morojele, Neo K, et al, 'Alcohol Use and the Risk of Communicable Diseases' (2021) 13(10) *Nutrients* 3317

Mozny, Martin, et al, 'Climate-Induced Decline in the Quality and Quantity of European Hops Calls for Immediate Adaptation Measures' (2023) 14(1) *Nature Communications* 6028

Murphy, Brenda, 'Pure Genius: Guinness Consumption and Irish Identity' (2003) 7(4) *New Hibernia Review* 50

Narziss, L, 'The German Beer Law' (1984) 90(6) *Journal of the Institute of Brewing* 351

Nutt, David J, Leslie A King and Lawrence D Phillips, 'Drug Harms in the UK: A Multicriteria Decision Analysis' (2010) 376(9752) *The Lancet* 1558

Ohly, Ansgar, 'Das neue UWG – Mehr Freiheit für den Wettbewerb? [The new UWG – More Freedom for Competition?]' (2004) *GRUR* 889

Popovici, Ioana, 'Alcohol Use and Crime: Findings from a Longitudinal Sample of U.S. Adolescents and Young Adults' (2012) 36(3) *Alcoholism, Clinical and Experimental Research* 532

Posner, Richard A, and William M Landes, 'The Economics of Trademark Law' (1988) 78 *Trademark Reporter* 267

Rogers, John D, and Thomas K Greenfield, 'Beer Drinking Accounts for Most of the Hazardous Alcohol Consumption Reported in the United States' (2015) 60(6) *Journal of Studies on Alcohol* 732

Room, Robin, Deborah Gleeson and Mia Miller, 'Alcoholic Beverages in Trade Agreements: Industry Lobbying and the Public Health Interest' (2021) 40(1) *Drug and Alcohol Review* 19

Room, Robin, et al, 'Supranational Changes in Drinking Patterns: Factors in Explanatory Models of Substantial and Parallel Social Change' (2020) 28(6) Addiction Research & Theory 467

Rusch, Neil, 'Controlled Fermentation, Honey, Bees and Alcohol: Archaeological and Ethnohistorical Evidence from Southern Africa' (2020) 33(1) *South African Humanities* 1

Schmidt, Aernout, 'Radbruch in Cyberspace: About Law-System Quality and ICT Innovation' (2009) 3(2) *Masaryk University Journal of Law and Technology* 195

Schweitzer, Michael, and Rudolf Streinz, 'Reinheitsgebot fur Bier und freier Warenverkehr' (1984) 39 *Recht der internationalen Wirtschaft* 41

Spinardi, Graham, 'Performance-based Design, Expertise Asymmetry, and Professionalism: Fire Safety Regulation in the Neoliberal Era' (2019) 13(4) *Regulation & Governance* 520

The Lancet Rheumatology, 'Alcohol and Health: All, None, or Somewhere In-between?' (2023) 5(4) *The Lancet Rheumatology* 167

Thomas, Diana W, 'Deregulation despite Transitional Gains: The Brewers Guild of Cologne 1461' (2009) 140(3/4) *Public Choice* 329

Thomas, Diana W, and Peter T Leeson, 'The Brewer, the Baker, and the Monopoly Maker' (2012) 1(1) *Journal of Entrepreneurship and Public Policy* 84

Timberg, Sigmund, 'Trademarks, Monopoly and the Restraint of Competition' (1949) 14(2) *Law and Contemporary Problems* 323

Tirado-Kulieva, Vicente Amirpasha, et al, 'A Comprehensive Review of the Benefits of Drinking Craft Beer: Role of Phenolic Content in Health and Possible Potential of the Alcoholic Fraction' (2023) 6 *Current Research in Food Science* 100477

Tomlinson, Monica F, et al, 'Recreational Drug Use and Human Aggressive Behavior: A Comprehensive Review since 2003' (2016) 27 *Aggression and Violent Behavior* 9

Tremblay, Victor J, et al, 'The Dynamics of Industry Concentration for US Micro and Macro Brewers' (2005) 26(3) *Review of Industrial Organization* 304

Vrana, Filip, 'Právovárečná měšťanstva – část 1: Historie a právní vývoj [Brewing-Law Burghers – Part 1: History and Legal Development]' (2018) 64(1) *Kvasný Průmysl* 29

Wilson, RG, 'Greene King: A Business and Family History' (1983) 58(4) *Business History Review* 639

Wright, Alexandra, Katherine E Smith and Mark Hellowell, 'Policy Lessons from Health Taxes: A Systematic Review of Empirical Studies' (2017) 17(1) *BMC Public Health* 583

Yeomans, Henry, 'Taxation, State Formation, and Governmentality: The Historical Development of Alcohol Excise Duties in England and Wales' (2018) 42(2) *Social Science History* 269

Yeomans, Martin R, et al, 'Alcohol and Food Intake' (2003) 6(6) *Current Opinion in Clinical Nutrition and Metabolic Care* 639

Zajíc, Libor, 'Pivo jako předmět bádání v rámci humanitních věd [Beer as an Object of Research in the Humanities]' (2023) 70(2) *Studia Historica Brunensia* 7
Zeigler, Donald W, 'The Alcohol Industry and Trade Agreements: A Preliminary Assessment' (2009) 104(1) *Addiction* 13
Zhuang, Shiwen et al, 'Brewing with 100% Unmalted Grains: Barley, Wheat, Oat and Rye' (2017) 243(3) *European Food Research & Technology* 447

REPORTS

BarthHaas, *BarthHaas Report 2023/2024* (Report, July 2024)
Foley, Anthony, *International Comparisons of Irish Alcohol Excise Taxation in the European Union and the UK in 2024* (Research Report, July 2024)
Paradis et al, *Canada's Guidance on Alcohol and Health* (Final Report, January 2023)
World Health Organization, *Global Status Report on Alcohol and Health and Treatment of Substance Use Disorders* (Global Report, 25 June 2024)
No place for Cheap Alcohol: The Potential Value of Minimum Pricing for Protecting Lives (Report, 2022)

ARTICLES (WEBSITES AND BLOGS)

'2023 Brewers Association Beer Style Guideline', *Brewers Association* (Web Page)
Acitelli, Tom, 'The Origins of America's First University Degree in Brewing', *All About Beer* (Web Page, 11 June 2015)
Advertising Ethics Jury, 'Communication Centre Launches New Educational Message on Alcohol Advertising, in Consultation with Industry', *JEP* (Web Page, 26 February 2024)
Albuquerque, William, 'Riding the Pink Elephant: A Kook at Delirium', *The Bowdoin Orient* (Web Page, 3 December 2010)
Allagash in Oregon, 'Results For "Coolship"', *Allagash Brewing Company* (Web Page)
Alworth, Jeff, 'The Complex, 500-Year-Old Story of Reinheitsgebot', *Beervana* (Web Page, 6 April 2021)
American Beverage Co Ambev, '20-F' for 12/31/04 – EX-4.17', *SEC Info* (Web Page)
Anderson, Kym, 'Beverage Market Disruptions and Their Trade Consequences', *CEPR* (Web Page, 16 February 2020)
Australia Competition and Consumer Commission, 'ACCC Releases Findings of Beer Taps Investigation', ACCC (Media Release, 13 July 2017)
'Ban on Regular Glass in High-risk Venues', *Business Queensland* (Web Page, 29 November 2017)
Bavaria NV, 'Final Victory in Italy for Dutch Brewery Bavaria in Trademark Battle', *PR Newswire* (Web Page, 24 September 2012)
'Bayerische Biergartenverordnung [Bavarian Beer Garden Ordinance]', (Web Page, 20 April 1999)
'Bayerisches Bier', *European Commission* (Web Page)
'Beer Consumption by Country 2024', *World Population Review* (Web Page)
'Beer Culture in Belgium', *UNESCO Intangible Heritage* (Web Page)
'Beers of Old', *Central European University* (Web Page, 16 June 2014)
'Belgian Beer Café', *Creneau International* (Web Page)
'Belgian Beer Café', *Franchise* (Web Page)
Belgian Beer Café Melbourne (Web Page)

Belgium Beer World (Web Page)
Bernstein, Adam, 'Joseph Owades Dies at 86; The Father of Light Beer', *The Washington Post* (Web Page, 21 December 2005)
'BJCP Style Guidelines', *Beer Judge Certification Program* (Web Page, 18 May 2023)
Björgúlfsdóttir, Helga Dís, 'Beer in Iceland: A Historical Overview', *Your Friend in Reykjavik* (Web Page, 3 August 2023)
Blake, Victoria Carollo, 'The Oxford Companion to Beer Definition of Hops', *Craft Beer & Brewing* (Web Page)
Blecher, Natalia, 'Bavaria NV v Bayerischer Brauerbund eV', *Lexology* (Web Page, 10 August 2009)
Boffey, Daniel, 'Belgian Bars Put the Boot into Tourists Who Steal Beer Glasses', *The Guardian* (Web Page, 15 March 2018)
Brewers Association, '2023 Beer Style Guidelines', *Brewers Association* (Web Page, 18 May 2023)
British Beer and Pub Association, 'Written Evidence Submitted by the British Beer and Pub Association', *UK Parliament* (Web Page, October 2022)
'British Beer History', *Beer Day Britain* (Web Page)
Brown, Pete, 'Who Really Owns/Brews Your Favourite Beer?', *Pete Brown* (Web Page, 16 December 2022)
'Budweiser Budvar Has Won Two Lawsuits in Italy', *Budweiser Budvar* (Web Page, 23 August 2023)
'Budweiser Trademark Dispute', *Wikipedia* (Web Page, 28 July 2024)
Burnet, Clare, 'Craft Beer Retailer in Trademark Battle with Coles', *Brews News* (Web Page, 12 May 2020)
'Canada – Tax Exemptions and Reductions for Wine and Beer', *World Trade Organization* (Web Page)
Canet, Julie, 'Tesla Has Beer but No Trademark', *Lexology* (Web Page, 16 October 2023)
Carlsberg Breweries A/S, 'Rebrewing the First Quality Beer Using Carlsberg's Original Purified Yeast', *Carlsberg Group* (Web Page)
Carlsberg Breweries, 'The Invention of the pH Scale', *Carlsberg Group* (Web Page)
Carpenter, Dave, 'Ask the Experts: Belgian Yeast Strains', *Craft Beer & Brewing* (Web Page, 13 March 2006)
'What Is the Difference between Ale and Lager?', *Craft Beer & Brewing* (Web Page, 18 May 2017)
'Causing a Brouhaha: Trade Secrets Disputes in the Craft Beer Industry', *Orrick* (Web Page, 4 February 2017)
Child, Ted, 'What Came First: The Beer or the Bread?', *The Growler* (Blog Post, 30 June 2023)
Chini, Maïthé, 'Bar Goers in Belgium Asked to Stop Stealing Beer Glasses', *The Brussels Times* (Web Page, 18 October 2022)
Cizmar, Martin, 'The Etiquette of Cooperation: 7 Simple Ground Rules for Successful Collaboration Beers', *BeerAdvocate* (Web Page, February 2016)
Clark, D, 'Tax Receipts in the United Kingdom from 2000/01 to 2023/24', *Statista* (Web Page, 3 July 2024)
Clun, Rachel, 'The Fight Brewing over the Beer Giants That Have Captured the Australian Market', *Sydney Morning Herald* (Web Page, 29 April 2024)
Cohen, Jennie, 'Did Beer Spur the Rise of Agriculture and Politics?', *History* (Web Page, 23 August 2018)
'Collaboration Not Litigation Ale', *BeerAdvocate* (Web Page)

'Collaborative Brewing Agreement', *Nebraska Liquor Control Commission* (Web Page)
'Contemporary Environmental Challenges and Opportunities within the Brewing Industry', *Donut Waste* (Web Page, 7 February 2023)
Conway, Jan, 'Annual Revenue from Beer Excise Duty in Germany from 2008 to 2022', *Statista* (Web Page, 2 May 2024)
'Leading Beer Importing Countries Worldwide in 2022, by Trade Value', *Statista* (Web Page, 22 May 2024)
Cornell, Martyn, 'The Porter Brewer and the Peterloo Massacre', *Zythophile* (Web Page, 22 November 2018)
Craft Beer, 'Seek the Seal™', *CraftBeer.com* (Web Page)
'Craft Beer Trademarks: Beer vs Wine', *David Lizerbram & Associates* (Blog Post, 2 December 2014)
Crafty Pint, 'Take Two', *The Crafty Pint* (Web Page, 16 November 2011)
'Criteria for Obtaining the ATP Label', *International Trappist Association* (Web Page)
'Das Reinheitsgebot [The Purity Law]', *Private Brauereien Bayern* (Web Page)
'Deutsche Brauwirtschaft in Zahlen [German Brewing Industry in Figures]', *Deutscher Brauer-Bund* (Web Page, 10 April 2024)
Delirium Café Brussels', *Delirium Village Brussels* (Web Page)
'Die Ursprünge des untergärigen Lagerbieres – Eine Theorie [The Origins of Bottom-Fermented Lager – A Theory]', *Schlenkerla* (Web Page)
Didora, Paige Latham, 'What's Fair in Beer and Litigation? – The Role of Noncompetes, Nondisclosures, and Trade Secrets in Brewing', *Good Beer Hunting* (Web Page, 18 February 2021)
Dimiter Toshkov, '30 Years of Socio-Economic Developments in Central and Eastern Europe', *Dimiter Toshkov* (Web Page, November 2019)
Donaldson, Michael, 'NZ Creation Phantasm Revolutionises Beer World', *Pursuit of Hoppiness* (Web Page, 1 September 2022)
Dornbusch, Horst, and Garrett Oliver, 'The Oxford Companion to Beer Definition of Weissbier', *Craft Beer & Brewing* (Web Page)
Dychmenko, Alan, Milan Gersl and Tomáš Gregor, 'Brewing Beer Using Bakery Leftovers as a Substitute for Malt', *Research Gate* (Web Page, February 2023)
Edda, Sæmund, and DL Ashliman (eds), 'Hávamál [The Words of Odin the High One]', (Web Page)
Eiken, Jens, 'The Oxford Companion to Beer Definition of Denmark', *Craft Beer & Brewing* (Web Page)
Ekelin, Svante, 'The Oxford Companion to Beer Definition of Finland', *Craft Beer & Brewing* (Web Page)
'Elon Musk-Backed Tesla GigaBier Beer Is Here, Pack of 3 Priced over Rs 8K', *The Economic Times* (Web Page, 31 March 2023)
Erb, Kelly Phillips, '13 Quirky Beer and Tax Facts on National Beer Day', *Forbes* (Web Page, 7 April 2015)
'15 Fun Facts about Beer and Taxes on National Beer Day', *Forbes* (Web Page, 7 April 2023)
'Erdinger Beer Glass: No Trademark Protection as 3D Mark', *Meyer-Dulheuer MD Legal Patentanwälte PartG mbB* (Web Page, 29 September 2020)
Evison, James, 'Drinking Habits Shift as UK Changes from Beer to Wine', *The Drinks Business* (Web Page, 27 November 2023)
Eymold, Ursula, 'Oktoberfest', *Historical Dictionary of Bavaria* (Web Page, 5 June 2013)

Fallon, Daniel, 'Why Belgian Beer Tastes Different (and Better) in Belgium', *Sydney Morning Herald* (Web Page, 11 August 2023)
Forman, Dan M, 'Courts Help Brewers Protect Their Recipes and Techniques from Employee Theft', *CDF Labor Law* (Blog Post)
'Galaxy', *Hop Products Australia* (Web Page)
Gapper, John, 'AB InBev Should Defy the Bud Light Culture War', *Financial Times* (Web Page, 28 April 2023)
Garshol, Lars Marius, 'A Small Dictionary of Finnish Drinking Words', *Larsblog* (Blog Post, 16 August 2020)
'Danish Farmhouse Ale', *Larsblog* (Blog Post, 16 August 2015)
'Gotlandsdricke – An Overview', *Larsblog* (Blog Post, 8 January 2017)
'Larsblog' (Blog Post)
'Nordic Grog', *Larsblog* (Blog Post, 9 February 2015)
'Raw Ale', *Larsblog* (Blog Post, 5 June 2015)
'The Early History of Hops', *Larsblog* (Blog Post, 6 December 2022)
'The True Meaning of Christmas', *Larsblog* (Blog Post, 15 December 2020)
'When Did People Start Reusing Yeast?', *Larsblog* (Blog Post, 29 April 2018)
'When Not Brewing Christmas Beer Was Illegal', *Larsblog* (Blog Post, 7 December 2019)
'Genieten van bier in een unieke brouwerij [Enjoying Beer in a Unique Brewery]', *Brouwerij Klein Kloosterke* (Web Page)
Gibbs, Alexandra, 'Why HSBC Chose to Move on from Being "The World's Local Bank"', *CNBC* (Web Page, 17 August 2016)
Global Health Observatory, 'Number of Standard Alcoholic Drinks Displayed on Containers', *World Health Organization* (Web Page)
'Taxes on Alcoholic Beverages', *World Health Organization* (Web Page, 2022)
Goethe, Johann Wolfgang von, 'The Project Gutenberg eBook of Faust [Part 1]. Translated into English in the Original Metres', *Gutenberg* (Web Page, 4 January 2005)
Graefe, L, 'Ausgeschenkte Menge Bier auf dem Oktoberfest in München von 1980 bis 2023 [Amount of Beer Served at the Oktoberfest in Munich from 1980 to 2023]', *Statista* (Web Page, 3 January 2024)
Gribbins, Keith 'Let's Talk Non-Compete Agreements in the Brewing Industry and Reflect on the Toppling Goliath Suit', *Craft Brewing Business* (Web Page, 6 August 2018)
Grimoldby, Stephanie N, 'Attorney Predicts Deceptive Labeling Class Actions Will Increase; Leffe Case Brewing in Florida', *Florida Record* (Web Page, 29 April 2016)
Grönvall, Camilla Waltersson, and Zandra Milton, 'Bättre förutsättningar för besöksnäringen i fråga om småskalig produktion av alkoholdrycker [Better Conditions for the Tourism Industry in Terms of Small-Scale Production of Alcoholic Beverages]', *Government Offices of Sweeden* (Web Page, 4 July 2024)
'Guinness through the Ages: The Story of Guinness', *Guinness Storehouse* (Web Page)
Hall, Nick, '13 Strongest Beers in the World for Serious Brew-Snobs', *Man of Many* (Web Page, 7 August 2023)
Herz, Julia, 'The Roots of American Craft Brewing', *CraftBeer.com* (Web Page, 15 May 2014)
Higgins, Tucker, 'Brewers Warn Supreme Court: Back the Clean Water Act, or Beer Will Taste Like Medicine', *CNBC* (Web Page, 15 October 2019)
'Historie piva v Čechách [History of Beer in Bohemia]', *BeerWeb* (Web Page)
'History of the Malting Process', *Great Western Malting* (Web Page)
'History of the UC Davis Master Brewers Certificate Program', *UC Davis* (Web Page)
'History', *Musée De La Bière Schaerbeekois* (Web Page)

'Hladina alkoholu v krvi řidiče vozidla do 0,2% [The Level of Alcohol in the Blood of the Driver of the Vehicle up to 0.2%]', *Policie České republiky* (Web Page, 2016)

HM Treasury, 'Chancellor Unveils a Budget for Growth', *Gov.UK* (Web Page, 15 March 2023)

Hofer, Franz D, 'The Munich Baker–Brewer Dispute: Yeast and the Emergence of Lager', *A Tempest in a Tankard* (Web Page, 23 April 2024)

Hoffer, Adam, 'Beer Taxes in Europe, 2023', *Tax Foundation* (Web Page, 19 September 2023)

'Beer Taxes by State, 2024', *Tax Foundation* (Web Page, 11 June 2024)

'Modernization of the Alcohol Tax', *Tax Foundation* (Web Page, December 2023)

House of Belgian Brewers 2024 (Web Page)

Ilic, Nikolina, 'So, Turns Out Beer Spas Are the Newest Thing in Wellness', *Australian Men's Health* (Web page, 18 October 2022)

Infante, Dave, 'When Brewers Enforce Non-Competes, Everybody Loses', *VinePair* (Web Page, 16 February 2024)

Infante, Jessica, 'Former Sales Reps Challenge Boston Beer's Non-Compete in Pair of Lawsuits, Allege Hostile Work Environment', *Brewbound* (Web Page, 7 February 2024)

Intergovernmental Committee for the Safeguarding of the Intangible Cultural Heritage, 'Decision of the Intergovernmental Committee: 11.COM 10.B.5', *UNESCO* (Web Page)

'Decision of the Intergovernmental Committee: 17.COM 7.B.4', *UNESCO* (Web Page)

Internet Archive, 'Beer Politics through the Ages', *The Wayback Machine* (Web Page)

'Jean De Clerck', *Wikipedia* (Web Page, 7 March 2024)

Jean, Hillary St, 'Key Legal Considerations for Breweries, Part I: Transactional and Contract Matters', *Rogoway Law Group* (Web Page, 15 March 2024)

Jikiun, Kjetil, 'The Oxford Companion to Beer Definition of Norway', *Craft Beer & Brewing* (Web Page)

Johnston, Katie, 'The Brewer behind Sam Adams Has Long Kept Former Employees on a Tight Leash. Now Some Are Suing to Break Free', *The Boston Globe* (Web Page, 8 March 2024)

Kain, Kevin, 'Rethinking Vienna Lager in Mexico', *Casket Beer* (Web Page, 11 November 2020)

Keene, Ben, 'The Oxford Companion to Beer Definition of Carter, James Earl, Jr', *Craft Beer & Brewing* (Web Page)

Keene, Celes, 'Theft of Trade Secrets: The Newest Chapter in the War of the Beer Companies', *Klemchuk LLP* (Blog Post, 30 October 2019)

Kendall, Justin, 'Anheuser-Busch Accuses MillerCoors of Stealing Confidential Beer Recipes', *Brewbound* (Web Page, 17 October 2019)

Kingdom of Belgians (Web Page)

Kix, Paul, 'How David Fincher, Sharon Stone and a Bunch of Scheming Canadians Conspired to Create Ice Beer', *Thrillist* (Web Page, 23 July 2015)

Klos, Mathieu, 'AB InBev and Heineken Settle Global Beer dispenser Dispute', *JUVE Patent* (Web Page, 5 May 2020)

Kolmar, Chris, 'The 10 Largest Beer Companies in the World', *Zippia* (Web Page, 19 April 2023)

Krupp, Allison, 'Could This Popular, Bitter Drink Have Healing Powers?', *healthline* (Web Page, 3 April 2020)

Laitinen, Mika, 'Sahti and Related Ancient Farmhouse Ales', *Brewing Nordic* (Web Page)

'LalBrew Abbaye™', *Lallemand Brewing* (Web Page)

Lamb, Karen, and David Farmer, 'The Genius at Guinness and His Statistical Legacy', *The Conversation* (Web Page, 16 March 2018)

Larsson, Mårten, 'Did You Know That... There Was a Law on Growing Hops in Sweden?', *Skåne Plus* (Web Page, 10 August 2023)

Lech, Mikołaj, 'The Oldest Registered Trademarks in the World', *Kancelaria Patentowa 'LECH'* (Web Page)

Lee-Weitz, Grace, '7 Indigenous Breweries to Support during Native American Heritage Month (and Forever)', *Hop Culture* (Web Page, 16 November 2021)

Lee, Gifford, 'Fears for Aussie Brewers over Euro Free Trade Deal', *Beer & Brewer* (Web Page, 13 October 2022)

'Leffe', *Wikipedia* (Web Page, 24 April 2024)

Linderborg, Tanja, et al, 'Standardregler för stor stark [Standard Rules for Large Strong]', *Sveriges Riksdag* (Web Page, 30 September 1999)

Ly, Chen, 'Guinness Yeasts Are Genetically Unique among Irish Beers', *New Scientist* (Web Page, 12 January 2024)

'Made in Italy Enhancement', *Asacert* (Web Page)

'Malt', *All About Beer* (Web Page)

Mark, Joshua J, 'Beer in the Ancient World', *World History Encyclopedia* (Web Page, 2 March 2011)

'Mexico Is the World's Leading Beer Exporter in the World', *MexicoNow* (Web Page, 15 August 2022)

'Michael Jackson (writer)', *Wikipedia* (Web Page, 27 September 2024)

'Monty Python Live at the Hollywood Bowl', *IMDb* (Web Page)

Moss, Candida, 'How Beer Ruled the Ancient World', *Daily Beast* (Web Page, 6 March 2021)

Neuscheler, Von Tillmann, 'Streit um Benediktiner-Bier [Dispute over Benedictine Beer]', *FRAZ.NET* (Web Page, 18 May 2023)

Nordic Council of Ministers, 'Nordic Nutrition Recommendations 2023 Alcohol' (Web Page, 2023)

'No Patents on Beer! Carlsberg Claims Barley and Beer as Its Invention', *No Patents on Seeds* (Web Page, 17 November 2016)

Obesity Evidence Hub, 'Countries That Have Taxes on Sugar-Sweetened Beverages (SSBs)', *Obesity Evidence Hub* (Web Page, 21 March 2024)

Office of Communications, 'Brewer's Notice', *Alcohol and Tobacco Tax and Trade Bureau US Department* (Web Page, 26 January 2020)

'Our Story', *New Belgium Brewing* (Web Page)

Pete Drinks, 'Import vs. Brewed under License', *Pete Drinks* (Web Page, 17 October 2014)

'Pizza', *Wikipedia* (Web Page, 7 October 2024)

'Postgraduate Programme Malting and Brewing Sciences', *KU Leuven* (Web Page)

Prensky, Hannah, 'Beer Spa: Health Hack or Tacky Tourist Trap?', *Columbia Science Review* (Web Page, 11 July 2019)

Ratebeer, 'Your Guide to the World of Beer' (Web Page)

Rath, Martin, 'Im Wendekreis des Malzbiers [In the Tropic of Malt Beer]', *Legal Tribune Online* (Web Page, 27 October 2019)

'Reglamento de la Ley General de Salud en Materia de Publicidad [Regulation of the General Law on Health in Matters of Advertising]' (Web Page, 4 May 2000)

'Reinheitsgebot [Purity Law]', *Wikipedia* (Web Page, 27 August 2024)

Renteria, Melissa, 'Executing a Global Strategy, Locally: Lessons from the World's Local Bank', *Columbia Business School* (Web Page, 15 March 2023)

'Restricting Digital Marketing in the Context of Tobacco, Alcohol, Food and Beverages, and Breast-Milk Substitutes: Existing Approaches and Policy Options', *World Health Organization* (Web Page, 2023)

Riley, Charles, 'AB InBev Accuses Rival of Obtaining the Secret Recipe for Bud Light', *CNN Business* (Web Page, 18 October 2019)

Rokka, Jussi, 'The Oxford Companion to Beer Definition of Finland', *Craft Beer & Brewing* (Web Page)

Ropes and Gray, 'Refusal to Register "Beer Glass and Stand" Mark Affirmed', *World Trademark Review* (Web Page, 24 September 2010)

Rupprecht, Klaus, 'Reinheitsgebot, 1516 [Purity Law, 1516]', *Historisches Lexikon Bayerns* (Web Page, 28 July 2016)

Ryanc, 'English Pale Ale: Exploring Its Unique Taste and History', *Brewers Union* (Web Page)

'Search the Oxford Companion to Beer', *Craft Beer & Brewing* (Web Page)

Sherlach, Tonia, 'How Old Are Taxes? Older than You Think', *National Geographic* (Web Page, 11 April 2024)

Shutterstock, 'Bottling a Brand: How Alcohol Branding Differs from Beer to Wine to Liquor', *Shutterstock* (Web Page, 5 July 2016)

Smale, Will, 'Italian Label Maybe but the Beer's British Brewed', *BBC* (Web page, 15 December 2022)

Snider, Mike, 'On National Beer Day 2024, the US Is Drinking More Modelo than Bud Light as NA Brews Rise', *USA Today* (Web Page, 6 April 2024)

Snowdon, Christopher, 'Nanny State Index', *Institute of Economic Affairs* (Web Page, 2023)

'Sovereign Right to Tax Goods in "Taxation"', *World Trade Organization* (Web Page)

Speak, Clare, 'How Italy's Government Wants to Rank Italian Restaurants Abroad', *The Local Italy* (Web Page, 9 May 2023)

Stafilidis, Tasso, et al, 'Med anledning av prop. 2003/04:38 En ny prisinformationslag m.m [In Connection with Bill 2003/04:38 A New Price Information Act, etc]', *Sveriges Riksdag* (Web Page, 2 December 2003)

Standlee, Emily 'A Brewery without Booze: How Anheuser-Busch Pivoted to Survive Prohibition', *Feast Magazine* (Web Page, 31 May 2023)

Statista Research Department, 'Average Price Per Unit of Beer in the Asia-Pacific Region in 2023 with a Forecast for 2024, by Country or Territory', *Statista* (Web Page, 11 September 2024)

Statista Research Department, 'Bierverbrauch pro Kopf in Deutschland in den Jahren 1950 bis 2023 [Beer Consumption Per Capita in Germany from 1950 to 2023]', *Statista* (Web Page, 26 June 2024)

Stella Artois (Web Page)

Strong, Gordon, and Kristen England, '2021 Beer Style Guidelines', *Beer Judge Certification Program* (Web Page)

Sturluson, Snorri, 'Heimskringla The Chronicle of the Kings of Norway', *Gutenberg* (Web Page, 27 November 2009)

Sugiura, Eri, 'AB InBev Chief Blames Social Media as Transgender Spat Drains Bud Light Sales', *Financial Times* (Web Page, 8 May 2023)

Svantesson, Dan, 'Australian Consumer Law Is Failing Beer Drinkers', *The Conversation* (Web Page, 11 October 2017)

'What Beer Brewing Can Teach Law Students about ChatGPT", *Bond University* (Blog Post, 2 February 2023)

'With Many "Foreign" Beers Now Brewed in Australia, Is It Time for Clearer Labels?', *ABC News* (Web Page, 11 October 2017)

Swedish Breweries, 'Bryggerirapport [Brewery Report]', *Swedish Breweries* (Web Page, 2023)

'Taste Test: Locally Brewed vs Imported', *Choice* (Web Page, 12 August 2014)

'Tax on Shopping and Services', *Gov.UK* (Web Page)

'Taxes in Europe Database v4', *European Commission* (Web Page)

'Tête De Mort [Skull]', *European Union Intellectual Property Office* (Web Page)

'The Beer and Pub Manifesto 2024', *British Beer and Pub Association* (Web Page)

The Brussels Times with Belga, 'Number of Belgian Breweries Drops for the First Time in 15 Years', *The Brussels Times* (Web Page, 13 January 2024)

'The Custom of Buying a Round', *Britain Explained* (Web Page)

'The Senate Overrides the President's Veto of the Volstead Act', *United States Senate* (Web Page, 28 October 1919)

'The Story of Guinness', *Guinness* (Web Page)

Thomas, Louis, 'Ten Countries that Drink the Most Beer', *The Drinks Business* (Web Page, 7 November 2022)

Törne, Lars von, 'Tradition des Vatertags: Als die Söhne saufen lernten [Father's Day Tradition: When the Sons Learned to Drink]', *Tagesspiegel* (Web Page, 14 May 2015)

'UC Davis Brewing Program History', *UC Davis* (Web Page)

United States Patent Office, 'Preparation of a Low Dextrin Beer by Using Amyloglucosidase' (Web Page)

Untapped, 'Find Beers You'll Love' (Web Page)

'US Beer Giant Loses Bud Trade Mark Battle', *Pinsent Masons* (Web Page, 18 February 2003)

Vasa Museet, 'Vasa – The Machine of War', *Vasa Museet* (Web Page, 18 June 2020)

Vasa Museet, '12. In Battle', *Vasa Museet* (Web Page, 13 October 2020)

Verive, John, 'Gearhead: Pasteurization's Place in Craft Beer's Battle', *Craft Beer & Brewing* (Web Page, 9 May 2020)

Verstl, Ina, 'Trust-Busters: Heineken Unit Brau Union Abuses Market Power', *BRAUWELT International 2024* (Web Page, 6 July 2024)

VinePair Staff, 'Top 20 Beer Producing Countries in the World', *VinePair* (Web Page, 22 July 2024)

Walch, Stephan, 'Jahresabschlussbericht 2016 [Annual Report]', *CVUA Karlsruhe* (Web Page, 2016)

'Welcome to Oktoberfest', *Oktoberfest Munich* (Web Page)

'Weyermann® Acidulated Malt', *Weyermann* (Web Page)

'Weyermann® Carahell®', *Weyermann* (Web Page)

'Weyermann® Isaria 1924®', *Weyermann* (Web Page)

'Weyermann® Munich Malt Type 2', *Weyermann* (Web Page)

'What Beer Brewing Can Teach Law Students about ChatGPT', *Bond University* (Blog Post, 2 February 2023)

'What Is Draught or Draft Beer? Everything You Need to Know', *Beer & Wine Guide* (Web Page, 18 April 2023)

'What Makes Irish Beer Special [2024]', *Best in Ireland* (Web Page, 14 November 2024)

'Why Iceland Banned Beer', *BBC* (Web Page, 1 March 2015)

'William Sealy Gosset', *Wikipedia* (Web Page, 16 August 2024)

Witte, Melissa De, 'An Ancient Thirst for Beer May Have Inspired Agriculture, Stanford Archaeologists Say', *Stanford Report* (Web Page, 12 September 2018)

World Health Organization, 'Controlling the Global Obesity Epidemic' (Web Page)

'No Level of Alcohol Consumption Is Safe for Our Health' (News Release, 4 January 2023)

Young, Andy, 'Top 10 Weirdest Beer Ingredients', *The Drinks Business* (Web Page, 22 February 2013)

Young, Robert G, 'The Secret Sauce: Protecting Brewing Recipes and Processes – The Role of Employee Agreements', *Bowditch & Dewey* (Blog Post, 8 December 2016)

Ysewijn, Regula, 'My Books: Belgian Café Culture', *Miss Foodwise* (Web Page, 20 October 2016)

'Žatec and the Landscape of Saaz Hops', *UNESCO* (Web Page)

بلجيان بير كافيه [Belgian Beer Café], *Visit Ras Al Khaimah* (Web Page)

LEGISLATION

An Act to Amend the Internal Revenue Code of 1954 with Respect to Excise Tax on Certain Trucks, Buses, Tractors, et Cetera, Home Production of Beer and Wine, Refunds of the Taxes on Gasoline and Special Fuels to Aerial Applicators, and Partial Rollovers of Lump Sum Distributions, Pub L No 95-458, 92 Stat 1255

Australia New Zealand Food Standards Code

Beerhouse Act 1830 (UK)

Council Decision (EU) 2021/651 of 19 April 2021 on the Signing, on Behalf of the Union, of the Agreement in the Form of an Exchange of Letters between the European Union and the Argentine Republic Pursuant to Article XXVIII of the General Agreement on Tariffs and Trade (GATT) 1994 Relating to the Modification of Concessions on All the Tariff-Rate Quotas Included in the EU Schedule CLXXV as a Consequence of the United Kingdom's Withdrawal from the European Union [2021] OJ L 135/01

Council Directive (EU) 2020/1151 of 29 July 2020 Amending Directive 92/83/EEC on the Harmonization of the Structures of Excise Duties on Alcohol and Alcoholic Beverages [2020] OJ L 256/1

Council Directive 92/83/EEC of 19 October 1992 on the Harmonization of the Structures of Excise Duties on Alcohol and Alcoholic Beverages [1992] OJ L 316/21

Council Directive 92/84/EEC of 19 October 1992 on the Approximation of the Rates of Excise Duty on Alcohol and Alcoholic Beverages [1992] OJ L 316/29

Craft Beverage Modernization Act of 2020 (USA)

Decision No 854/2005/EC of the European Parliament and of the Council of 11 May 2005 Establishing a Multiannual Community Programme on Promoting Safer Use of the Internet and New Online Technologies [2005] OJ L 149/1

Directive 2004/22/EC of the European Parliament and of the Council of 31 March 2004 on Measuring Instruments [2004] OJ L 135/1

Directive 2005/29/EC of the European Parliament and of the Council of 11 May 2005 Concerning Unfair Business-to-Consumer Commercial Practices in the Internal Market and Amending Council Directive 84/450/EEC, Directives 97/7/EC, 98/27/EC and 2002/65/EC of the European Parliament and of the Council and Regulation (EC) No 2006/2004 of the European Parliament and of the Council [2005] OJ L 149/22

Directive 2006/114/EC of the European Parliament and of the Council of 12 December 2006 Concerning Misleading and Comparative Advertising [2006] OJ L 376/21

Excise Ordinance 202-14 (22 July 1643)

Excise Tariff Act 1921 (Cth)

Food and Drug Regulations CRC (C)

Licensing Act 2003 (UK)

Magna Carta 1215

Public Health (Alcohol) Act 2018 (Ireland)

Public Health (Alcohol) (Labelling) Regulations 2023 (Ireland)

Regulation (EC) No 1333/2008 of the European Parliament and of the Council of 16 December 2008 on Food Additives [2008] OJ L 354/16

Regulation (EC) No 178/2002 of the European Parliament and of the Council of 28 January 2002 Laying Down the General Principles and Requirements of Food Law, Establishing the European Food Safety Authority and Laying Down Procedures in Matters of Food Safety [2002] OJ L 31/1

Regulation (EC) No 1924/2006 of the European Parliament and of the Council of 20 December 2006 on Nutrition and Health Claims Made on Foods [2006] OJ L 404/9

Regulation (EU) 2018/848 of the European Parliament and of the Council of 30 May 2018 on Organic Production and Labelling of Organic Products and Repealing Council Regulation (EC) No 834/2007 [2018] OJ L 150/1

Regulation (EU) No 1169/2011 of the European Parliament and of the Council of 25 October 2011 on the Provision of Food Information to Consumers, Amending Regulations (EC) No 1924/2006 and (EC) No 1925/2006 of the European Parliament and of the Council, and Repealing Commission Directive 87/250/EEC, Council Directive 90/496/EEC, Commission Directive 1999/10/EC, Directive 2000/13/EC of the European Parliament and of the Council, Commission Directives 2002/67/EC and 2008/5/EC and Commission Regulation (EC) No 608/2004 Text with EEA Relevance [2011] OJ L 304/18

Regulation (EU) No 251/2014 of the European Parliament and of the Council of 26 February 2014 on the Definition, Description, Presentation, Labelling and the Protection of Geographical Indications of Aromatised Wine Products and Repealing Council Regulation (EEC) No 1601/91 [2014] OJ L 84/14

Reinheitsgebot 1516 (Germany)

CASES

Alpirsbacher Klosterbräu Glauner GmbH & Co KG v European Union Intellectual Property Office (T 844/16) [2017] Judgment of the General Court (Ninth Chamber)

Anheuser-Busch, Inc v Budějovick [yacute] Budvar, Národní Podnik & Ors [2002] FCA 390

Anheuser-Busch, Inc v John Labatt Limited, 89 F 3d 1339 (8th Cir, 1996)

Bavaria NV v Bayerischer Brauerbund eV [2009] FCA 428

Bayerischer V erwaltungsgerichtshof [Bavarian Administrative Court], (22 CS 23.1265, 22 August 2023)

Bundesgerichtshof [German Federal Court of Justice], I ZR 106/89, GRUR, 21 February 1992

Bundesgerichtshof [German Federal Court of Justice], I ZR 136/84, 10 December 1987 reported in GRUR 1987

Bundesgerichtshof [German Federal Court of Justice], I ZR 252/16, 17 May 2018 reported in GRUR 2018

Bundesgerichtshof [German Federal Court of Justice], I ZR 276/99, 7 November 2002 reported in GRUR 2003

Bundesgerichtshof [German Federal Court of Justice], I ZR 30/81, 21 April 1983 reported in GRUR 1983

Bundesgerichtshof [German Federal Court of Justice], I ZR 33/04, 26 October 2006 reported in NJW 2007

Bundesgerichtshof [German Federal Court of Justice], I ZR 97/04, 26 October 2006 reported in GRUR 2007

Bundesgerichtshof [German Supreme Court] NJW, I ZR 54/96, 19 September 2002

Bundesgerichtshof [German Federal Court of Justice] 2 StR 80/57, 1958

Bundesverband der Verbraucherzentralen und Verbraucherverbände – Verbraucherzentrale Bundesverband eV v Teekanne GmbH & Co KG (C-195/14) [2012] CJEU 361

Cantarella Bros Pty Ltd v Modena Trading Pty Ltd (2014) 254 CLR 337

Commission of the European Communities v Federal Republic of Germany (C-178/84) [1987] ECJ 1227

Court of Appeal of Antwerp, (A&M, 29 June 2009)

Criminal Proceedings against Harry Franzén (C-189/95) [1997] CJEU 504

Decision of the Fourth Board of Appeal of 21 January 2010 (Case R 385/2008-4) OHIM

Deutsches Weintor eG v Land Rheinland-Pfalz (C–544/10) [2012] Judgment of the Court (Third Chamber)

E & J Gallo Winery v Lion Nathan Australia Pty Limited (2009) 175 FCR 386
Eurocermex SA v Office for Harmonisation in the Internal Market (Trade Marks and Designs) (OHIM) (C-286/04 P) [2005] CJEU 422
Federal Administrative Court (Germany), 3 C 5/04, NJW, 24 February 2005
Getty Images (US) Inc & Ors v Stability AI Ltd [2023] EWHC 3090
Google France SARL and Google Inc v Louis Vuitton Malletier SA (C-236/08), *Google France SARL v Viaticum SA and Luteciel SARL* (C-237/08) and *Google France SARL v Centre national de recherche en relations humaines (CNRRH) SARL and Others* (C-238/08) [2010] CJEU 159
Hauser Weinimport GmbH v Freistaat Bayern (C-216/23) [2024] CJEU 393
Hessischer VGH [Hesse Higher Administrative Court] 6 B 31/09, 25 February 2009
L'Oréal SA and Others v eBay International AG and Others (C-324/09) [2011] 474
Landgericht Nürnberg-Fürth [Regional Court Nürnberg-Fürth], 4 HK O 5207/19, 23 July 2021
Oberlandesgericht [German High Court], 4 U 19/14, 20 May 2014 reported in GRUR-RR 2014
Oberlandesgericht München [Munich Court of Appeal], 29 U 3187/15, GRUR-RR, 17 March 2016
Oberlandesgericht München [Munich Court of Appeal], 29 U 885/17, 1 February 2018 reported in GRUR-RR 2018
PrenzMarien GmbH v European Union Intellectual Property Office (T-766/20) [2022] CJEU 123
Purely Creative Ltd and Others v Office of Fair Trading [2012] (C-428/11) CJEU 651
Revue de droit intellectuel [Brussels Commercial Court], 6 September 1985
Rewe-Zentral AG v Federal Monopoly Administration for Spirits (C-120/78) [1979] ECJ 649
Sackett v Environmental Protection Agency (2023) 598 US 651
Schutzverband gegen Unwesen in der Wirtschaft eV v Warsteiner Brauerei Haus Cramer GmbH & Co KG (C-312/98) [2000] EuZW 2001
Stone & Wood Group Pty Ltd v Intellectual Property Development Corporation Pty Ltd [2016] FCA 820
The Coca-Cola Company v Office for Harmonisation in the Internal Market (Trade Marks and Designs) (OHIM) (T-411/14) [2016] Judgment of the General Court (Eighth Chamber)
Unión de Cervecerías Peruanas Backus y Johnston SAA v Office for Harmonisation in the Internal Market (Trade Marks and Designs) (OHIM) (T-323/11) [2012] Judgment of the General Court (Sixth Chamber)
Voss of Norway ASA v Office for Harmonisation in the Internal Market (Trade Marks and Designs) (C-445/13 P) [2015] CJEU 303

OTHER

Brussels.belgianbeercafe, 'Brussels Belgian Beer Café' (Instagram)
Decree of the Ministry of Agriculture No 335/1997
'Excise Duties: Commission Moves against Sweden Over Tax Discrimination Against Wine', *European Commission* (Press Release, IP/01/819, 12 June 2001)
Larsson, Gabriela Bjarne, 'Stadgelagstiftning i senmedeltidens Sverige [Statutory Legislation in Late Medieval Sweden]' (Doctoral Thesis, Stockholm University, 1994)
Madsen, Erik Strøjer, and Yanqing Wu, 'Advertising and Concentration in the Brewing Industry' (Economics Working Papers, Aarhus University, October 2014)
Persyn, Damiaan, Johan Swinnen and Stijn Vanormelingen, *Belgian Beers: Where History Meets Globalization* (Discussion Paper No 271, LICOS Centre for Institutions and Economic Performance, October 2010)

Room, Robin (ed), *The Effects of Nordic Alcohol Policies: What Happens to Drinking and Harm When Alcohol Controls Change* (Nordic Alcohol and Drug Council No 42, 2002)

Scott, Mary Elizabeth, 'A Herefordshire Nunnery, A Calendar, with Introduction, of the Aconbury Cartulary' (MPhil Thesis, University of Southampton, 2001)

UNESCO, 'Beer Culture in Belgium' (Video)

World Health Organization, *Global Status Report on Alcohol and Health* 2018, WHO Doc CC BY-NCSA 3.0 IGO (2018)

World Health Organization, *Global Status Report on Alcohol and Health and Treatment of Substance Use Disorders*, WHO Doc CC BY-NC-SA 3.0 IGO (25 June 2024)

Index

For EU product safety concerns, contact us at Calle de José Abascal, 56–1°, 28003 Madrid, Spain or eugpsr@cambridge.org.

www.ingramcontent.com/pod-product-compliance
Lightning Source LLC
LaVergne TN
LVHW091528200926
848483LV00002B/330

* 9 7 8 1 0 0 9 6 3 2 5 7 7 *